DSA®
DRIVING STANDARDS AGENCY

the official DSA®
THEORY
TEST for Car Drivers

and the
Highway Code

Approved by
Plain
English
Campaign

London: TSO

Written and compiled by the Publications Unit of the Driving Standards Agency (DSA).

Questions and answers are compiled by the Question Development Team of the DSA.

Published with the permission of the Driving Standards Agency on behalf of the Controller of Her Majesty's Stationery Office.

First published 1996
Eighth edition 2005
Second impression 2006

ISBN 011 552660 9

A CIP catalogue record for this book is available from the British Library.

Other titles in the Driving Skills series

The Official DSA Theory Test for Motorcyclists
The Official DSA Theory Test for Drivers of Large Vehicles
The Official DSA Theory Test Revision Papers for Car Drivers
The Official DSA Guide to Learning to Drive
Helping Learners to Practise - the official DSA guide
The Official DSA Guide to Driving - the essential skills
The Official DSA Guide to Learning to Ride
The Official DSA Guide to Riding - the essential skills
The Official DSA Guide to Driving Buses and Coaches
The Official DSA Guide to Driving Goods Vehicles
The Official DSA Guide to Tractor and Specialist Vehicle Driving Tests
The Official DSA Theory Test for Car Drivers (CD-Rom)
The Official DSA Theory Test for Motorcyclists (CD-Rom)
The Official DSA Guide to Hazard Perception (DVD) (also available on VHS)
The Official DSA Guide to Learning to Drive (DVD)

Acknowledgements
The Driving Standards Agency would like to thank their staff and the following organisations for their contribution to the production of this publication:

Transport Research Laboratory

Department for Transport

Driver and Vehicle Testing Agency, Northern Ireland

Every effort has been made to ensure that the information contained in this publication is accurate at the time of going to press. The Stationery Office cannot be held responsible for any inaccuracies. Information in this book is for guidance only.

All metric and imperial conversions in this book are approximate.

Directgov

Directgov is the place to find all government motoring information and services. From Logbooks to licensing, from driving tests to road tax, go to:

www.direct.gov.uk/motoring

Theory and practical tests
(Bookings and enquiries)

Online **www.dsa.gov.uk**
DSA **0870 0101 372**
Fax **0870 0104 372**
Minicom **0870 0106 372**
Welsh speakers **0870 0100 372**

DVTA (Northern Ireland)
Theory test **0845 600 6700**
Practical test **0870 247 2471**

Driving Standards Agency
(Headquarters)

www.dsa.gov.uk

Stanley House, 56 Talbot Street, Nottingham NG1 5GU

Tel **0115 901 2500**
Fax **0115 901 2510**

Driver & Vehicle Testing Agency
(Headquarters)

www.dvtani.gov.uk

Balmoral Road, Belfast BT12 6QL

Tel **02890 681 831**
Fax **02890 665 520**

Driver & Vehicle Licensing Agency
(GB Licence Enquiries)

www.dvla.gov.uk

Longview Road, Swansea SA6 7JL

Tel **0870 240 0009**
Fax **01792 783 071**
Minicom **01792 782 787**

Driver & Vehicle Licensing in Northern Ireland

www.dvlni.gov.uk

County Hall, Castlerock Road, Coleraine BT51 3TB

Tel **02870 341 469**
24 hour tel **0345 111 222**
Minicom **02870 341 380**

The Driving Standards Agency (DSA) is an executive agency of the Department for Transport. You'll see its logo at test centres.

DSA aims to promote road safety through the advancement of driving standards, by

- establishing and developing high standards and best practice in driving and riding on the road; before people start to drive, as they learn, and after they pass their test
- ensuring high standards of instruction for different types of driver and rider
- conducting the statutory theory and practical tests efficiently, fairly and consistently across the country
- providing a centre of excellence for driver training and driving standards
- developing a range of publications and other publicity material designed to promote safe driving for life.

The Driving Standards Agency recognises and values its customers. We will treat all our customers with respect, and deliver our services in an objective, polite and fair way.

www.dsa.gov.uk

The Driver and Vehicle Testing Agency (DVTA) is an executive agency within the Department of the Environment for Northern Ireland.

Its primary aim is to promote and improve road safety through the advancement of driving standards and implementation of the Government's policies for improving the mechanical standards of vehicles.

www.dvtani.gov.uk

CONTENTS

introduction
ABOUT THE THEORY TEST

This section covers:

- getting started
- the theory test
- after the theory test
- Pass Plus
- using the questions and answers section

A message from the Chief Driving Examiner

With the ever-increasing volume of traffic on the roads today, it's important to make sure that new drivers have a broad spread of driving knowledge. Since July 1996 all new drivers have had to pass a separate theory test before obtaining a full driving licence. In November 2002 the original multiple choice test was extended to include a hazard perception part. The introduction of the theory test has been a major step towards improving road safety in the UK.

All aspects of the theory test are continually monitored, and the bank of questions is regularly updated to take account of changes to legislation and best driving practices. This book contains the whole theory test question bank, set out in an easy-to-read style, with explanations as to why the answers are correct.

However, to prepare properly for the test, you should study the source material; this consists of

The Highway Code

Know Your Traffic Signs

**The Official DSA Guide to Driving
- the essential skills**

To help you practise for the multiple choice questions, *The Official DSA Theory Test for Car Drivers* (CD-Rom) contains the full question bank and allows you to take mock multiple choice tests.

You can prepare for the hazard perception part of the test by working through *The Official DSA Guide to Hazard Perception* (DVD) which is also available as a VHS and booklet pack.

Using these training aids will give you an extensive knowledge of driving theory, and will help you towards a better understanding of practical driving skills.

You'll never know all the answers. Throughout your driving career there will always be more to learn. Remember, any passengers you carry will be your responsibility. By being reliable, efficient and safe you'll be on your way to becoming a good driver.

Chief Driving Examiner
Driving Standards Agency

Getting started

Applying for your licence

You must be at least 17 years old to drive a car. As an exception, if you receive Disability Living Allowance at the higher rate, you're allowed to start driving at 16. You must have a valid provisional driving licence before you can drive on the road.

Driving licences are issued by the Driver and Vehicle Licensing Agency (DVLA). Application forms D1 and D750 can be obtained from any Post Office. In Northern Ireland the issuing authority is Driver and Vehicle Licensing Northern Ireland and the form is a DL1.

The forms should be sent to the appropriate office, which is shown on the form. You must enclose the required passport-type photos, as all provisional licences now issued are photocard licences.

When you receive your provisional licence, check that all details are correct before you drive on the road. If you need to contact DVLA, their telephone number is 0870 240 0009 (DVLNI is 02870 341469).

You will need to show your provisional licence when you take your theory test.

Residency requirements

You can't take a test or obtain a full licence unless you are normally resident in this country. Normal residence means the place where you reside because of personal or occupational ties. However, if you moved to the United Kingdom (UK) having recently been permanently resident in another state of the EC/EEA (European Economic Area), you must have been normally resident in the UK for 185 days in the 12 months prior to your application for a driving test or full driving licence.

Choosing an instructor

DSA in Great Britain, and DVTA in Northern Ireland, approve instructors who are then able to teach learner drivers in return for payment. These instructors have their standards checked regularly.

Approved Driving Instructors (ADIs) must

- pass a series of difficult examinations
- reach a high standard of instruction
- be registered with DSA or DVTA
- display an Approved Driving Instructor's certificate (except in Northern Ireland).

These professional driving instructors will give you guidance on

- your practical skills
- how to study and practise
- when you're ready for your tests
- further training after your practical test under the *Pass Plus* scheme.

DSA and DVTA regulate ADIs and both organisations place great emphasis on professional standards and business ethics. A code of practice has been created, setting a framework within which all instructors should operate. Details of this can be obtained from DSA (tel 0115 901 2500).

About the theory test

The theory test is a screen-based test, and consists of two parts. It has been devised to test your knowledge of driving theory, in particular the rules of the road and best driving practice.

Your knowledge of this information is tested in the first part, as a series of multiple choice questions. More information about this part of the test is given on page 15 and the questions are given in the main part of the book, beginning on page 22.

The second part is called the hazard perception part, more information about this is given on page 17.

Can I take the practical test first?

No. You have to pass your theory test before you can book a practical test.

Does everyone have to take the theory test?

Most people in the UK who are learning to drive will have to sit a theory test. However, you won't have to if

- you're upgrading in the same category i.e. B (car) to B+E (car with trailer)
- you already have a full B1 entitlement because you have a full motorcycle licence issued before 1 February 2001 (not applicable in Northern Ireland).

Any enquiries about whether you have to take a theory test should be addressed to the Customer Service Unit, DSA, Stanley House, 56 Talbot Street, Nottingham, NG1 5GU, tel 0115 901 2500 (for Northern Ireland address enquiries to DVTA Theory Test Section, Balmoral Road, Belfast BT12, tel 02890 681 831).

Foreign licence holders: If you hold a foreign driving licence issued outside the EC/EEA, first check with the Driver Vehicle Licensing Agency (tel 0870 240 0009, for Northern Ireland call 02870 341 469) to see whether you can exchange your driving licence. If you cannot exchange your licence, you will need to apply for a provisional licence and take a theory and practical driving test.

Preparing for your theory test

Although you have to pass your theory test before you can take your practical test, it's recommended that you start studying for your theory test, but don't actually take it until you have some practical driving experience.

To prepare for the multiple choice part of the theory test, we strongly recommend that you study the books from which the questions are taken, as well as the questions themselves. These books are:

The Highway Code - This is essential reading for all drivers. It contains the most up-to-date advice on road safety and the laws which apply to all road users. The *Theory Test Companion* is available packaged with *The Highway Code*. It presents the contents of the theory test in an easy to use format which includes a question paper.

Know Your Traffic Signs - This contains most of the signs and road markings that you are likely to come across.

The Official DSA Guide to Driving - the essential skills - This is the official reference, giving practical advice and best driving practice for all drivers.

These books will help you to answer the questions correctly and will also help you when studying for your practical test. The information in them will be relevant throughout your driving life so make sure you always have an up-to-date copy that you can refer to.

It's important that you study, not just to pass the test, but to become a safer driver

Other study aids

The Official DSA Theory Test for Car Drivers (CD-Rom) - This is an alternative way of preparing for the multiple choice part of the theory test. It contains all the questions and answers and also allows you to take mock tests.

The Official DSA Guide to Hazard Perception (DVD) - We strongly recommend that you use this, preferably with your instructor, to prepare for the hazard perception part of the test. Alternatively, this is available as a VHS and booklet pack.

The DVD is packed with useful tips, quizzes and expert advice. It also includes interactive hazard perception clips, with feedback on your performance.

The Official DSA Complete Theory Test Kit for Car Drivers - This contains both the above products, giving you all the information you need to prepare for the complete theory test, at a reduced price.

Why do the questions keep changing?

To make sure that all candidates are being tested fairly, questions and video clips are under continuous review.

Some of the questions may be changed as a result of customer feedback. They may also be changed to reflect revised legislation, and the publications listed here are updated to reflect such changes.

Can I take a mock test?

You can take a mock test for the multiple choice part of the theory test online at **www.dsa.gov.uk**

All the training materials listed are available by mail order from **0870 241 4523**. They are also available, together with relevant products from other publishers, from bookshops and selected computer software retailers.

You can purchase official titles online at **www.dsa.gov.uk**

The theory test

Booking your theory test

The easiest ways to book your test are online or by phone, but you can also book by post.

Booking online or by telephone - by using these methods you'll be given the date and time of your test immediately.

Book online at www.direct.gov.uk/motoring (for Northern Ireland use www.dvtani.gov.uk).

To book by telephone, call 0870 0101 372 (0845 600 6700 for Northern Ireland).

If you're deaf and use a minicom machine, call 0870 0106 372 and if you are a Welsh speaker, call 0870 0100 372.

You will need your

- DVLA or DVLNI driving licence number
- credit or debit card details (the card holder must book the test). We accept Mastercard, Visa, Delta, Switch, Maestro, Electron and Solo.

You'll be given a booking number and should receive an appointment letter within eight days.

How do I cancel or postpone my test?

To cancel or postpone your theory test appointment you must give at least **three clear working days** before your test date, otherwise you'll lose your fee. You can do this online or by telephone. Only in exceptional circumstances, such as documented ill-health or family bereavement, can this rule be waived.

What if I don't receive an acknowledgement?

If you don't receive an acknowledgement within the time specified above, please contact the booking office online or by telephone to check that an appointment has been made. We can't take responsibility for postal delays. If you miss your test appointment you'll lose your fee.

Where can I take the test?

There are over 150 theory test centres throughout England, Scotland and Wales, and six in Northern Ireland.

Most people have a test centre within 20 miles of their home, but this will vary depending on the density of population in your area (see page 418).

When are test centres open?

Test centres are usually open on weekdays, some evenings and Saturdays.

Booking by post - If you prefer to book by post, you'll need to fill in an application form. These are available from theory test centres or driving test centres, or your instructor may have one.

If you require a theory test in a language other than English or provision for special needs please turn to page 14.

You should normally receive an appointment letter within ten days of posting your application form.

Taking your theory test

Arriving at the test centre - You must make sure that when you arrive at the test centre you have all the relevant documents with you, or you won't be able to take your test and you'll lose your fee.

You'll need either

- your signed photocard licence and paper counterpart; or
- your signed driving licence and valid passport (your passport doesn't have to be British).

No other form of identification is accepable.

Different rules apply in Northern Ireland (see page 422).

All documents must be original. We can't accept photocopies.

The test centre staff will check your documents and make sure that you take the right category of test.

Make sure that you arrive in plenty of time so you aren't rushed. If you arrive after the session has started you may not be allowed to take the test.

Remember, if you don't bring your documents your test will be cancelled.

You'll then be ready to start your test. It's a screen-based test and is made up of a multiple choice part and a hazard perception part.

Languages other than English

You can listen through a headset to the test being read out in one of 20 other languages as well as English. These are: Albanian, Arabic, Bengali, Cantonese, Dari, Farsi, Gujarati, Hindi, Kashmiri, Kurdish, Mirpuri, Polish, Portuguese, Punjabi, Pushto, Spanish, Tamil, Turkish, Urdu and Welsh.

In Wales, and at theory test centres on the Welsh borders, you can take your theory test with Welsh text on screen.

To take your test in a language other than those listed above, you may bring a translator with you to certain theory test centres. The translator must be approved by DSA and you must make arrangements when you book your test. You have to arrange and pay for the services of the translator yourself.

Tests with translators can be taken at the following test centres: Aldershot, Birkenhead, Birmingham, Cardiff, Derby, Edinburgh, Glasgow, Ipswich, Leeds, Milton Keynes, Preston, Southgate and all test centres in Northern Ireland.

Provision for special needs

Every effort is made to ensure that the theory test can be taken by all candidates. It's important that you state your needs when you book your test so that the necessary arrangements can be made.

Reading difficulties - There's an English language voiceover, on a headset, to help you if you have reading difficulties or dyslexia.

You can ask for up to twice the normal time to take the multiple choice part of the test.

If you need extra time you will be asked to provide a letter from a suitable independent person who knows about your reading ability (such as a teacher or employer). Please check with the Special Needs section on the normal booking number (see p12) if you're unsure who to ask.

We can't guarantee to return any original documents, so please send copies only.

Hearing difficulties - If you're deaf or have other hearing difficulties, the multiple choice part and the introduction to the hazard perception part of the test can be delivered in British Sign Language (BSL) by an on-screen signer.

A BSL interpreter or lip speaker can be provided if requested at the time of booking. If you have any other requirements please call the Special Needs section on the normal booking number (see p12).

Physical disabilities - If you have a physical disability which would make it difficult for you to use a mouse button to respond to the clips in the hazard perception part of the test, we may be able to make special arrangements for you to use a different method if you let us know when you book your test.

Multiple choice questions

The first part of the theory test consists of 35 multiple choice questions. You select your answers for this part of the test by simply touching the screen. This 'touch screen' has been carefully designed to make it easy to use.

Before you start you'll be given the chance to work through a practice session for up to 15 minutes to get used to the system. Staff at the test centre will be available to help you if you have any difficulties.

The questions will cover a variety of topics relating to road safety, the environment and documentation. Only one question will appear on the screen at a time.

Most questions will ask you to mark one correct answer from four possible answers given. Some questions may ask for two or more correct answers from a selection, but this is shown clearly on the screen. If you try to move on without marking the correct number of answers you'll be reminded that more answers are needed.

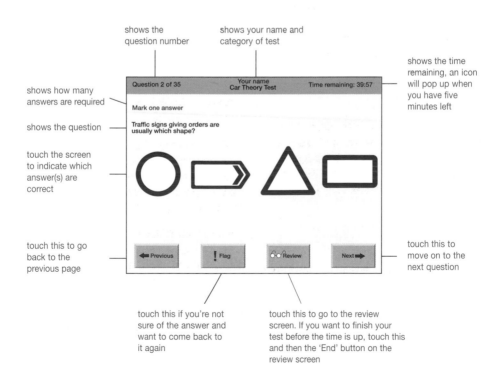

shows the question number

shows your name and category of test

shows the time remaining, an icon will pop up when you have five minutes left

shows how many answers are required

shows the question

touch the screen to indicate which answer(s) are correct

touch this to go back to the previous page

touch this to move on to the next question

touch this if you're not sure of the answer and want to come back to it again

touch this to go to the review screen. If you want to finish your test before the time is up, touch this and then the 'End' button on the review screen

To answer, you need to touch the box alongside the answer or answers you think are correct. If you change your mind and don't want that answer to be selected, touch it again. You can then choose another answer.

Take your time and read the questions carefully. You're given 40 minutes for this part of the test, so relax and don't rush. Extra time can be provided if you have special needs and you let us know when you book your test.

Some questions will take longer to answer than others, but there are no trick questions. The time remaining is displayed on screen.

You'll be able to move backwards and forwards through the questions and you can also 'flag' questions that you'd like to look at again. It's easy to change your answer if you want to.

Try to answer all the questions. If you're well prepared you shouldn't find them difficult.

Before you finish this part of the test, if you have time, you can use the 'review' feature to check your answers. If you want to finish your test before the full time, touch the 'review' button and then the 'end' button on the review screen. When you touch the review button you will see the following screen.

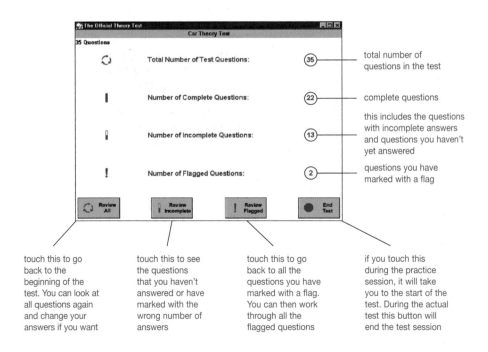

total number of questions in the test

complete questions

this includes the questions with incomplete answers and questions you haven't yet answered

questions you have marked with a flag

touch this to go back to the beginning of the test. You can look at all questions again and change your answers if you want

touch this to see the questions that you haven't answered or have marked with the wrong number of answers

touch this to go back to all the questions you have marked with a flag. You can then work through all the flagged questions

if you touch this during the practice session, it will take you to the start of the test. During the actual test this button will end the test session

Hazard perception

After you've finished the multiple choice part, there is a break of up to three minutes before you start the hazard perception part of the test. You cannot leave your seat during this break. This part of the test will consist of a series of film clips, shown from a driver's point of view.

Before you start this part of the test you'll be shown a short tutorial video that explains how the test works and gives you a chance to see a sample film clip. This will help you to understand what you need to do. You can run this video a second time if you want to.

During the hazard perception part of the test you'll be shown 14 film clips. Each clip contains one or more developing hazards. You should respond by pressing the mouse button **as soon as you see** a hazard

developing that may result in you, the driver, having to take some action, such as changing speed or direction. The earlier you notice a developing hazard and make a response, the higher your score. There are 15 scoreable hazards in total.

Your response will not cause the scene in the video to change in any way. However, a red flag will appear on the bottom of the screen to show that your response has been noted.

Before each clip starts, there will be a 10-second pause to allow you to see the new road situation.

The hazard perception part of the test lasts about 20 minutes. For this part of the test there is no extra time available, and you can't repeat any of the clips - you don't get a second chance to see a hazard when you're driving on the road.

Trial questions

We're constantly checking the questions and clips to help us decide whether to use them in future tests. After the hazard perception part of the test you may be asked to try a few trial questions and clips. You don't have to do these if you don't want to, and if you answer them they won't count towards your final score.

Customer satisfaction survey

We want to ensure our customers are completely satisfied with the service they receive. At the end of your test you'll be shown some questions designed to give us information about you and how happy you are with the service you received from us.

Your answers will be treated in the strictest confidence. They are not part of the test and they won't be used in determining your final score or for marketing purposes. You'll be asked if you want to complete the survey, there's no obligation to do so.

The result

You should receive your result at the test centre within 10 minutes of completing the test.

You'll be given a score for each part of the test (the multiple choice part and the hazard perception part). You'll need to pass both parts to pass the theory test. If you fail one of the parts you'll have to take the whole test again.

What's the pass mark?

To pass the multiple choice part of the theory test you must answer at least 30 questions correctly. For learner car drivers and bike riders the pass mark for the hazard perception part is 44 out of 75.

If I don't pass, when can I take the test again?

If you fail your test, you've shown that you're not fully prepared. You'll have to wait at least three clear working days before you take the theory test again.

Good preparation will save you time and money.

Why do I have to retake both parts of the test if I only fail one?

It's really only one test. The theory test has always included questions relating to hazard awareness – the second part simply tests the same skills in a more effective way. The two parts are only presented separately in the theory test because different scoring methods are used.

After the theory test

When you pass your theory test you'll be given a certificate. Keep this carefully, you'll need it when you go for your practical test.

This certificate has a life of two years from the date of your test. This means that you have to take and pass the practical test within this two-year period. If you don't, you'll have to take and pass the theory test again before you can book your practical test.

Your practical driving test

Your next step is to prepare for and take your practical driving test. To help you we have produced a DVD and book called *The Official DSA Guide to Learning to Drive*.

These products explain the standards required to pass the practical driving test. They include information about each of the 24 key skills examined within the test, with tips from the experts, and they explain what the examiner is looking for during the test.

The DVD also shows a test in action so that you can see what's in store.

Pass Plus

After passing the practical driving test you are at greater risk of being involved in a road accident. That risk is reflected in car insurance premiums.

There may be many driving situations which you have not experienced during your lessons. The *Pass Plus* scheme can help with this by showing you how to deal with these situations so that you can drive with confidence.

Pass Plus is aimed at improving your driving skills and making you a safer driver. It can also lead to insurance discounts.

Pass Plus will take you through driving:

- in town
- on rural roads
- in all weathers
- on dual carriageways and motorways
- in the dark.

The structured syllabus gives you the extra experience you need at a time when you're most likely to have an accident, it builds on your existing skills and there's no test to take at the end.

The amount of money you save on insurance could cover the cost of the course. More than 60% of car insurers recognise the benefits of the scheme and most will give you substantial discounts when you insure your car.

To find out more about the *Pass Plus* scheme, insurance discounts and *Pass Plus* instructors in your area

- ask your driving instructor
- check out the ads in *Drive On* magazine
- visit **www.passplus.org.uk**
- call the *Pass Plus* hotline on **0115 901 2633**
- email **passplus@dsa.gsi.gov.uk**

You can take the *Pass Plus* course at any time in your driving career, but it's mainly aimed at you as a new driver, in the first year after passing your test.

Saving money on your car insurance should bring a smile to your face

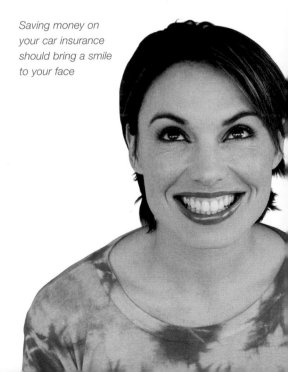

Using the questions and answers section

The following part of the book contains all the questions that could be used in the multiple choice part of the theory test.

For easy reference, and to help you study, the questions have been divided into topics and put into sections. Although this isn't how you'll find them in your test, it's helpful if you want to refer to particular subjects.

The questions are in the left-hand column with a choice of answers beneath. On the right-hand side of the page you'll find the correct answers and a brief explanation of why they are correct. There will also be some advice on correct driving procedures.

Don't just learn the answers. It's important that you know why the answers are correct. This will help you with your practical skills and prepare you to become a safe and confident driver.

Taking exams or tests is rarely a pleasant experience, but you can make your test less stressful by being confident that you have the knowledge to answer the questions correctly.

Make studying more enjoyable by involving friends and relatives. Take part in a question-and-answer game. Test those 'experienced' drivers who've had their licence a while: they might learn something too!

Best wishes with your theory test. Once you're on the road, don't forget everything you've learnt

Some of the questions in this book will not be used in Northern Ireland theory tests. These questions are marked as follows: *NI EXEMPT*

section one
ALERTNESS

This section covers:

- observation
- anticipation
- concentration
- awareness
- distraction
- boredom

1.1
*Mark **one** answer*

Windscreen pillars can obstruct your view. You should take particular care when

- driving on a motorway
- driving on a dual carriageway
- approaching a one-way street
- approaching bends and junctions

⊙ **approaching bends and junctions**

Windscreen pillars can obstruct your view, particularly at bends and junctions. Look out for other road users, particularly cyclists and pedestrians, as they can be hard to see.

1.2
*Mark **one** answer*

When emerging from junctions, which is most likely to obstruct your view?

- Windscreen pillars
- Steering wheel
- Interior mirror
- Windscreen wipers

⊙ **Windscreen pillars**

Windscreen pillars can block your view, particularly at junctions. Those road users most at risk of not being seen are cyclists, motorcyclists and pedestrians. Never rely on just a quick glance.

1.3
*Mark **one** answer*

You cannot see clearly behind when reversing. What should you do?

- Open your window to look behind
- Open the door and look behind
- Look in the nearside mirror
- Ask someone to guide you

⊙ **Ask someone to guide you**

If you want to turn your car around try to find a place where you have good all-round vision. If this isn't possible and you're unable to see clearly, then get someone to guide you.

1.4
*Mark **one** answer*

Which of the following should you do before stopping?

- Sound the horn
- Use the mirrors
- Select a higher gear
- Flash your headlights

⊙ **Use the mirrors**

Before pulling up check the mirrors to see what is happening behind you. Also assess what is ahead and make sure you give the correct signal if it helps other road users.

When you are moving off from behind a parked car you should

- ⊙ look round before you move off
- ⊙ use all the mirrors on the vehicle
- ⊙ look round after moving off
- ⊙ use the exterior mirrors only
- ⊙ give a signal if necessary
- ⊙ give a signal after moving off

⊙ **look round before you move off**

⊙ **use all the mirrors on the vehicle**

⊙ **give a signal if necessary**

Before moving off you should use all the mirrors to check if the road is clear. Look round to check the blind spots and give a signal if it is necessary to warn other road users of your intentions.

You are waiting to emerge from a junction. The windscreen pillar is restricting your view. What should you be particularly aware of?

- ⊙ Lorries
- ⊙ Buses
- ⊙ Motorcyclists
- ⊙ Coaches

⊙ **Motorcyclists**

Windscreen pillars can completely block your view of pedestrians, motorcyclists and pedal cyclists. You should particularly watch out for these road users; don't just rely on a quick glance. Where possible make eye contact with them so you can be sure they have seen you too.

You are driving on a wet road. You have to stop your vehicle in an emergency. You should

- ⊙ apply the handbrake and footbrake together
- ⊙ keep both hands on the wheel
- ⊙ select reverse gear
- ⊙ give an arm signal

⊙ **keep both hands on the wheel**

As you drive, look well ahead and all around so that you're ready for any hazards that might occur. There may be occasions when you have to stop in an emergency. React as soon as you can whilst keeping control of the vehicle.

1.8
Mark **one** answer

You are turning right onto a dual carriageway. What should you do before emerging?

- ◉ Stop, apply the handbrake and then select a low gear
- ◉ Position your vehicle well to the left of the side road
- ◉ Check that the central reservation is wide enough for your vehicle
- ◉ Make sure that you leave enough room for a vehicle behind

◉ **Check that the central reservation is wide enough for your vehicle**

Before emerging right onto a dual carriageway make sure that the central reservation is wide enough to protect your vehicle. If it's not, you should treat it as one road and check that it's clear in both directions before pulling out. Neglecting to do this could place part or all of your vehicle in the path of approaching traffic and cause an accident.

1.9
Mark **one** answer

Before you make a U-turn in the road, you should

- ◉ give an arm signal as well as using your indicators
- ◉ signal so that other drivers can slow down for you
- ◉ look over your shoulder for a final check
- ◉ select a higher gear than normal

◉ **look over your shoulder for a final check**

If you want to make a U-turn, slow down and ensure that the road is clear in both directions. Make sure that the road is wide enough to carry out the manoeuvre safely.

1.10
Mark **two** answers

On a long motorway journey boredom can cause you to feel sleepy. You should

- ◉ leave the motorway and find a safe place to stop
- ◉ keep looking around at the surrounding landscape
- ◉ drive faster to complete your journey sooner
- ◉ ensure a supply of fresh air into your vehicle
- ◉ stop on the hard shoulder for a rest

◉ **leave the motorway and find a safe place to stop**

◉ **ensure a supply of fresh air into your vehicle**

Plan your journey to include suitable rest stops. You should take all possible precautions against feeling sleepy while driving. Any lapse of concentration could have serious consequences.

1.11 Mark four answers

Which of the following may cause loss of concentration on a long journey?

- ⊙ Loud music
- ⊙ Arguing with a passenger
- ⊙ Using a mobile phone
- ⊙ Putting in a cassette tape
- ⊙ Stopping regularly to rest
- ⊙ Pulling up to tune the radio

- ⊙ **Loud music**
- ⊙ **Arguing with a passenger**
- ⊙ **Using a mobile phone**
- ⊙ **Putting in a cassette tape**

You should not allow yourself to be distracted when driving. You need to concentrate fully in order to be safe on the road. Loud music could mask other sounds, such as the audible warning of an emergency vehicle.

Any distraction which causes you to take your hands off the steering wheel or your eyes off the road could be dangerous.

1.12 Mark one answer

What does the term 'blind spot' mean for a driver?

- ⊙ An area covered by your right-hand mirror
- ⊙ An area not covered by your headlights
- ⊙ An area covered by your left-hand mirror
- ⊙ An area not covered by your mirrors

- ⊙ **An area not covered by your mirrors**

Modern vehicles provide the driver with well-positioned mirrors which are essential to safe driving. However, they cannot see every angle of the scene behind and to the sides of the vehicle. This is why it is essential that you check over your shoulder, so that you are aware of any hazards not reflected in your mirrors.

1.13 Mark two answers

You are most likely to lose concentration when driving if you

- ⊙ use a mobile phone
- ⊙ listen to very loud music
- ⊙ switch on the heated rear window
- ⊙ look at the door mirrors

- ⊙ **use a mobile phone**
- ⊙ **listen to very loud music**

Distractions which cause you to take your hands off the steering wheel or your eyes off the road are potentially dangerous. You must be in full control of your vehicle at all times.

1.14
Mark *four* answers

Which FOUR are most likely to cause you to lose concentration while you are driving?

⊙ Using a mobile phone
⊙ Talking into a microphone
⊙ Tuning your car radio
⊙ Looking at a map
⊙ Checking the mirrors
⊙ Using the demisters

⊙ **Using a mobile phone**

⊙ **Talking into a microphone**

⊙ **Tuning your car radio**

⊙ **Looking at a map**

Planning your journey is important. A few sensible precautions will allow you to

• tune your radio into frequencies in your area of travel before setting off

• take planned breaks (which can be used for phone calls)

• plan your route (make notes of road numbers and junction numbers if necessary).

This will avoid the need to look at maps or use a mobile phone while driving.

1.15
Mark *three* answers

As you approach this bridge you should

⊙ move into the middle of the road to get a better view
⊙ slow down
⊙ get over the bridge as quickly as possible
⊙ consider using your horn
⊙ find another route
⊙ beware of pedestrians

⊙ **slow down**

⊙ **consider using your horn**

⊙ **beware of pedestrians**

This sign gives you a warning. The brow of the hill prevents you seeing oncoming traffic so you must be cautious.

The bridge is narrow and there may not be enough room for you to pass an oncoming vehicle at this point.

There is no footpath, so pedestrians may be walking in the road.

Consider the hidden hazards and be ready to react if necessary.

You lose your way on a busy road. What is the best action to take?

⊙ Stop at traffic lights and ask pedestrians

⊙ Shout to other drivers to ask them the way

⊙ Turn into a side road, stop and check a map

⊙ Check a map, and keep going with the traffic flow

⊙ **Turn into a side road, stop and check a map**

It's easy to lose your way in an unfamiliar area. If you need to check a map or ask for directions, first find a safe place to stop.

This road marking warns

⊙ drivers to use the hard shoulder

⊙ overtaking drivers there is a bend to the left

⊙ overtaking drivers to move back to the left

⊙ drivers that it is safe to overtake

⊙ **overtaking drivers to move back to the left**

You should plan your overtaking to take into account any hazards ahead. In this picture the marking indicates that you are approaching a junction. You will not have time to overtake and move back to the left safely.

Objects hanging from your interior mirror may

⊙ restrict your view

⊙ improve your driving

⊙ distract your attention

⊙ help your concentration

⊙ **restrict your view**

⊙ **distract your attention**

Ensure that you can see clearly through the windscreen of your vehicle. Stickers or hanging objects could affect your field of vision or draw your eyes away from the road.

1.19
*Mark **two** answers*

You are driving at dusk. You should switch your lights on

⊙ even when street lights are not lit
⊙ so others can see you
⊙ only when others have done so
⊙ only when street lights are lit

⊙ **even when street lights are not lit**

⊙ **so others can see you**

Your headlights and tail lights help others on the road to see you. It may be necessary to turn on your lights during the day if visibility is reduced, for example due to heavy rain. In these conditions the light might fade before the street lights are timed to switch on. Be seen to be safe.

1.20
*Mark **one** answer*

You are travelling along this narrow country road. When passing the cyclist you should go

⊙ slowly, sounding the horn as you pass
⊙ quickly, leaving plenty of room
⊙ slowly, leaving plenty of room
⊙ quickly, sounding the horn as you pass

⊙ **slowly, leaving plenty of room**

Look well ahead and only pull out if it is safe. You will need to use all of the road to pass the cyclist, so be extra-cautious. Look out for entrances to fields where tractors or other farm machinery could be waiting to pull out.

1.21
*Mark **one** answer*

In which of these situations should you avoid overtaking?

⊙ Just after a bend
⊙ In a one-way street
⊙ On a 30 mph road
⊙ Approaching a dip in the road

⊙ **Approaching a dip in the road**

As you begin to think about overtaking, ask yourself if it's really necessary. If you can't see well ahead stay back and wait for a safer place to pull out.

Why are these yellow lines painted across the road?

⊙ To help you choose the correct lane

⊙ To help you keep the correct separation distance

⊙ To make you aware of your speed

⊙ To tell you the distance to the roundabout

⊙ **To make you aware of your speed**

These lines are often found on the approach to a roundabout or a dangerous junction. They give you extra warning to adjust your speed. Look well ahead and do this in good time.

Using a mobile phone while you are driving

⊙ is acceptable in a vehicle with power steering

⊙ will reduce your field of vision

⊙ could distract your attention from the road

⊙ will affect your vehicle's electronic systems

⊙ **could distract your attention from the road**

Driving today requires all of your attention, all of the time. Any distraction, however brief, is potentially dangerous and could lead to you losing control of your vehicle.

To answer a call on your mobile phone while travelling you should

⊙ reduce your speed wherever you are

⊙ stop in a proper and convenient place

⊙ keep the call time to a minimum

⊙ slow down and allow others to overtake

⊙ **stop in a proper and convenient place**

No phone call is important enough to risk endangering lives. If you must be contactable when driving, plan your route to include breaks where you can catch up on telephone messages in safety. Always choose a proper and convenient place to take a break, such as a lay-by or service area.

1.25
*Mark **one** answer*

When following a large vehicle you should keep well back because this

- ⊙ allows you to corner more quickly
- ⊙ helps the large vehicle to stop more easily
- ⊙ allows the driver to see you in the mirrors
- ⊙ helps you to keep out of the wind

⊙ **allows the driver to see you in the mirrors**

If you're following a large vehicle but are so close to it that you can't see the exterior mirrors, the driver can't see you.

Keeping well back will also allow you to see the road ahead by looking past either side of the large vehicle.

1.26
*Mark **one** answer*

Your mobile phone rings while you are travelling. You should

- ⊙ stop immediately
- ⊙ answer it immediately
- ⊙ pull up in a suitable place
- ⊙ pull up at the nearest kerb

⊙ **pull up in a suitable place**

Always use the safe option. It is not worth taking the risk of endangering other road users.

If you need to use a mobile phone, make sure that you pull up in a place that does not obstruct other road users. Using a message service will enable you to complete your journey without interruptions and you can catch up with your calls when you take your rest breaks.

1.27
*Mark **one** answer*

You should ONLY use a mobile phone when

- ⊙ receiving a call
- ⊙ suitably parked
- ⊙ driving at less than 30 mph
- ⊙ driving an automatic vehicle

⊙ **suitably parked**

It is far more convenient for you, as well as being safer, if you have parked in a safe and convenient place before receiving or making a call or using text messaging. You will also be free to take notes or refer to papers, which would be not be possible while driving.

Your vehicle is fitted with a hand-held telephone. To use the telephone you should

⊙ reduce your speed
⊙ find a safe place to stop
⊙ steer the vehicle with one hand
⊙ be particularly careful at junctions

⊙ **find a safe place to stop**

Your attention should be on your driving at all times. Never attempt to dial or reach out for your phone while on the move. This could mean taking your eyes off the road and at 60 mph your vehicle will travel about 27 metres every second.

What is the safest way to use a mobile phone in your vehicle?

⊙ Use hands-free equipment
⊙ Find a suitable place to stop
⊙ Drive slowly on a quiet road
⊙ Direct your call through the operator

⊙ **Find a suitable place to stop**

If the use of a mobile phone causes you to drive in a careless or dangerous manner, you could be prosecuted for those offences. The penalties include an unlimited fine, disqualification and up to two years' imprisonment.

Your mobile phone rings while you are on the motorway. Before answering you should

⊙ reduce your speed to 30 mph
⊙ pull up on the hard shoulder
⊙ move into the left-hand lane
⊙ stop in a safe place

⊙ **stop in a safe place**

When driving on motorways, you can't just pull up to answer your mobile phone. If you need to be contactable, plan your journey to include breaks so you can pick up any phone messages.

You are approaching traffic lights that have been on green for some time. You should

⊙ accelerate hard
⊙ maintain your speed
⊙ be ready to stop
⊙ brake hard

⊙ **be ready to stop**

The longer traffic lights have been on green, the greater the chance of them changing. Always allow for this on approach and be prepared to stop.

1.32
Mark **one** answer

You should not use a mobile phone
while driving

- until you are satisfied that no other
  traffic is near
- unless you are able to drive one-handed
- because it might distract your attention
  from the road ahead
- because reception is poor when the
  engine is running

⊙ **because it might distract your
attention from the road ahead**

Driving requires your total attention and
concentration at all times. Using a mobile
phone will distract you and will increase
your chances of having an accident.

Be safe, switch off your phone while driving
and pick up any messages when you stop
for a break.

1.33
Mark **one** answer

Your vehicle is fitted with a hands-free
phone system. Using this equipment whilst
driving

- is quite safe as long as you slow down
- could distract your attention from the
  road
- is recommended by *The Highway Code*
- could be very good for road safety

⊙ **could distract your attention
from the road**

Using a hands-free system doesn't mean
that you can safely drive and use a mobile
phone. This type of mobile phone can
still distract your attention from the road.
As a driver, it is your responsibility to
keep yourself and other road users safe
at all times.

1.34
Mark **one** answer

Using a hands-free phone is likely to

- improve your safety
- increase your concentration
- reduce your view
- divert your attention

⊙ **divert your attention**

Unlike someone in the car with you,
the person on the other end of the line is
unable to see the traffic situations you are
dealing with. They will not stop speaking to
you even if you are approaching a hazardous
situation. You need to be concentrating on
your driving all of the time, but especially
so when dealing with a hazard.

section two
ATTITUDE

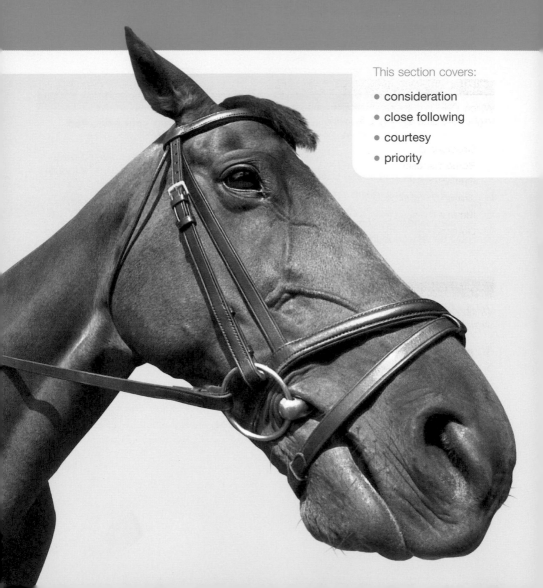

This section covers:

- consideration
- close following
- courtesy
- priority

2.1 Mark *one* answer

When being followed by an ambulance showing a flashing blue beacon you should

- pull over as soon as soon as possible to let it pass
- accelerate hard to get away from it
- maintain your speed and course
- brake harshly and immediately stop in the road

⊙ **pull over as soon as safely possible to let it pass**

Pull over in a place where the ambulance can pass safely. Check that there are no bollards or obstructions in the road that will prevent it from doing so.

2.2 Mark *three* answers

Which THREE of these emergency services might have blue flashing beacons?

- Coastguard
- Bomb disposal
- Gritting lorries
- Animal ambulances
- Mountain rescue
- Doctors' cars

⊙ **Coastguard**

⊙ **Bomb disposal**

⊙ **Mountain rescue**

When attending an emergency these vehicles will be travelling at speed. You should help their progress by pulling over and allowing them to pass. Do so safely. Don't stop suddenly or in a dangerous position.

2.3 Mark *one* answer

Which instrument panel warning light would show that headlights are on full beam?

⊙

You should be aware of where all the warning lights and visual aids are on the vehicle you are driving. If you are driving a vehicle for the first time you should take time to check all the controls.

A vehicle pulls out in front of you at a junction. What should you do?

- Swerve past it and sound your horn
- Flash your headlights and drive up close behind
- Slow down and be ready to stop
- Accelerate past it immediately

⊙ **Slow down and be ready to stop**

Try to be ready for the unexpected. Plan ahead and learn to anticipate hazards. You'll then give yourself more time to react to any problems that might occur.

Be tolerant of the behaviour of other road users who don't behave correctly.

You are approaching unmarked crossroads. How should you deal with this type of junction?

- Accelerate and keep to the middle
- Slow down and keep to the right
- Accelerate looking to the left
- Slow down and look both ways

⊙ **Slow down and look both ways**

Be extra-cautious, especially when your view is restricted by hedges, bushes, walls and large vehicles etc. In the summer months these junctions can become more difficult to deal with when growing foliage may obscure your view.

If your vehicle uses diesel fuel, take extra care when refuelling. Diesel fuel when spilt is

- sticky
- odourless
- clear
- slippery

⊙ **slippery**

If you are using diesel or are at a pump which has a diesel facility be aware that there may be spilt fuel on the ground. Fuel contamination on the soles of your shoes may cause them to slip when using the foot pedals.

You are driving at night on an unlit road behind another vehicle. You should

- flash your headlights
- use dipped beam headlights
- switch off your headlights
- use full beam headlights

⊙ **use dipped beam headlights**

If you follow another vehicle with your headlights on full beam they could dazzle the driver. Leave a safe distance and ensure that the light from your dipped beam falls short of the vehicle in front.

2.8　　　　　*Mark one answer*

What type of emergency vehicle is fitted with a green flashing beacon?

- Fire engine
- Road gritter
- Ambulance
- Doctor's car

⊙ **Doctor's car**

A green flashing beacon on a vehicle means the driver or passenger is a doctor on an emergency call. Give way to them if it's safe to do so. Be aware that the vehicle may be travelling quickly or may stop in a hurry.

2.9　　　　　*Mark one answer*

A flashing green beacon on a vehicle means

- police on non-urgent duties
- doctor on an emergency call
- road safety patrol operating
- gritting in progress

⊙ **doctor on an emergency call**

If you see a vehicle with a flashing green beacon approaching, allow it to pass when you can do so safely. Be aware that someone's life could depend on the driver making good progress through traffic.

2.10　　　*Mark three answers*

Which of the following vehicles will use blue flashing beacons?

- Motorway maintenance
- Bomb disposal
- Blood transfusion
- Police patrol
- Breakdown recovery

⊙ **Bomb disposal**

⊙ **Blood transfusion**

⊙ **Police patrol**

When you see emergency vehicles with blue flashing beacons move out of the way as soon as it is safe to do so.

2.11　　　　*Mark one answer*

When overtaking a horse and rider you should

- sound your horn as a warning
- go past as quickly as possible
- flash your headlights as a warning
- go past slowly and carefully

⊙ **go past slowly and carefully**

Horses can become startled by the sound of a car engine or the rush of air caused by passing too closely. Keep well back and only pass when it is safe; leave them plenty of room. You may have to use the other side of the road to go past: if you do, first make sure there is no oncoming traffic.

2.12 *Mark **two** answers*

You are driving along a country road.
A horse and rider are approaching. What
should you do?

- ⊙ Increase your speed
- ⊙ Sound your horn
- ⊙ Flash your headlights
- ⊙ Drive slowly past
- ⊙ Give plenty of room
- ⊙ Rev your engine

⊙ **Drive slowly past**

⊙ **Give plenty of room**

It's important that you reduce your speed.
Passing too closely at speed could startle
the horse and unseat the rider.

2.13 *Mark **one** answer*

A person herding sheep asks you to stop.
You should

- ⊙ ignore them as they have no authority
- ⊙ stop and switch off your engine
- ⊙ continue on but drive slowly
- ⊙ try and get past quickly

⊙ **stop and switch off your engine**

Allow the sheep to clear the road before
you proceed. Animals are unpredictable
and startle easily; they could turn and run
into your path or into the path of another
moving vehicle.

2.14 *Mark **one** answer*

You should ONLY flash your headlights to
other road users

- ⊙ to show that you are giving way
- ⊙ to show that you are about to turn
- ⊙ to tell them that you have right
  of way
- ⊙ to let them know that you are there

⊙ **to let them know that you
  are there**

You should only flash your headlights to
warn others of your presence. Don't use
them to

- • greet others
- • show impatience
- • give up your priority.

Other road users could misunderstand
your signal.

2.15
*Mark **two** answers*

You have a loose filler cap on your diesel fuel tank. This will

- ⊙ waste fuel and money
- ⊙ make roads slippery for other road users
- ⊙ improve your vehicles' fuel consumption
- ⊙ increase the level of exhaust emissions

⊙ **waste fuel and money**

⊙ **make roads slippery for other road users**

Diesel fuel is especially slippery if spilled on a wet road. At the end of a dry spell of weather you should be aware that the road surfaces may have a high level of diesel spillage that hasn't been washed away by rain.

2.16
*Mark **one** answer*

To avoid spillage after refuelling, you should make sure that

- ⊙ your tank Is only three quarters full
- ⊙ you have used a locking filler cap
- ⊙ you check your fuel gauge is working
- ⊙ your filler cap is securely fastened

⊙ **your filler cap is securely fastened**

When learning to drive it is a good idea to practise filling your car with fuel. Ask your instructor if you can use a petrol station and fill the fuel tank yourself. You need to know where the filler cap is located on the car you are driving in order to park on the correct side of the pump. Take care not to overfill the tank or spill fuel. Make sure you secure the filler cap as soon as you have replaced the fuel nozzle.

2.17
*Mark **one** answer*

A vehicle has a flashing green beacon. What does this mean?

- ⊙ A doctor is answering an emergency call
- ⊙ The vehicle is slow-moving
- ⊙ It is a motorway police patrol vehicle
- ⊙ The vehicle is carrying hazardous chemicals

⊙ **A doctor is answering an emergency call**

A doctor attending an emergency may show a green flashing beacon on their vehicle. Give way to them when you can do so safely as they will need to reach their destination quickly. Be aware that they might pull over suddenly.

A bus lane on your left shows no times of operation. This means it is

- ☉ not in operation at all
- ☉ only in operation at peak times
- ☉ in operation 24 hours a day
- ☉ only in operation in daylight hours

☉ in operation 24 hours a day

Don't drive or park in a bus lane when it's in operation. This can cause disruption to traffic and delays to public transport.

You are driving on a clear night. There is a steady stream of oncoming traffic. The national speed limit applies. Which lights should you use?

- ☉ Full beam headlights
- ☉ Sidelights
- ☉ Dipped headlights
- ☉ Fog lights

☉ Dipped headlights

Use the full beam headlights only when you can be sure that you won't dazzle other road users.

You are waiting in a traffic queue at night. To avoid dazzling following drivers you should

- ☉ apply the handbrake only
- ☉ apply the footbrake only
- ☉ switch off your headlights
- ☉ use both the handbrake and footbrake

☉ apply the handbrake only

You should consider the driver behind; brake lights can dazzle. However, if you are driving in fog it's safer to keep your foot on the footbrake. In this case it will give the vehicle behind extra warning of your presence.

2.21 *Mark **one** answer*

You are driving behind a large goods vehicle. It signals left but steers to the right. You should

- ⊙ slow down and let the vehicle turn
- ⊙ drive on, keeping to the left
- ⊙ overtake on the right of it
- ⊙ hold your speed and sound your horn

⊙ **slow down and let the vehicle turn**

Large, long vehicles need extra room when making turns at junctions. They may move out to the right in order to make a left turn. Keep well back and don't attempt to pass on the left.

2.22 *Mark **one** answer*

A long, heavily-laden lorry is taking a long time to overtake you. What should you do?

- ⊙ Speed up
- ⊙ Slow down
- ⊙ Hold your speed
- ⊙ Change direction

⊙ **Slow down**

A long lorry with a heavy load will need more time to pass you than a car, especially on an uphill stretch of road. Slow down and allow the lorry to pass.

2.23 *Mark **one** answer*

You are driving along this road. The red van cuts in close in front of you. What should you do?

- ⊙ Accelerate to get closer to the red van
- ⊙ Give a long blast on the horn
- ⊙ Drop back to leave the correct separation distance
- ⊙ Flash your headlights several times

⊙ **Drop back to leave the correct separation distance**

There are times when other drivers make incorrect or ill-judged decisions. Be tolerant and try not to retaliate or react aggressively.

Always consider the safety of other road users, your passengers and yourself.

2.24

*Mark **one** answer*

You are travelling at the legal speed limit. A vehicle comes up quickly behind, flashing its headlights. You should

- ⊙ accelerate to make a gap behind you
- ⊙ touch the brakes sharply to show your brake lights
- ⊙ maintain your speed to prevent the vehicle from overtaking
- ⊙ allow the vehicle to overtake

⊙ **allow the vehicle to overtake**

Don't enforce the speed limit by blocking another vehicle's progress. This will only lead to the other driver becoming more frustrated. Allow the other vehicle to pass when you can do so safely.

2.25

*Mark **one** answer*

You are driving in traffic at the speed limit for the road. The driver behind is trying to overtake. You should

- ⊙ move closer to the car ahead, so the driver behind has no room to overtake
- ⊙ wave the driver behind to overtake when it is safe
- ⊙ keep a steady course and allow the driver behind to overtake
- ⊙ accelerate to get away from the driver behind

⊙ **keep a steady course and allow the driver behind to overtake**

Keep a steady course to give the driver behind an opportunity to overtake safely. If necessary, slow down. Reacting incorrectly to another driver's impatience can lead to danger.

2.26

*Mark **one** answer*

You are driving a slow-moving vehicle on a narrow winding road. You should

- ⊙ keep well out to stop vehicles overtaking dangerously
- ⊙ wave following vehicles past you if you think they can overtake quickly
- ⊙ pull in safely when you can, to let following vehicles overtake
- ⊙ give a left signal when it is safe for vehicles to overtake you

⊙ **pull in safely when you can, to let following vehicles overtake**

Try not to hold up a queue of traffic. Other road users may become impatient and this could lead to reckless actions. If you're driving a slow-moving vehicle and the road is narrow, look for a safe place to pull in. DON'T wave other traffic past since this could be dangerous if you or they haven't seen an oncoming vehicle.

2.27
*Mark **one** answer*

At a pelican crossing the flashing amber light means you MUST

- ⊙ stop and wait for the green light
- ⊙ stop and wait for the red light
- ⊙ give way to pedestrians waiting to cross
- ⊙ give way to pedestrians already on the crossing

⊙ **give way to pedestrians already on the crossing**

Pelican crossings are signal-controlled crossings operated by pedestrians. Push-button controls change the signals. Pelican crossings have no red-and-amber stage before green. Instead, they have a flashing amber light, which means you must give way to pedestrians already on the crossing, but if it is clear, you may continue.

2.28
*Mark **one** answer*

You should never wave people across at pedestrian crossings because

- ⊙ there may be another vehicle coming
- ⊙ they may not be looking
- ⊙ it is safer for you to carry on
- ⊙ they may not be ready to cross

⊙ **there may be another vehicle coming**

If people are waiting to use a pedestrian crossing, slow down and be prepared to stop. Don't wave them across the road since another driver may not

- have seen them
- have seen your signal
- be able to stop safely.

2.29
*Mark **one** answer*

At which type of crossing are cyclists allowed to ride across with pedestrians?

- ⊙ Toucan
- ⊙ Puffin
- ⊙ Pelican
- ⊙ Zebra

⊙ **Toucan**

A toucan crossing is designed to allow pedestrians and cyclists to cross at the same time. Look out for cyclists approaching the crossing at speed.

You are approaching a zebra crossing. Pedestrians are waiting to cross. You should

⊙ give way to the elderly and infirm only

⊙ slow down and prepare to stop

⊙ use your headlights to indicate they can cross

⊙ wave at them to cross the road

⊙ **slow down and prepare to stop**

Zebra crossings have

- flashing amber beacons on both sides of the road
- black and white stripes on the crossing
- white zigzag markings on both sides of the crossing.

Where you can see pedestrians are waiting to cross, slow down and prepare to stop.

You stop for pedestrians waiting to cross at a zebra crossing. They do not start to cross. What should you do?

⊙ Be patient and wait

⊙ Sound your horn

⊙ Carry on

⊙ Wave them to cross

⊙ **Be patient and wait**

If you stop for pedestrians and they don't start to cross don't wave them across or sound your horn.

This could be dangerous if another vehicle is approaching and hasn't seen or heard your signal.

You are approaching a red light at a puffin crossing. Pedestrians are on the crossing. The red light will stay on until

⊙ you start to edge forward on to the crossing

⊙ the pedestrians have reached a safe position

⊙ the pedestrians are clear of the front of your vehicle

⊙ a driver from the opposite direction reaches the crossing

⊙ **the pedestrians have reached a safe position**

The electronic device will automatically detect that the pedestrians have reached a safe position. Don't proceed until the green light shows it is safe for vehicles to do so.

2.33
*Mark **one** answer*

You are following a vehicle on a wet road. You should leave a time gap of at least

- one second
- two seconds
- three seconds
- four seconds

⊙ **four seconds**

Wet roads will reduce your tyres' grip on the road. The safe separation gap of at least two seconds in dry conditions should be doubled in wet weather.

2.34
*Mark **one** answer*

At a puffin crossing, which colour follows the green signal?

- Steady red
- Flashing amber
- Steady amber
- Flashing green

⊙ **Steady amber**

Puffin crossings have infra-red sensors which detect when pedestrians are crossing and hold the red traffic signal until the crossing is clear. The use of a sensor means there is no flashing amber phase as there is with a pelican crossing.

2.35
*Mark **one** answer*

At puffin crossings, which light will not show to a driver?

- Flashing amber
- Red
- Steady amber
- Green

⊙ **Flashing amber**

A flashing amber light is shown at pelican crossings, but puffin crossings are different. They are controlled electronically and automatically detect when pedestrians are on the crossing. The phase is shortened or lengthened according to the position of the pedestrians.

2.36
*Mark **one** answer*

You are in a one-way street and want to turn right. You should position yourself

- in the right-hand lane
- in the left-hand lane
- in either lane, depending on the traffic
- just left of the centre line

⊙ **in the right-hand lane**

If you're travelling in a one-way street and wish to turn right you should take up a position in the right-hand lane. This will enable other road users not wishing to turn to proceed on the left. Indicate your intention and take up your position in good time.

45

You wish to turn right ahead. Why should you take up the correct position in good time?

- ⊙ To allow other drivers to pull out in front of you
- ⊙ To give a better view into the road that you're joining
- ⊙ To help other road users know what you intend to do
- ⊙ To allow drivers to pass you on the right

⊙ **To help other road users know what you intend to do**

If you wish to turn right into a side road take up your position in good time. Move to the centre of the road when it's safe to do so. This will allow vehicles to pass you on the left. Early planning will show other traffic what you intend to do.

Following this vehicle too closely is unwise because

- ⊙ your brakes will overheat
- ⊙ your view ahead is increased
- ⊙ your engine will overheat
- ⊙ your view ahead is reduced

⊙ **your view ahead is reduced**

Staying back will increase your view of the road ahead. This will help you to see any hazards that might occur and allow you more time to react.

You are approaching a pelican crossing. The amber light is flashing. You must

- ⊙ give way to pedestrians who are crossing
- ⊙ encourage pedestrians to cross
- ⊙ not move until the green light appears
- ⊙ stop even if the crossing is clear

⊙ **give way to pedestrians who are crossing**

While the pedestrians are crossing don't encourage them to cross by waving or flashing your headlights: other road users may misunderstand your signal.

Don't harass them by creeping forward or revving your engine.

2.40
*Mark **one** answer*

'Tailgating' means

- ⊙ using the rear door of a hatchback car
- ⊙ reversing into a parking space
- ⊙ following another vehicle too closely
- ⊙ driving with rear fog lights on

⊙ **following another vehicle too closely**

'Tailgating' is used to describe this dangerous practice, often seen in fast-moving traffic and on motorways. Following the vehicle in front too closely is dangerous because it

- • restricts your view of the road ahead
- • leaves you no safety margin if the vehicle in front slows down or stops suddenly.

2.41
*Mark **one** answer*

You are following this lorry. You should keep well back from it to

- ⊙ give you a good view of the road ahead
- ⊙ stop following traffic from rushing through the junction
- ⊙ prevent traffic behind you from overtaking
- ⊙ allow you to hurry through the traffic lights if they change

⊙ **give you a good view of the road ahead**

By keeping well back you will increase your width of vision around the rear of the lorry. This will allow you to see further down the road and be prepared for any hazards.

2.42
*Mark **one** answer*

What should you use your horn for?

- ⊙ To alert others to your presence
- ⊙ To allow you right of way
- ⊙ To greet other road users
- ⊙ To signal your annoyance

⊙ **To alert others to your presence**

Your horn must not be used between 11.30 pm and 7.00 am in a built-up area or when you are stationary, unless a moving vehicle poses a danger. Its function is to alert other road users to your presence.

You are in a line of traffic. The driver behind you is following very closely. What action should you take?

- ⊙ Ignore the following driver and continue to travel within the speed limit
- ⊙ Slow down, gradually increasing the gap between you and the vehicle in front
- ⊙ Signal left and wave the following driver past
- ⊙ Move over to a position just left of the centre line of the road

⊙ **Slow down, gradually increasing the gap between you and the vehicle in front**

It can be worrying to see that the car behind is following you too closely. Give yourself a greater safety margin by easing back from the vehicle in front.

You should leave at least a two-second gap between your vehicle and the one in front when conditions are

- ⊙ wet
- ⊙ good
- ⊙ damp
- ⊙ foggy

⊙ **good**

In good, dry conditions an alert driver who's driving a vehicle with tyres and brakes in good condition needs to keep a distance of at least two seconds from the car in front.

The conditions are good and dry. You could use the 'two-second rule'

- ⊙ before restarting the engine after it has stalled
- ⊙ to keep a safe gap from the vehicle in front
- ⊙ before using the 'Mirror-Signal-Manoeuvre' routine
- ⊙ when emerging on wet roads

⊙ **to keep a safe gap from the vehicle in front**

To measure this, choose a fixed reference point such as a bridge, sign or tree. When the vehicle ahead passes the object, say to yourself 'Only a fool breaks the two-second rule.' If you reach the object before you finish saying this, you're TOO CLOSE.

2.46 *Mark one answer*

A bus has stopped at a bus stop ahead of you. Its right-hand indicator is flashing. You should

⊙ flash your headlights and slow down

⊙ slow down and give way if it is safe to do so

⊙ sound your horn and keep going

⊙ slow down and then sound your horn

⊙ **slow down and give way if it is safe to do so**

Give way to buses whenever you can do so safely, especially when they signal to pull away from bus stops. Look out for people leaving the bus and crossing the road.

2.47 *Mark one answer*

Diamond-shaped signs give instructions to

⊙ tram drivers

⊙ bus drivers

⊙ lorry drivers

⊙ taxi drivers

⊙ **tram drivers**

These signs only apply to trams. They are directed at tram drivers but you should know their meaning so that you're aware of the priorities and are able to anticipate the actions of the driver.

2.48 *Mark one answer*

On a road where trams operate, which of these vehicles will be most at risk from the tram rails?

⊙ Cars

⊙ Cycles

⊙ Buses

⊙ Lorries

⊙ **Cycles**

The narrow wheels of a bicycle can become stuck in the tram rails, causing the cyclist to stop suddenly, wobble or even lose balance altogether.

The tram lines are also slippery which could cause a cyclist to slide or fall off.

section three
SAFETY AND YOUR VEHICLE

This section covers:

- fault detection
- defects
- safety equipment
- emissions
- noise

3.1 Mark *one* answer

The main cause of brake fade is

⊙ the brakes overheating
⊙ air in the brake fluid
⊙ oil on the brakes
⊙ the brakes out of adjustment

⊙ **the brakes overheating**

If your vehicle is fitted with drum brakes they can get hot and lose efficiency. This happens when they're used continually, such as on a long, steep, downhill stretch of road. Using a lower gear will assist the braking and help prevent the vehicle gaining momentum.

3.2 Mark *one* answer

Your anti-lock brakes warning light stays on. You should

⊙ check the brake fluid level
⊙ check the footbrake free play
⊙ check that the handbrake is released
⊙ have the brakes checked immediately

⊙ **have the brakes checked immediately**

Only drive to a garage if it is safe to do so. Consult the vehicle handbook or garage before driving the vehicle.

3.3 Mark *one* answer

What will reduce the risk of neck injury resulting from a collision?

⊙ An air-sprung seat
⊙ Anti-lock brakes
⊙ A collapsible steering wheel
⊙ A properly adjusted head restraint

⊙ **A properly adjusted head restraint**

If you're involved in a collision, head restraints will reduce the risk of neck injury. They must be properly adjusted. Make sure they aren't positioned too low – in an accident this could cause damage to the neck.

3.4 Mark *one* answer

Car passengers MUST wear a seat belt if one is available, unless they are

⊙ under 14 years old
⊙ under 1.5 metres (5 feet) in height
⊙ sitting in the rear seat
⊙ exempt for medical reasons

⊙ **exempt for medical reasons**

If you have adult passengers it is their responsibility to wear a seat belt, but you should still remind them to put them on as they get in the car.

51

Your vehicle pulls to one side when braking. You should

- ⊙ change the tyres around
- ⊙ consult your garage as soon as possible
- ⊙ pump the pedal when braking
- ⊙ use your handbrake at the same time

⊙ **consult your garage as soon as possible**

The brakes on your vehicle must be effective and properly adjusted. If your vehicle pulls to one side when braking, take it to be checked by a qualified mechanic. Don't take risks.

While driving, this warning light on your dashboard comes on. It means

- ⊙ a fault in the braking system
- ⊙ the engine oil is low
- ⊙ a rear light has failed
- ⊙ your seat belt is not fastened

⊙ **a fault in the braking system**

Don't ignore this warning light. A fault in your braking system could have dangerous consequences.

The pictured vehicle is 'environmentally friendly' because it

- ⊙ reduces noise pollution
- ⊙ uses diesel fuel
- ⊙ uses electricity
- ⊙ uses unleaded fuel
- ⊙ reduces parking spaces
- ⊙ reduces town traffic

⊙ **reduces noise pollution**

⊙ **uses electricity**

⊙ **reduces town traffic**

Trams are powered by electricity and therefore do not emit exhaust fumes. They are also much quieter than petrol or diesel engines and can carry a large number of passengers.

3.8

You are carrying two 13 year old children and their parents in your car. Who is responsible for seeing that the children wear seat belts?

- ⊙ The childrens' parents
- ⊙ You, the driver
- ⊙ The front-seat passenger
- ⊙ The children

⊙ **You, the driver**

Seat belts save lives and reduce the risk of injury. If you are carrying passengers under 14 years of age, it's your responsibility as the driver to ensure that their seat belts are fastened or they are seated in an approved child restraint.

3.9

The most important reason for having a properly adjusted head restraint is to

- ⊙ make you more comfortable
- ⊙ help you to avoid neck injury
- ⊙ help you to relax
- ⊙ help you to maintain your driving position

⊙ **help you to avoid neck injury**

The restraint should be adjusted so that it gives maximum protection to the head and neck. This will help in the event of a rear-end collision.

3.10

You are driving the children of a friend home from school. They are both under 14 years old. Who is responsible for making sure they wear a seat belt?

- ⊙ An adult passenger
- ⊙ The children
- ⊙ You, the driver
- ⊙ Your friend

⊙ **You, the driver**

Child passengers should always be secured and safe. They should be encouraged to fasten their seat belts themselves from an early age so that it becomes a matter of routine. As the driver you must check that the seat belts are fastened securely; it's your responsibility.

3.11

Rear-facing baby seats should NEVER be used on a seat protected with

- ⊙ an airbag
- ⊙ seat belts
- ⊙ head restraints
- ⊙ seat covers

⊙ **an airbag**

NEVER fit a rear-facing baby seat in a seat protected by an airbag. In an accident the airbag would hit the baby seat with great force and the child would be at risk of receiving serious or possibly fatal injuries.

3.12
Mark one answer

Supertrams or Light Rapid Transit (LRT) systems are environmentally friendly because

- they use diesel power
- they use quieter roads
- they use electric power
- they do not operate during rush hour

⊙ **they use electric power**

This means that they do not emit toxic fumes, which add to city pollution problems. They are also a lot quieter and smoother to ride on.

3.13
Mark one answer

The purpose of a catalytic converter is to reduce

- fuel consumption
- the risk of fire
- toxic exhaust gases
- engine wear

⊙ **toxic exhaust gases**

Catalytic converters are designed to reduce toxic emissions by up to 90%. They work more efficiently when the engine has reached its normal working temperature.

3.14
Mark one answer

A roof rack fitted to your car will

- reduce fuel consumption
- improve the road handling
- make your car go faster
- increase fuel consumption

⊙ **increase fuel consumption**

If you are carrying anything on a roof rack, make sure that any cover is securely fitted and does not flap about while driving. Aerodynamically designed roof boxes are available which reduce wind resistance and in turn fuel consumption.

3.15
Mark one answer

When a roof rack is not in use it should be removed. Why is this?

- It will affect the suspension
- It is illegal
- It will affect your braking
- It will waste fuel

⊙ **It will waste fuel**

We are all responsible for the environment we live in. If each driver takes responsibility for conserving fuel, together it will make a difference.

3.16   Mark *one* answer

Catalytic converters are fitted to make the

⊙ engine produce more power
⊙ exhaust system easier to replace
⊙ engine run quietly
⊙ exhaust fumes cleaner

⊙ **exhaust fumes cleaner**

Harmful gases in the exhaust system pollute the atmosphere. These gases are reduced by up to 90% if a catalytic converter is fitted. Cleaner air benefits everyone, especially people who live or work near congested roads.

3.17   Mark *two* answers

How should you dispose of a used battery?

⊙ Take it to a local authority site
⊙ Put it in the dustbin
⊙ Break it up into pieces
⊙ Leave it on waste land
⊙ Take it to a garage
⊙ Burn it on a fire

⊙ **Take it to a local authority site**

⊙ **Take it to a garage**

Batteries contain acid which is hazardous and must be disposed of safely.

3.18   Mark *one* answer

What is most likely to cause high fuel consumption?

⊙ Poor steering control
⊙ Accelerating around bends
⊙ Staying in high gears
⊙ Harsh braking and accelerating

⊙ **Harsh braking and accelerating**

Accelerating and braking gently and smoothly will help to save fuel, reduce wear on your vehicle and is better for the environment.

3.19   Mark *one* answer

New petrol-engined cars must be fitted with catalytic converters. The reason for this is to

⊙ control exhaust noise levels
⊙ prolong the life of the exhaust system
⊙ allow the exhaust system to be recycled
⊙ reduce harmful exhaust emissions

⊙ **reduce harmful exhaust emissions**

We should all be concerned about the effect traffic has on our environment. Fumes from vehicles are polluting the air around us. Catalytic converters act like a filter, removing some of the toxic waste from exhaust gases.

Driving at 70 mph uses more fuel than driving at 50 mph by up to

- 10%
- 30%
- 75%
- 100%

30%

Your vehicle will be cheaper to run if you avoid heavy acceleration. The higher the engine revs, the more fuel you will use.

How can you, as a driver, help the environment?

- By reducing your speed
- By gentle acceleration
- By using leaded fuel
- By driving faster
- By harsh acceleration
- By servicing your vehicle properly

By reducing your speed

By gentle acceleration

By servicing your vehicle properly

Rapid acceleration and heavy braking lead to greater fuel consumption. They also increase wear and tear on your vehicle.

Having your vehicle regularly serviced means your engine will maintain its efficiency, produce cleaner emissions and lengthen its life.

Which THREE things can you, as a road user, do to help the environment?

- Cycle when possible
- Drive on under-inflated tyres
- Use the choke for as long as possible on a cold engine
- Have your vehicle properly tuned and serviced
- Watch the traffic and plan ahead
- Brake as late as possible without skidding

Cycle when possible

Have your vehicle properly tuned and serviced

Watch the traffic and plan ahead

Although the car is a convenient form of transport it can also cause damage to health and the environment, especially when used on short journeys. Before you travel consider other types of transport. Walking and cycling are better for your health and public transport can be quicker, more convenient and less stressful than driving.

3.23 *Mark **three** answers*

To help the environment, you can avoid wasting fuel by

- having your vehicle properly serviced
- making sure your tyres are correctly inflated
- not over-revving in the lower gears
- driving at higher speeds where possible
- keeping an empty roof rack properly fitted
- servicing your vehicle less regularly

◉ **having your vehicle properly serviced**

◉ **making sure your tyres are correctly inflated**

◉ **not over-revving in the lower gears**

If you don't have your vehicle serviced regularly, the engine will not burn all the fuel efficiently. This will cause excess gases to be discharged into the atmosphere.

3.24 *Mark **three** answers*

To reduce the volume of traffic on the roads you could

- use public transport more often
- share a car when possible
- walk or cycle on short journeys
- travel by car at all times
- use a car with a smaller engine
- drive in a bus lane

◉ **use public transport more often**

◉ **share a car when possible**

◉ **walk or cycle on short journeys**

Walking or cycling are good ways to get exercise. Using public transport also gives the opportunity for exercise if you walk to the railway station or bus stop. Leave the car at home whenever you can.

3.25 *Mark **three** answers*

Which THREE of the following are most likely to waste fuel?

- Reducing your speed
- Carrying unnecessary weight
- Using the wrong grade of fuel
- Under-inflated tyres
- Using different brands of fuel
- A fitted, empty roof rack

◉ **Carrying unnecessary weight**

◉ **Under-inflated tyres**

◉ **A fitted, empty roof rack**

Wasting fuel costs you, the driver, hard-earned cash. It also causes unnecessary pollution to the atmosphere.

Failing to carry out basic maintenance checks, such as tyre pressures, can affect the handling of your vehicle as well as increasing fuel consumption. It is also an offence for which you can be prosecuted.

57

To help protect the environment you
should NOT

⊙ remove your roof rack when unloaded

⊙ use your car for very short journeys

⊙ walk, cycle, or use public transport

⊙ empty the boot of unnecessary weight

⊙ **use your car for very
short journeys**

Try not to use your car as a matter of
routine. For shorter journeys, consider
walking or cycling instead – this is much
better for both you and the environment.

Your vehicle has a catalytic converter.
Its purpose is to reduce

⊙ exhaust noise

⊙ fuel consumption

⊙ exhaust emissions

⊙ engine noise

⊙ **exhaust emissions**

Catalytic converters reduce the harmful
gases given out by the engine. The gases
are changed by a chemical process as they
pass through a special filter.

You service your own vehicle. How should
you get rid of the old engine oil?

⊙ Take it to a local authority site

⊙ Pour it down a drain

⊙ Tip it into a hole in the ground

⊙ Put it into your dustbin

⊙ **Take it to a local
authority site**

It is illegal to pour engine oil down any
drain. Oil is a pollutant and harmful to
wildlife. Dispose of it safely at an authorised
site.

It is important to wear suitable shoes when
you are driving. Why is this?

⊙ To prevent wear on the pedals

⊙ To maintain control of the pedals

⊙ To enable you to adjust your seat

⊙ To enable you to walk for assistance
if you break down

⊙ **To maintain control of
the pedals**

When you're going to drive, ensure that
you're wearing suitable clothing.

Comfortable shoes will ensure that you
have proper control of the foot pedals.

3.30 *Mark **two** answers*

Which TWO of the following will improve fuel consumption?

⊙ Reducing your road speed
⊙ Planning well ahead
⊙ Late and harsh braking
⊙ Driving in lower gears
⊙ Short journeys with a cold engine
⊙ Rapid acceleration

⊙ **Reducing your road speed**

⊙ **Planning well ahead**

Harsh braking, constant gear changes and harsh acceleration increase fuel consumption. An engine uses less fuel when travelling at a constant low speed.

You need to look well ahead so you are able to anticipate hazards early. Easing off the accelerator and timing your approach at junctions, for example, could actually improve the fuel consumption of your vehicle.

3.31 *Mark **one** answer*

Why do MOT tests include a strict exhaust emission test?

⊙ To recover the cost of expensive garage equipment
⊙ To help protect the environment against pollution
⊙ To discover which fuel supplier is used the most
⊙ To make sure diesel and petrol engines emit the same fumes

⊙ **To help protect the environment against pollution**

Emission tests are carried out to ensure your vehicle's engine is operating efficiently. This ensures the pollution produced by the engine is kept to a minimum.

If your vehicle is not serviced regularly, it may fail the annual MOT test.

3.32 *Mark **two** answers*

A properly serviced vehicle will give

⊙ lower insurance premiums
⊙ you a refund on your road tax
⊙ better fuel economy
⊙ cleaner exhaust emissions

⊙ **better fuel economy**

⊙ **cleaner exhaust emissions**

When you purchase your vehicle, check at what intervals you should have it serviced. This can vary depending on model and manufacturer. Use the service manual and keep it up to date. The cost of a service may well be less than the cost of running a poorly maintained vehicle.

To reduce the damage your vehicle causes to the environment you should

- use narrow side streets
- avoid harsh acceleration
- brake in good time
- anticipate well ahead
- use busy routes

- **avoid harsh acceleration**
- **brake in good time**
- **anticipate well ahead**

By looking well ahead and recognising hazards early you can avoid last-minute harsh braking. Watch the traffic flow and look well ahead for potential hazards so you can control your speed accordingly. Avoid over-revving the engine and accelerating harshly as this increases wear to the engine and uses more fuel.

You must NOT sound your horn

- between 10 pm and 6 am in a built-up area
- at any time in a built-up area
- between 11.30 pm and 7 am in a built-up area
- between 11.30 pm and 6 am on any road

- **between 11.30 pm and 7 am in a built-up area**

Vehicles can be noisy. Every effort must be made to prevent excessive noise, especially in built-up areas at night. Don't

- rev the engine
- sound the horn

unnecessarily. It is illegal to sound your horn in a built-up area between 11.30 pm and 7 am, except when another vehicle poses a danger.

Driving with under-inflated tyres can affect

- engine temperature
- fuel consumption
- braking
- oil pressure

- **fuel consumption**
- **braking**

Keeping your vehicle's tyres correctly inflated is a legal requirement.

Driving with correctly inflated tyres will use less fuel and your vehicle will brake more safely.

3.36
*Mark **three** answers*

Motor vehicles can harm the environment. This has resulted in

- ⊙ air pollution
- ⊙ damage to buildings
- ⊙ less risk to health
- ⊙ improved public transport
- ⊙ less use of electrical vehicles
- ⊙ using up of natural resources

- ⊙ **air pollution**
- ⊙ **damage to buildings**
- ⊙ **using up of natural resources**

Exhaust emissions are harmful to health and this form of pollution, together with vibration from heavy traffic, causes damage to buildings.

Petrol and diesel fuels come from a finite and non-renewable source. Anything you can do to reduce the amount of these fuels that you use will help the environment.

3.37
*Mark **two** answers*

As a driver you can cause more damage to the environment by

- ⊙ choosing a fuel-efficient vehicle
- ⊙ making a lot of short journeys
- ⊙ driving in as high a gear as possible
- ⊙ accelerating as quickly as possible
- ⊙ having your vehicle regularly serviced

- ⊙ **making a lot of short journeys**
- ⊙ **accelerating as quickly as possible**

For short journeys it may be quicker to walk or cycle, which is far better for your health. Time spent stationary in traffic with the engine running is damaging to health, the environment and expensive in fuel costs.

3.38
*Mark **one** answer*

As a driver, you can help reduce pollution levels in town centres by

- ⊙ driving more quickly
- ⊙ over-revving in a low gear
- ⊙ walking or cycling
- ⊙ driving short journeys

- ⊙ **walking or cycling**

Using a vehicle for short journeys means the engine does not have time to reach its normal running temperature. When an engine is running below its normal running temperature it produces increased amounts of pollution.

Walking and cycling do not create pollution and have health benefits as well.

Mark **one** answer

When should you NOT use your horn in a built-up area?

- Between 8 pm and 8 am
- Between 9 pm and dawn
- Between dusk and 8 am
- Between 11.30 pm and 7 am

⊙ **Between 11.30 pm and 7 am**

Only sound your horn to prevent an accident. If you need to let someone know you are there, you could flash your headlights instead.

Mark **one** answer

'Red routes' in major cities have been introduced to

- raise the speed limits
- help the traffic flow
- provide better parking
- allow lorries to load more freely

⊙ **help the traffic flow**

Traffic jams today are often caused by the volume of traffic. However, inconsiderate parking can lead to the closure of an inside lane or traffic having to wait for oncoming vehicles. Driving slowly in traffic increases fuel consumption and causes a build-up of exhaust fumes.

Mark **one** answer

Road humps, chicanes, and narrowings are

- always at major road works
- used to increase traffic speed
- at toll-bridge approaches only
- traffic calming measures

⊙ **traffic calming measures**

Traffic calming measures help keep vehicle speeds low in sensitive areas.

A pedestrian is much more likely to survive an accident with a motor vehicle travelling at 20 mph than at 40 mph.

Mark **one** answer

On a vehicle, where would you find a catalytic converter?

- In the fuel tank
- In the air filter
- On the cooling system
- On the exhaust system

⊙ **On the exhaust system**

Although carbon dioxide is still produced, a catalytic converter reduces the toxic and polluting gases by up to 90%. Unleaded fuel must be used in vehicles fitted with a catalytic converter.

3.43

You enter a road where there are road humps. What should you do?

- ⊙ Maintain a reduced speed throughout
- ⊙ Accelerate quickly between each one
- ⊙ Always keep to the maximum legal speed
- ⊙ Drive slowly at school times only

⊙ **Maintain a reduced speed throughout**

The humps are there for a reason – to reduce the speed of the traffic. Don't accelerate harshly between them as this means you will only have to brake harshly to negotiate the next hump. Harsh braking and accelerating uses more fuel.

3.44

Which TWO are badly affected if the tyres are under-inflated?

- ⊙ Braking
- ⊙ Steering
- ⊙ Changing gear
- ⊙ Parking

⊙ **Braking**

⊙ **Steering**

Your tyres are your only contact with the road so it is very important to ensure that they are free from defects, have sufficient tread depth and are correctly inflated. Correct tyre pressures help reduce the risk of skidding and provide a safer and more comfortable drive or ride.

3.45

It is essential that tyre pressures are checked regularly. When should this be done?

- ⊙ After any lengthy journey
- ⊙ After travelling at high speed
- ⊙ When tyres are hot
- ⊙ When tyres are cold

⊙ **When tyres are cold**

When you check the tyre pressures do so when the tyres are cold. This will give you a more accurate reading. The heat generated from a long journey will raise the pressure inside the tyre.

3.46
Mark **one** answer

You will use more fuel if your tyres are

- under-inflated
- of different makes
- over-inflated
- new and hardly used

⊙ **under-inflated**

Check your tyre pressures frequently – normally once a week. If pressures are lower than those recommended by the manufacturer, there will be more 'rolling resistance'. The engine will have to work harder to overcome this, leading to increased fuel consumption.

3.47
Mark **two** answers

Excessive or uneven tyre wear can be caused by faults in the

- gearbox
- braking system
- suspension
- exhaust system

⊙ **braking system**

⊙ **suspension**

Uneven wear on your tyres can be caused by the condition of your vehicle. Having it serviced regularly will ensure that the brakes, steering and wheel alignment are maintained in good order.

3.48
Mark **one** answer

It is illegal to drive with tyres that

- have been bought second-hand
- have a large deep cut in the side wall
- are of different makes
- are of different tread patterns

⊙ **have a large deep cut in the side wall**

When checking your tyres for cuts and bulges in the side walls don't forget the inner walls (ie. those facing each other under the vehicle).

3.49
Mark **one** answer

The legal minimum depth of tread for car tyres over three quarters of the breadth is

- 1 mm
- 1.6 mm
- 2.5 mm
- 4 mm

⊙ **1.6 mm**

Tyres must have sufficient depth of tread to give them a good grip on the road surface. The legal minimum for cars is 1.6 mm.

This depth should be across the central three quarters of the breadth of the tyre and around the entire circumference.

3.50
*Mark **one** answer*

What can cause heavy steering?

- Driving on ice
- Badly worn brakes
- Over-inflated tyres
- Under-inflated tyres

⊙ **Under-inflated tyres**

If your tyres don't have enough air in them they'll drag against the surface of the road and this makes the steering feel heavy.

As well as steering, under-inflated tyres can affect

- braking
- cornering
- fuel consumption.

It is an offence to drive with tyres that are not properly inflated.

3.51
*Mark **one** answer*

When should you especially check the engine oil level?

- Before a long journey
- When the engine is hot
- Early in the morning
- Every 6000 miles

⊙ **Before a long journey**

During long journeys an engine can use more oil than on shorter trips. Insufficient oil is potentially dangerous: it can lead to excessive wear and expensive repairs.

Most cars have a dipstick to allow the oil level to be checked. If not, you should refer to the vehicle's handbook. Also make checks on

- fuel
- water
- tyres.

3.52
*Mark **three** answers*

Excessive or uneven tyre wear can be caused by faults in which THREE of the following?

- The gearbox
- The braking system
- The accelerator
- The exhaust system
- Wheel alignment
- The suspension

⊙ **The braking system**

⊙ **Wheel alignment**

⊙ **The suspension**

Regular servicing will help to detect faults at an early stage and this will avoid the risk of minor faults becoming serious or even dangerous.

The fluid level in your battery is low.
What should you top it up with?

⊙ Battery acid

⊙ Distilled water

⊙ Engine oil

⊙ Engine coolant

⊙ **Distilled water**

Some modern batteries are maintenance-free. Check your vehicle handbook and, if necessary, make sure that the plates in each battery cell are covered.

You have too much oil in your engine.
What could this cause?

⊙ Low oil pressure

⊙ Engine overheating

⊙ Chain wear

⊙ Oil leaks

⊙ **Oil leaks**

Too much oil in the engine will create excess pressure and could damage engine seals and cause oil leaks. Any excess oil should be drained off.

You are testing your suspension. You notice that your vehicle keeps bouncing when you press down on the front wing. What does this mean?

⊙ Worn tyres

⊙ Tyres under-inflated

⊙ Steering wheel not located centrally

⊙ Worn shock absorbers

⊙ **Worn shock absorbers**

If you find that your vehicle bounces as you drive around a corner or bend in the road, the shock absorbers might be worn. Press down on the front wing and if the vehicle continues to bounce, take it to be checked by a qualified mechanic.

You need to top up your battery. What level should you fill to?

⊙ The top of the battery

⊙ Half-way up the battery

⊙ Just below the cell plates

⊙ Just above the cell plates

⊙ **Just above the cell plates**

Top up the battery with distilled water and make sure each cell plate is covered.

3.57

*Mark **three** answers*

Which THREE does the law require you to keep in good condition?

- ⊙ Gears
- ⊙ Transmission
- ⊙ Headlights
- ⊙ Windscreen
- ⊙ Seat belts

⊙ **Headlights**

⊙ **Windscreen**

⊙ **Seat belts**

Also check the

- lights – get someone to help you check the brake lights
- indicators
- battery – this may be maintenance-free and not need topping up
- steering – check for 'play' in the steering
- oil
- water
- suspension.

Once you've moved off, check that the speedometer is working.

3.58

*Mark **one** answer*

Unbalanced wheels on a car may cause

- ⊙ the steering to pull to one side
- ⊙ the steering to vibrate
- ⊙ the brakes to fail
- ⊙ the tyres to deflate

⊙ **the steering to vibrate**

If your wheels are out of balance it will cause the steering to vibrate at certain speeds. It is not a fault that will rectify itself. You will have to take your vehicle to a garage or tyre fitting firm as this is specialist work.

3.59

*Mark **one** answer*

You have to leave valuables in your car. It would be safer to

- ⊙ put them in a carrier bag
- ⊙ park near a school entrance
- ⊙ lock thcm out of sight
- ⊙ park near a bus stop

⊙ **lock them out of sight**

If you have to leave valuables in your car, always lock them out of sight. If you can see them, so can a thief.

67

Which FOUR of these must be in good working order for your car to be roadworthy?

- The temperature gauge
- The speedometer
- The windscreen washers
- The windscreen wipers
- The oil warning light
- The horn

- **The speedometer**
- **The windscreen washers**
- **The windscreen wipers**
- **The horn**

You should also regularly check

- lights (you may need to get someone to help you with this)
- indicators
- battery electrolyte level (if necessary)
- steering
- oil
- water and other fluid levels
- suspension.

Turning the steering wheel while your car is stationary can cause damage to the

- gearbox
- engine
- brakes
- steering
- tyres

- **steering**
- **tyres**

Turning the steering wheel when the car is not moving can cause unnecessary wear to the tyres and steering mechanism. This is known as 'dry' steering.

How could you deter theft from your car when leaving it unattended?

- Leave valuables in a carrier bag
- Lock valuables out of sight
- Put valuables on the seats
- Leave valuables on the floor

- **Lock valuables out of sight**

If you can see valuables in your car so can a thief. If you can't take them with you lock them out of sight or you risk losing them, as well as having your car damaged.

3.63

Which of the following may help to deter a thief from stealing your car?

- ⊙ Always keeping the headlights on
- ⊙ Fitting reflective glass windows
- ⊙ Always keeping the interior light on
- ⊙ Etching the car number on the windows

⊙ **Etching the car number on the windows**

Having your car registration number etched on all your windows is a cheap and effective way to deter professional car thieves.

3.64

Which of the following should not be kept in your vehicle?

- ⊙ A first aid kit
- ⊙ A road atlas
- ⊙ The tax disc
- ⊙ The vehicle documents

⊙ **The vehicle documents**

Never leave the vehicles documents inside it. They would help a thief dispose of the vehicle more easily.

3.65

What should you do when leaving your vehicle?

- ⊙ Put valuable documents under the seats
- ⊙ Remove all valuables
- ⊙ Cover valuables with a blanket
- ⊙ Leave the interior light on

⊙ **Remove all valuables**

When leaving your vehicle unattended it is best to take valuables with you. If you can't, then lock them out of sight in the boot. If you can see valuables in your car, so can a thief.

3.66

Which of these is most likely to deter the theft of your vehicle?

- ⊙ An immobiliser
- ⊙ Tinted windows
- ⊙ Locking wheel nuts
- ⊙ A sun screen

⊙ **An immobiliser**

An immobiliser makes it more difficult for your vehicle to be driven off by a thief. It is a particular deterrent to opportunist thieves.

When parking and leaving your car
you should

⊙ park under a shady tree

⊙ remove the tax disc

⊙ park in a quiet road

⊙ engage the steering lock

⊙ **engage the steering lock**

When you leave your car always engage
the steering lock. This increases the
security of your vehicle, as the ignition key
is needed to release the steering lock.

When leaving your vehicle parked and
unattended you should

⊙ park near a busy junction

⊙ park in a housing estate

⊙ remove the key and lock it

⊙ leave the left indicator on

⊙ **remove the key and lock it**

An unlocked car is an open invitation to
thieves.

Leaving the keys in the ignition not only
makes your car easy to steal, it could also
invalidate your insurance.

When leaving your car unattended for
a few minutes you should

⊙ leave the engine running

⊙ switch the engine off but leave
the key in

⊙ lock it and remove the key

⊙ park near a traffic warden

⊙ **lock it and remove the key**

Always switch off the engine, remove the
key and lock your car, even if you are only
leaving it for a few minutes.

When parking and leaving your car for
a few minutes you should

⊙ leave it unlocked

⊙ lock it and remove the key

⊙ leave the hazard warning lights on

⊙ leave the interior light on

⊙ **lock it and remove the key**

Always remove the key and lock your car
even if you only leave it for a few minutes.

3.71

You are having difficulty finding a parking space in a busy town. You can see there is space on the zigzag lines of a zebra crossing. Can you park there?

- No, unless you stay with your car
- Yes, in order to drop off a passenger
- Yes, if you do not block people from crossing
- No, not in any circumstances

⊙ **No, not in any circumstances**

It's an offence to park there. You will be causing an obstruction by obscuring the view of both pedestrians and drivers.

3.72

You are parked on the road at night. Where must you use parking lights?

- Where there are continuous white lines in the middle of the road
- Where the speed limit exceeds 30 mph
- Where you are facing oncoming traffic
- Where you are near a bus stop

⊙ **Where the speed limit exceeds 30 mph**

When parking at night, park in the direction of the traffic. This will enable other road users to see the reflectors on the rear of your vehicle. Use your parking lights if the speed limit is over 30 mph.

3.73

Which of these, if allowed to get low, could cause an accident?

- Anti-freeze level
- Brake fluid level
- Battery water level
- Radiator coolant level

⊙ **Brake fluid level**

You should carry out frequent checks on all fluid levels but particularly brake fluid. As the friction material on your brake shoes or pads wears down, the brake fluid level will fall. If it falls below the minimum mark on the fluid reservoir, air could enter the hydraulic system and this would lead to loss of braking efficiency.

3.74

*Mark **one** answer*

When leaving your vehicle where should you park if possible?

- ⊙ Opposite a traffic island
- ⊙ In a secure car park
- ⊙ On a bend
- ⊙ At or near a taxi rank

⊙ **In a secure car park**

Whenever possible leave your car in a secure car park. This will help stop thieves.

3.75

*Mark **one** answer*

You are leaving your vehicle parked on a road. When may you leave the engine running?

- ⊙ If you will be parking for less than five minutes
- ⊙ If the battery is flat
- ⊙ When in a 20 mph zone
- ⊙ Never on any occasion

⊙ **Never on any occasion**

When you leave your vehicle parked on a road

- switch off the engine
- make sure that there aren't any valuables visible
- shut all the windows
- lock the vehicle
- set the alarm if it has one
- use an anti-theft device such as a steering wheel lock.

3.76

*Mark **three** answers*

In which THREE places would parking your vehicle cause danger or obstruction to other road users?

- ⊙ In front of a property entrance
- ⊙ At or near a bus stop
- ⊙ On your driveway
- ⊙ In a marked parking space
- ⊙ On the approach to a level crossing

⊙ **In front of a property entrance**

⊙ **At or near a bus stop**

⊙ **On the approach to a level crossing**

Don't park your vehicle where parking restrictions apply. Think carefully before you slow down and stop. Look at road markings and signs to ensure that you aren't parking illegally.

3.77 — *Mark **three** answers*

In which THREE places would parking cause an obstruction to others?

- Near the brow of a hill
- In a lay-by
- Where the kerb is raised
- Where the kerb has been lowered for wheelchairs
- At or near a bus stop

- ⊙ **Near the brow of a hill**

- ⊙ **Where the kerb has been lowered for wheelchairs**

- ⊙ **At or near a bus stop**

Think about the effect your parking will have on other road users. Don't forget that not all vehicles are the size of a car. Large vehicles will need more room to pass and might need more time too.

Parking out of the view of traffic, such as before the brow of a hill, causes unnecessary risks. Think before you park.

3.78 — *Mark **one** answer*

You are away from home and have to park your vehicle overnight. Where should you leave it?

- Opposite another parked vehicle
- In a quiet road
- Opposite a traffic island
- In a secure car park

- ⊙ **In a secure car park**

When leaving your vehicle unattended, use a secure car park whenever possible.

3.79 — *Mark **one** answer*

You are parking on a two-way road at night. The speed limit is 40 mph. You should park on the

- left with parking lights on
- left with no lights on
- right with parking lights on
- right with dipped headlights on

- ⊙ **left with parking lights on**

On a two-way road you may only park at night, without leaving the vehicle's lights on, if you're facing in the direction of the traffic flow, the road has a speed limit of 30 mph or less and you're at least 10 metres (32 feet) away from any junction.

3.80

3.80 *Mark **one** answer*

Wherever possible, which one of the following should you do when parking at night?

⊙ Park in a quiet car park

⊙ Park in a well-lit area

⊙ Park facing against the flow of traffic

⊙ Park next to a busy junction

⊙ **Park in a well-lit area**

If you are away from home, try to avoid leaving your vehicle unattended in poorly-lit areas. If possible park in a secure, well-lit car park.

3.81 *Mark **one** answer*

How can you lessen the risk of your vehicle being broken into at night?

⊙ Leave it in a well-lit area

⊙ Park in a quiet side road

⊙ Don't engage the steering lock

⊙ Park in a poorly-lit area

⊙ **Leave it in a well-lit area**

Having your vehicle broken into or stolen can be very distressing and inconvenient. Avoid leaving your vehicle unattended in poorly-lit areas.

3.82 *Mark **one** answer*

To help keep your car secure you could join a

⊙ vehicle breakdown organisation

⊙ vehicle watch scheme

⊙ advanced driver's scheme

⊙ car maintenance class

⊙ **vehicle watch scheme**

The vehicle watch scheme helps reduce the risk of having your car stolen. By displaying high visibility vehicle watch stickers in your car you are inviting the police to stop your vehicle if seen in use between midnight and 5 am.

3.83 *Mark **one** answer*

When leaving your car to help keep it secure you should

- ⊙ leave the hazard warning lights on
- ⊙ lock it and remove the key
- ⊙ park on a one-way street
- ⊙ park in a residential area

⊙ **lock it and remove the key**

To help keep your car secure when you leave it, you should always remove the key from the ignition, lock it and take the key with you. Don't make it easy for thieves.

3.84 *Mark **one** answer*

How can you reduce the chances of your car being broken into when leaving it unattended?

- ⊙ Take all valuables with you
- ⊙ Park near a taxi rank
- ⊙ Place any valuables on the floor
- ⊙ Park near a fire station

⊙ **Take all valuables with you**

When leaving your car take all valuables with you if you can, otherwise lock them out of sight.

3.85 *Mark **one** answer*

How can you help to prevent your car radio being stolen?

- ⊙ Park in an unlit area
- ⊙ Hide the radio with a blanket
- ⊙ Park near a busy junction
- ⊙ Install a security-coded radio

⊙ **Install a security-coded radio**

A security-coded radio can deter thieves as it is likely to be of little use when removed from the vehicle.

3.86
*Mark **one** answer*

You are parking your car. You have some valuables which you are unable to take with you. What should you do?

⊙ Park near a police station

⊙ Put them under the driver's seat

⊙ Lock them out of sight

⊙ Park in an unlit side road

⊙ **Lock them out of sight**

Your vehicle is like a shop window for thieves. Either remove all valuables or lock them out of sight.

3.87
*Mark **one** answer*

Before starting a journey it is wise to plan your route. How can you do this?

⊙ Look at a map

⊙ Contact your local garage

⊙ Look in your vehicle handbook

⊙ Check your vehicle registration document

⊙ **Look at the map**

Planning your journey before you set out can help to make it much easier, more pleasant and ease traffic congestion. Look at a map to help you to do this. You may need different scale maps depending on where and how far you're going. Printing or writing out the route can also help.

3.88   *NI EXEMPT*
*Mark **one** answer*

It can help to plan your route before starting a journey. You can do this by contacting

⊙ your local filling station

⊙ a motoring organisation

⊙ the Driver Vehicle Licensing Agency

⊙ your vehicle manufacturer

⊙ **a motoring organisation**

Most motoring organisations will give you a detailed plan of your trip showing directions and distance. Some will also include advice on rest and fuel stops. The Highways Agency website will also give you information on roadworks and accidents and gives expected delay times.

3.89   *Mark one answer*

How can you plan your route before starting a long journey?

- ⊙ Check your vehicle's workshop manual
- ⊙ Ask your local garage
- ⊙ Use a route planner on the internet
- ⊙ Consult your travel agents

⊙ **Use a route planner on the internet**

Various route planners are available on the internet. Most of them give you various options allowing you to choose the most direct, quickest or scenic route. They can also include rest and fuel stops and distances. Print them off and take them with you.

3.90   *Mark one answer*

Planning your route before setting out can be helpful. How can you do this?

- ⊙ Look in a motoring magazine
- ⊙ Only visit places you know
- ⊙ Try to travel at busy times
- ⊙ Print or write down the route

⊙ **Print or write down the route**

Print or write down your route before setting out. Some places are not well signed so using place names and road numbers may help you avoid problems en route. Try to get an idea of how far you're going before you leave. You can also use it to re-check the next stage at each rest stop.

3.91   *Mark one answer*

Why is it a good idea to plan your journey to avoid busy times?

- ⊙ You will have an easier journey
- ⊙ You will have a more stressful journey
- ⊙ Your journey time will be longer
- ⊙ It will cause more traffic congestion

⊙ **You will have an easier journey**

No one likes to spend time in traffic queues. Try to avoid busy times related to school or work travel. As well as moving vehicles you should also consider congestion caused by parked cars, buses and coaches around schools.

3.92 *Mark **one** answer*

Planning your journey to avoid busy times has a number of advantages. One of these is

⊙ your journey will take longer
⊙ you will have a more pleasant journey
⊙ you will cause more pollution
⊙ your stress level will be greater

⊙ **you will have a more pleasant journey**

Having a pleasant journey can have safety benefits. You will be less tired and stressed and this will allow you to concentrate more on your driving or riding.

3.93 *Mark **one** answer*

It is a good idea to plan your journey to avoid busy times. This is because

⊙ your vehicle will use more fuel
⊙ you will see less road works
⊙ it will help to ease congestion
⊙ you will travel a much shorter distance

⊙ **it will help to ease congestion**

Avoiding busy times means that you are not adding needlessly to traffic congestion. Other advantages are that you will use less fuel and feel less stressed.

3.94 *Mark **one** answer*

By avoiding busy times when travelling

⊙ you are more likely to be held up
⊙ your journey time will be longer
⊙ you will travel a much shorter distance
⊙ you are less likely to be delayed

⊙ **you are less likely to be delayed**

If possible, avoid the early morning and late afternoon and early evening 'rush hour'. Doing this should allow you to travel in a more relaxed frame of mind, concentrate solely on what you're doing and arrive at your destination feeling less stressed.

3.95 Mark *one* answer

It can help to plan your route before starting a journey. Why should you also plan an alternative route?

- ⊙ Your original route may be blocked
- ⊙ Your maps may have different scales
- ⊙ You may find you have to pay a congestion charge
- ⊙ Because you may get held up by a tractor

⊙ **Your original route may be blocked**

It can be frustrating and worrying to find your planned route is blocked by roadworks or diversions. If you have planned an alternative you will feel less stressed and able to concentrate fully on your driving or riding. If your original route is mostly on motorways it's a good idea to plan an alternative using non-motorway roads. Always carry a map with you just in case you need to refer to it.

3.96 Mark *one* answer

As well as planning your route before starting a journey, you should also plan an alternative route. Why is this?

- ⊙ To let another driver overtake
- ⊙ Your first route may be blocked
- ⊙ To avoid a railway level crossing
- ⊙ In case you have to avoid emergency vehicles

⊙ **Your first route may be blocked**

It's a good idea to plan an alternative route in case your original route is blocked for any reason. You're less likely to feel worried and stressed if you've got an alternative in mind. This will enable you to concentrate fully on your driving or riding. Always carry a map that covers the area you will travel in.

3.97 Mark *one* answer

Who of these will not have to pay Congestion Charges in London?

- ⊙ A van driver making deliveries
- ⊙ A rider of a two-wheeled vehicle
- ⊙ A car driver whose vehicle is more than 1000 cc
- ⊙ A driver who just wants to park in the area

⊙ **A rider of a two-wheeled vehicle**

Congestion charging schemes have been introduced in the London area. Some road users are exempt from the charges. These include two-wheeled vehicle users, residents living within the zone and disabled people who hold a blue badge. So they are not unfairly penalised, NHS staff, firefighters and patients too ill to use public transport, may be able to claim reimbursement.

3.98

You are making an appointment and will have to travel a long distance. You should

- ⊙ allow plenty of time for your journey
- ⊙ plan to go at busy times
- ⊙ avoid all national speed limit roads
- ⊙ prevent other drivers from overtaking

⊙ **allow plenty of time for your journey**

Always allow plenty of time for your journey in case of unforeseen problems. Anything can happen, punctures, breakdowns, road closures, diversions etc. You will feel less stressed and less inclined to take risks if you are not 'pushed for time'.

3.99

You will find that driving smoothly can

- ⊙ reduce journey times by about 15%
- ⊙ increase fuel consumption by about 15%
- ⊙ reduce fuel consumption by about 15%
- ⊙ increase journey times by about 15%

⊙ **reduce fuel consumption by about 15%**

Not only will you save fuel, by about 15%, by driving smoothly but you will also reduce the amount of wear and tear on your vehicle and reduce pollution. You will also feel more relaxed and have a more pleasant journey.

3.100

You can save fuel when conditions allow by

- ⊙ using lower gears as often as possible
- ⊙ accelerating sharply in each gear
- ⊙ using each gear in turn
- ⊙ missing out some gears

⊙ **missing out some gears**

Missing out intermediate gears when appropriate, reduces the amount of time spent accelerating and decelerating - the time when your vehicle uses most fuel.

3.101
*Mark **one** answer*

Congestion Charges apply in the London area. Who of these will NOT have to pay?

- ⊙ A person who lives in the area
- ⊙ A driver making deliveries
- ⊙ A person who is just driving through the area
- ⊙ A driver with no other passengers in the vehicle

⊙ **A person who lives in the area**

Congestion charging has been introduced in the London area to help traffic flow. Some road users are exempt from the charges. These include, residents living within the zone, riders of two-wheelers and disabled people who hold a blue badge. Other people may be able to claim reimbursement, for example NHS staff, firefighters and patients too ill to use public transport.

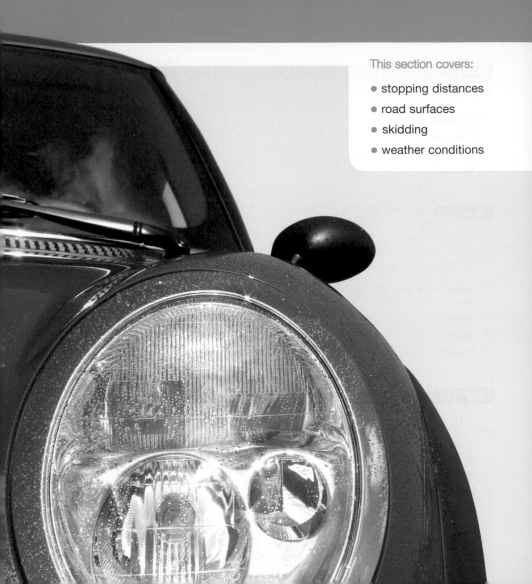

section four
SAFETY MARGINS

This section covers:

- stopping distances
- road surfaces
- skidding
- weather conditions

4.1 Mark **one** answer

What is the most common cause
of skidding?

⊙ Worn tyres

⊙ Driver error

⊙ Other vehicles

⊙ Pedestrians

⊙ **Driver error**

A skid happens when the driver changes
the speed or direction of their vehicle so
suddenly that the tyres can't keep their
grip on the road.

Remember that the risk of skidding on
wet or icy roads is much greater than in
dry conditions.

4.2 Mark **one** answer

Skidding is mainly caused by

⊙ the weather

⊙ the driver

⊙ the vehicle

⊙ the road

⊙ **the driver**

You should always consider the conditions
and drive accordingly.

4.3 Mark **one** answer

You are turning left on a slippery road.
The back of your vehicle slides to the right.
You should

⊙ brake firmly and not turn the steering
wheel

⊙ steer carefully to the left

⊙ steer carefully to the right

⊙ brake firmly and steer to the left

⊙ **steer carefully to the right**

This should stop the sliding and allow you
to regain control. Don't use the

• accelerator

• the brakes

• the clutch.

4.4 Mark **one** answer

Anti-lock brakes reduce the chances of
a skid occurring particularly when

⊙ driving down steep hills

⊙ braking during normal driving

⊙ braking in an emergency

⊙ driving on good road surfaces

⊙ **braking in an emergency**

The anti-lock braking system will operate
when the brakes have been applied
harshly.

It will reduce the chances of your car
skidding, but it is not a miracle cure
for careless driving.

Anti-lock brakes prevent wheels from locking. This means the tyres are less likely to

- ⊙ aquaplane
- ⊙ skid
- ⊙ puncture
- ⊙ wear

⊙ **skid**

If an anti-lock braking system (ABS) is fitted it activates automatically when maximum braking pressure is applied or when it senses that the wheels are about to lock. ABS prevents the wheels from locking so you can continue to steer the vehicle during braking.

ABS does not remove the need for good driving practices such as anticipation and correct speed for the conditions.

Vehicles fitted with anti-lock brakes

- ⊙ are impossible to skid
- ⊙ can be steered while you are braking
- ⊙ accelerate much faster
- ⊙ are not fitted with a handbrake

⊙ **can be steered while you are braking**

Preventing the wheels from locking means that the vehicle's steering and stability can be maintained, leading to safer stopping. However, you must ensure that the engine does not stall, as this could disable the power steering. When stopping in an emergency and braking harshly, depress the clutch pedal as you brake.

Driving a vehicle fitted with anti-lock brakes allows you to

- ⊙ brake harder because it is impossible to skid
- ⊙ drive at higher speeds
- ⊙ steer and brake at the same time
- ⊙ pay less attention to the road ahead

⊙ **steer and brake at the same time**

Anti-lock brakes will help you continue to steer when braking, but in poor weather conditions this will be less effective. You need to depress the clutch pedal to prevent the car stalling because the power steering system uses an engine-driven pump and will only operate when the engine is running.

4.8 Mark *two* answers

Anti-lock brakes may not work as effectively if the road surface is

⊙ dry
⊙ loose
⊙ wet
⊙ good
⊙ firm

⊙ **loose**

⊙ **wet**

Poor contact with the road surface could cause one or more of the tyres to lose grip on the road. This is more likely to happen when braking in poor weather conditions, when the road surface is uneven or has loose chippings.

4.9 Mark *one* answer

Anti-lock brakes are of most use when you are

⊙ braking gently
⊙ driving on worn tyres
⊙ braking excessively
⊙ driving normally

⊙ **braking excessively**

Anti-lock brakes will not be required when braking normally. Looking well down the road and anticipating possible hazards could prevent you having to brake late and harshly.

Knowing that you have anti-lock brakes is not an excuse to drive in a careless or reckless way.

4.10 Mark *one* answer

Anti-lock brakes can greatly assist with

⊙ a higher cruising speed
⊙ steering control when braking
⊙ control when accelerating
⊙ motorway driving

⊙ **steering control when braking**

If the wheels of your vehicle lock they will not grip the road and you will lose steering control. In good conditions the anti-lock system will prevent the wheels locking and allow you to retain steering control.

4.11 Mark *one* answer

How can you use your vehicle's engine as a brake?

⊙ By changing to a lower gear
⊙ By selecting reverse gear
⊙ By changing to a higher gear
⊙ By selecting neutral gear

⊙ **By changing to a lower gear**

When driving on downhill stretches of road selecting a lower gear gives increased engine braking. This will prevent excess use of the brakes, which become less effective if they overheat.

You are driving a vehicle fitted with anti-lock brakes. You need to stop in an emergency. You should apply the footbrake

- slowly and gently
- slowly but firmly
- rapidly and gently
- rapidly and firmly

⊙ **rapidly and firmly**

Look well ahead down the road as you drive and give yourself time and space to react safely to any hazards. You may have to stop in an emergency due to a misjudgement by another driver or a hazard arising suddenly such as a child running out into the road. In this case, if your vehicle has anti-lock brakes, you should apply the brakes immediately and keep them firmly applied until you stop.

Your vehicle has anti-lock brakes, but they may not always prevent skidding. This is most likely to happen when driving

- in foggy conditions
- on surface water
- on loose road surfaces
- on dry tarmac
- at night on unlit roads

⊙ **on surface water**

⊙ **on loose road surfaces**

In very wet weather water can build up between the tyre and the road surface. As a result your vehicle actually rides on a thin film of water and your tyres will not grip the road. Gravel or shingle surfaces also offer less grip and can present problems when braking. An anti-lock braking system may be ineffective in these conditions.

You are braking on a wet road. Your vehicle begins to skid. It does not have anti-lock brakes. What is the FIRST thing you should do?

- Quickly pull up the handbrake
- Release the footbrake fully
- Push harder on the brake pedal
- Gently use the accelerator

⊙ **Release the footbrake fully**

If the skid has been caused by braking too hard for the conditions, release the brake. This will allow the wheels to turn and so limit the skid.

Skids are much easier to get into than they are to get out of. Prevention is better than cure.

Stay alert to the road and weather conditions. Never drive so fast that you can't stop within the distance that you can see to be clear.

4.15   *Mark **one** answer*

Anti-lock brakes are most effective
when you

- keep pumping the foot brake to
  prevent skidding
- brake normally, but grip the steering
  wheel tightly
- brake promptly and firmly until
  you have slowed down
- apply the handbrake to reduce
  the stopping distance

- **brake promptly and firmly until
  you have slowed down**

Releasing the brake before you have
slowed right down will disable the system.
If you have to brake in an emergency
ensure that you keep your foot firmly
on the brake pedal until the vehicle
has stopped.

4.16   *Mark **one** answer*

Your car is fitted with anti-lock brakes. You
need to stop in an emergency. You should

- brake normally and avoid turning the
  steering wheel
- press the brake pedal promptly and
  firmly until you have stopped
- keep pushing and releasing the foot
  brake quickly to prevent skidding
- apply the handbrake to reduce
  the stopping distance

- **press the brake pedal
  promptly and firmly until
  you have stopped**

Keep pressure on the brake pedal until
you have come to a stop. The anti-lock
mechanism will activate automatically if
it senses the wheels are about to lock.

4.17   *Mark **one** answer*

When would an anti-lock braking system
start to work?

- After the parking brake has
  been applied
- Whenever pressure on the brake pedal
  is applied
- Just as the wheels are about to lock
- When the normal braking system fails to
  operate

- **Just as the wheels are
  about to lock**

The anti-lock braking system has sensors
that detect when the wheels are about
to lock. It releases the brakes momentarily
to allow the wheels to revolve and grip,
then automatically reapplies them.
This cycle is repeated several times a
second to maximise braking performance.

4.18

Your vehicle is fitted with anti-lock brakes. To stop quickly in an emergency you should

- ⊙ brake firmly and pump the brake pedal on and off
- ⊙ brake rapidly and firmly without releasing the brake pedal
- ⊙ brake gently and pump the brake pedal on and off
- ⊙ brake rapidly once and immediately release the brake pedal

⊙ **brake rapidly and firmly without releasing the brake pedal**

Once you have applied the brake keep your foot firmly on the pedal. Releasing the brake and reapplying it will disable the anti-lock brake system.

4.19

When approaching a right-hand bend you should keep well to the left. Why is this?

- ⊙ To improve your view of the road
- ⊙ To overcome the effect of the road's slope
- ⊙ To let faster traffic from behind overtake
- ⊙ To be positioned safely if you skid

⊙ **To improve your view of the road**

Doing this will give you an earlier view around the bend and enable you to see any hazards sooner.

It also reduces the risk of collision with an oncoming vehicle that may have drifted over the centre line while taking the bend.

4.20

'Coasting' the vehicle

- ⊙ improves the driver's control
- ⊙ makes steering easier
- ⊙ reduces the driver's control
- ⊙ uses more fuel

⊙ **reduces the driver's control**

'Coasting' is the term used when the clutch is held down or the gear lever is in neutral and the vehicle is allowed to freewheel. This reduces the driver's control of the vehicle. When you coast, the engine can't drive the wheels to pull you through a corner. Coasting also removes the assistance of engine braking that helps to slow the car.

4.21

Anti-lock brakes will take effect when

⊙ you do not brake quickly enough
⊙ maximum brake pressure has been applied
⊙ you have not seen a hazard ahead
⊙ speeding on slippery road surfaces

⊙ **maximum brake pressure has been applied**

If your car is fitted with anti-lock brakes they will take effect when you use them very firmly in an emergency. The system will only activate when it senses the wheels are about to lock.

4.22

Your overall stopping distance will be much longer when driving

⊙ in the rain
⊙ in fog
⊙ at night
⊙ in strong winds

⊙ **in the rain**

Extra care should be taken in wet weather as on wet roads your stopping distance could be double that in dry conditions.

4.23

You are on a good, dry road surface. Your vehicle has good brakes and tyres. What is the BRAKING distance at 50 mph?

⊙ 38 metres (125 feet)
⊙ 14 metres (46 feet)
⊙ 24 metres (79 feet)
⊙ 55 metres (180 feet)

⊙ **38 metres (125 feet)**

The braking distance does not include the thinking distance or reaction time.

4.24

You are on a long, downhill slope. What should you do to help control the speed of your vehicle?

⊙ Select neutral
⊙ Select a lower gear
⊙ Grip the handbrake firmly
⊙ Apply the parking brake gently

⊙ **Select a lower gear**

Selecting a low gear when travelling downhill will help you to control your speed. The engine will assist the brakes and help prevent your vehicle gathering speed.

You are about to go down a steep hill. To control the speed of your vehicle you should

⊙ select a high gear and use the brakes carefully

⊙ select a high gear and use the brakes firmly

⊙ select a low gear and use the brakes carefully

⊙ select a low gear and avoid using the brakes

⊙ **select a low gear and use the brakes carefully**

When travelling down a steep hill your vehicle will tend to increase speed. This will make it more difficult for you to stop. To maintain control and prevent the vehicle running away

• select a lower gear – the engine will then help to control your speed

• use the brakes carefully.

You should not overtake when

⊙ intending to turn left shortly afterwards

⊙ in a one-way street

⊙ approaching a junction

⊙ going up a long hill

⊙ the view ahead is blocked

⊙ **intending to turn left shortly afterwards**

⊙ **approaching a junction**

⊙ **the view ahead is blocked**

Before you overtake you should ask yourself if it's really necessary. Arriving safely is more important than taking unnecessary risks.

You are travelling at 50 mph on a good, dry road. What is your shortest overall stopping distance?

⊙ 36 metres (120 feet)

⊙ 53 metres (175 feet)

⊙ 75 metres (245 feet)

⊙ 96 metres (315 feet)

⊙ **53 metres (175 feet)**

Even in good conditions it will take you further than you think for your car to stop. Don't just learn the figures – understand how far the distance is.

4.28
*Mark **one** answer*

You are on a good, dry, road surface and your vehicle has good brakes and tyres. What is the typical overall stopping distance at 40 mph?

⊙ 23 metres (75 feet)
⊙ 36 metres (120 feet)
⊙ 53 metres (175 feet)
⊙ 96 metres (315 feet)

⊙ **36 metres (120 feet)**

Factors that affect how long it takes you to stop include

- how fast you're going
- whether you're travelling on the level, uphill or downhill
- the weather and road conditions
- the condition of tyres, brakes and suspension
- your reaction time.

4.29
*Mark **one** answer*

Your indicators may be difficult to see in bright sunlight. What should you do?

⊙ Put your indicator on earlier
⊙ Give an arm signal as well as using your indicator
⊙ Touch the brake several times to show the stop lights
⊙ Turn as quickly as you can

⊙ **Give an arm signal as well as using your indicator**

You should always ensure that other road users are aware of your intentions. If you think your indicator might not be seen, then give an arm signal as well.

4.30
*Mark **one** answer*

You have just gone through deep water. To dry off the brakes you should

⊙ accelerate and keep to a high speed for a short time
⊙ go slowly while gently applying the brakes
⊙ avoid using the brakes at all for a few miles
⊙ stop for at least an hour to allow them time to dry

⊙ **go slowly while gently applying the brakes**

Water on the brakes will act as a lubricant, causing them to work less efficiently. Using the brakes lightly as you go along will dry them out.

In good conditions, what is the typical stopping distance at 70 mph?

⊙ 53 metres (175 feet)
⊙ 60 metres (197 feet)
⊙ 73 metres (240 feet)
⊙ 96 metres (315 feet)

⊙ **96 metres (315 feet)**

Note that this is the typical stopping distance. It will take at least this distance to think, brake and stop in good conditions. In poor conditions it will take much longer.

What is the shortest overall stopping distance on a dry road at 60 mph?

⊙ 53 metres (175 feet)
⊙ 58 metres (190 feet)
⊙ 73 metres (240 feet)
⊙ 96 metres (315 feet)

⊙ **73 metres (240 feet)**

This distance is the equivalent of 18 car lengths. Try pacing out 73 metres and then look back. It's probably further than you think.

In windy conditions you need to take extra care when

⊙ using the brakes
⊙ making a hill start
⊙ turning into a narrow road
⊙ passing pedal cyclists

⊙ **passing pedal cyclists**

You should always give cyclists plenty of room when overtaking. When it's windy, a sudden gust could blow them off course.

Braking distances on ice can be

⊙ twice the normal distance
⊙ five times the normal distance
⊙ seven times the normal distance
⊙ ten times the normal distance

⊙ **ten times the normal distance**

In icy and snowy weather, your stopping distance will increase by up to ten times compared to good, dry conditions.

Take extra care when braking, accelerating and steering, to cut down the risk of skidding.

4.35
*Mark **one** answer*

You are on a fast, open road in good conditions. For safety, the distance between you and the vehicle in front should be

- ⊙ a two-second time gap
- ⊙ one car length
- ⊙ 2 metres (6 feet 6 inches)
- ⊙ two car lengths

⊙ **a two-second time gap**

One useful method of checking that you've allowed enough room between you and the vehicle in front is the two-second rule.

To check for a two-second time gap, choose a stationary object ahead, such as a bridge or road sign. When the car in front passes the object say 'Only a fool breaks the two-second rule'. If you reach the object before you finish saying it you're too close.

4.36
*Mark **one** answer*

You are following a vehicle at a safe distance on a wet road. Another driver overtakes you and pulls into the gap you have left. What should you do?

- ⊙ Flash your headlights as a warning
- ⊙ Try to overtake safely as soon as you can
- ⊙ Drop back to regain a safe distance
- ⊙ Stay close to the other vehicle until it moves on

⊙ **Drop back to regain a safe distance**

Wet weather will affect the time it takes for you to stop and can affect your control.

Your speed should allow you to stop safely and in good time. If another vehicle pulls into the gap you've left, ease back until you've regained your stopping distance.

4.37
*Mark **one** answer*

You are driving in a built-up area. You approach a speed hump. You should

- ⊙ move across to the left-hand side of the road
- ⊙ wait for any pedestrians to cross
- ⊙ slow your vehicle right down
- ⊙ stop and check both pavements

⊙ **slow your vehicle right down**

Many towns have speed humps to slow down traffic. They're often found where there are pedestrians, so

- • slow right down when driving over them
- • look out for pedestrians.

They might affect your steering and suspension if you drive too fast.

4.38 Mark **two** answers

You wish to park facing DOWNHILL. Which TWO of the following should you do?

- Turn the steering wheel towards the kerb
- Park close to the bumper of another car
- Park with two wheels on the kerb
- Put the handbrake on firmly
- Turn the steering wheel away from the kerb

- **Turn the steering wheel towards the kerb**

- **Put the handbrake on firmly**

Turning the wheels towards the kerb will allow it to act as a chock, preventing any forward movement of the vehicle.

4.39 Mark **one** answer

Freezing conditions will affect the distance it takes you to come to a stop. You should expect stopping distances to increase by up to

- two times
- three times
- five times
- ten times

- **ten times**

Your tyre grip is greatly reduced on icy roads and you need to allow up to ten times the normal stopping distance.

4.40 Mark **four** answers

Before starting a journey in freezing weather you should clear ice and snow from your vehicle's

- aerial
- windows
- bumper
- lights
- mirrors
- number plates

- **windows**

- **lights**

- **mirrors**

- **number plates**

Don't travel unless you really have to. Making unnecessary journeys will increase the risk of an accident.

It is important that you can see and be seen. Make sure any snow or ice is cleared from lights, mirrors, number plates and windows.

4.41   Mark **one** answer

You are trying to move off on snow.
You should use

⊙ the lowest gear you can
⊙ the highest gear you can
⊙ a high engine speed
⊙ the handbrake and footbrake together

⊙ **the highest gear you can**

If you attempt to move in a low gear,
such as first, the engine will rev at a higher
speed. This could cause the wheels to
spin and dig further into the snow.

4.42   Mark **one** answer

When driving in falling snow you should

⊙ brake firmly and quickly
⊙ be ready to steer sharply
⊙ use sidelights only
⊙ brake gently in plenty of time

⊙ **brake gently in plenty of time**

Braking on snow can be extremely
dangerous. Be gentle with both the
accelerator and brake to prevent
wheel-spin.

4.43   Mark **one** answer

The MAIN benefit of having four-wheel drive
is to improve

⊙ road holding
⊙ fuel consumption
⊙ stopping distances
⊙ passenger comfort

⊙ **road holding**

By driving all four wheels there is improved
grip, but this does not replace the skills
you need to drive safely. The extra grip
helps prevent skidding when travelling on
slippery or uneven roads.

4.44   Mark **one** answer

You are driving on an icy road. How can you
avoid wheelspin?

⊙ Drive at a slow speed in as high
    a gear as possible
⊙ Use the handbrake if the wheels start to
    slip
⊙ Brake gently and repeatedly
⊙ Drive in a low gear at all times

⊙ **Drive at a slow speed in as
    high a gear as possible**

If you're travelling on an icy road extra
caution will be required to avoid loss of
control. Keeping your speed down and
using the highest gear you can will reduce
the risk of the tyres losing their grip on this
slippery surface.

When driving in fog, which of the following are correct?

- ⊙ Use dipped headlights
- ⊙ Use headlights on full beam
- ⊙ Allow more time for your journey
- ⊙ Keep close to the car in front
- ⊙ Slow down
- ⊙ Use side lights only

- ⊙ **Use dipped headlights**

- ⊙ **Allow more time for your journey**

- ⊙ **Slow down**

Don't venture out if your journey is not necessary. If you have to travel and someone is expecting you at the other end, let them know that you will be taking longer than usual for your journey. This will stop them worrying if you don't turn up on time and will also take the pressure off you, so you don't feel you have to rush.

You are driving along a country road. You see this sign. AFTER dealing safely with the hazard you should always

- ⊙ check your tyre pressures
- ⊙ switch on your hazard warning lights
- ⊙ accelerate briskly
- ⊙ test your brakes

- ⊙ **test your brakes**

Deep water can affect your brakes, so you should check that they're working properly before you build up speed again. Before you do this, remember to check your mirrors and consider what's behind you.

You are driving in heavy rain. Your steering suddenly becomes very light. You should

- ⊙ steer towards the side of the road
- ⊙ apply gentle acceleration
- ⊙ brake firmly to reduce speed
- ⊙ ease off the accelerator

- ⊙ **ease off the accelerator**

If the steering becomes light in these conditions it is probably due to a film of water that has built up between your tyres and the road surface. Easing off the accelerator should allow your tyres to displace the film of water and they should then regain their grip on the road.

4.48 Mark *one* answer

How can you tell when you are driving over black ice?

- ⊙ It is easier to brake
- ⊙ The noise from your tyres sounds louder
- ⊙ You see black ice on the road
- ⊙ Your steering feels light

⊙ **Your steering feels light**

Sometimes you may not be able to see that the road is icy. Black ice makes a road look damp. The signs that you're travelling on black ice can be that

- the steering feels light
- the noise from your tyres suddenly goes quiet.

4.49 Mark *one* answer

The roads are icy. You should drive slowly

- ⊙ in the highest gear possible
- ⊙ in the lowest gear possible
- ⊙ with the handbrake partly on
- ⊙ with your left foot on the brake

⊙ **in the highest gear possible**

Driving at a slow speed in a high gear will reduce the likelihood of wheel spin and help your vehicle maintain the best possible grip.

4.50 Mark *one* answer

You are driving along a wet road. How can you tell if your vehicle is aquaplaning?

- ⊙ The engine will stall
- ⊙ The engine noise will increase
- ⊙ The steering will feel very heavy
- ⊙ The steering will feel very light

⊙ **The steering will feel very light**

If you drive at speed in very wet conditions your steering may suddenly feel 'light'. This means that the tyres have lifted off the surface of the road and are skating on the surface of the water. This is known as aquaplaning. Reduce speed by easing off the accelerator, but don't brake until your steering returns to normal.

4.51 Mark *one* answer

You have driven through a flood. What is the first thing you should do?

- ⊙ Stop and check the tyres
- ⊙ Stop and dry the brakes
- ⊙ Check your exhaust
- ⊙ Test your brakes

⊙ **Test your brakes**

Before you test you brakes you must check for following traffic. If it is safe, gently apply the brakes to clear any water that may be covering the braking surfaces.

4.52   *Mark **two** answers*

How can you tell if you are driving on ice?

- ⊙ The tyres make a rumbling noise
- ⊙ The tyres make hardly any noise
- ⊙ The steering becomes heavier
- ⊙ The steering becomes lighter

⊙ **The tyres make hardly any noise**

⊙ **The steering becomes lighter**

Drive extremely carefully when the roads are icy. When travelling on ice, tyres make virtually no noise and the steering feels unresponsive.

In icy conditions, avoid harsh braking, acceleration and steering.

4.53   *Mark **one** answer*

You are driving along a wet road. How can you tell if your vehicle's tyres are losing their grip on the surface?

- ⊙ The engine will stall
- ⊙ The steering will feel very heavy
- ⊙ The engine noise will increase
- ⊙ The steering will feel very light

⊙ **The steering will feel very light**

If you drive at speed in very wet conditions your steering may suddenly feel lighter than usual. This means that the tyres have lifted off the surface of the road and are skating on the surface of the water. This is known as aquaplaning. Reduce speed but don't brake until your steering returns to a normal feel.

4.54   *Mark **two** answers*

You are driving in freezing conditions. What should you do when approaching a sharp bend?

- ⊙ Slow down before you reach the bend
- ⊙ Gently apply your handbrake
- ⊙ Firmly use your footbrake
- ⊙ Coast into the bend
- ⊙ Avoid sudden steering movements

⊙ **Slow down before you reach the bend**

⊙ **Avoid sudden steering movements**

Harsh use of the accelerator, brakes or steering are likely to lead to skidding, especially on slippery surfaces. Avoid steering and braking at the same time.

In icy conditions it's very important that you constantly assess what's ahead, so that you can take appropriate action in plenty of time.

4.55   Mark **two** answers

In very hot weather the road surface can become soft. Which TWO of the following will be most affected?

⊙ The suspension

⊙ The grip of the tyres

⊙ The braking

⊙ The exhaust

⊙ **The grip of the tyres**

⊙ **The braking**

Only a small part of your tyres is in contact with the road. This is why you must consider the surface you're travelling on, and alter your speed to suit the road conditions.

4.56   Mark **one** answer

Where are you most likely to be affected by a side wind?

⊙ On a narrow country lane

⊙ On an open stretch of road

⊙ On a busy stretch of road

⊙ On a long, straight road

⊙ **On an open stretch of road**

In windy conditions, care must be taken on exposed roads. A strong gust of wind can blow you off course. Watch out for other road users who are particularly likely to be affected, such as

• cyclists

• motorcyclists

• high-sided lorries

• vehicles towing trailers.

4.57   Mark **one** answer

You are on a wet motorway with surface spray. You should use

⊙ hazard flashers

⊙ dipped headlights

⊙ rear fog lights

⊙ sidelights

⊙ **dipped headlights**

When surface spray reduces visibility switch on your dipped headlights. This will help other road users to see you.

section five
HAZARD AWARENESS

This section covers:

- anticipation
- attention
- speed and distance
- reaction time
- alchohol and drugs
- tiredness

5.1
*Mark **one** answer*

Why must you take extra care when turning right at this junction?

- ⊙ Road surface is poor
- ⊙ Footpaths are narrow
- ⊙ Road markings are faint
- ⊙ There is reduced visibility

⊙ **There is reduced visibility**

You may have to pull forward slowly until you can see up and down the road. Be aware that the traffic approaching the junction can't see you either. If you don't know that it's clear, don't go.

5.2
*Mark **one** answer*

When approaching this bridge you should give way to

- ⊙ bicycles
- ⊙ buses
- ⊙ motorcycles
- ⊙ cars

⊙ **buses**

A double-deck bus or high-sided lorry will have to take up a position in the centre of the road so that it can clear the bridge. There is normally a sign to indicate this.

Look well down the road, through the bridge and be aware you may have to stop and give way to an oncoming large vehicle.

5.3
*Mark **one** answer*

What type of vehicle could you expect to meet in the middle of the road?

- ⊙ Lorry
- ⊙ Bicycle
- ⊙ Car
- ⊙ Motorcycle

⊙ **Lorry**

The highest point of the bridge is in the centre so a large vehicle might have to move to the centre of the road to allow it enough room to pass under the bridge.

At this blind junction you must stop

⊙ behind the line, then edge forward to see clearly

⊙ beyond the line at a point where you can see clearly

⊙ only if there is traffic on the main road

⊙ only if you are turning to the right

⊙ **behind the line, then edge forward to see clearly**

The 'stop' sign has been put here because there is a poor view into the main road. You must stop because it will not be possible to assess the situation on the move, however slowly you are travelling.

Why should the junction on the left be kept clear?

⊙ To allow vehicles to enter and emerge

⊙ To allow the bus to reverse

⊙ To allow vehicles to make a 'U' turn

⊙ To allow vehicles to park

⊙ **To allow vehicles to enter and emerge**

You should always try to keep junctions clear. If you are in queuing traffic make sure that when you stop you leave enough space for traffic to flow in and out of the junction.

When driving a car fitted with automatic transmission what would you use 'kick down' for?

⊙ Cruise control

⊙ Quick acceleration

⊙ Slow braking

⊙ Fuel economy

⊙ **Quick acceleration**

'Kick down' selects a lower gear, enabling the vehicle to accelerate faster.

5.7

You should reduce your speed when driving along this road because

- ⊙ there is a staggered junction ahead
- ⊙ there is a low bridge ahead
- ⊙ there is a change in the road surface
- ⊙ the road ahead narrows

⊙ **there is a staggered junction ahead**

Traffic could be turning off to the left or right ahead of you.

Traffic turning left will be slowing down before the junction and any turning right may have to stop to allow oncoming traffic to clear. Be prepared for this as you might have to slow down or stop behind them.

5.8

You are driving at 60 mph. As you approach this hazard you should

- ⊙ maintain your speed
- ⊙ reduce your speed
- ⊙ take the next right turn
- ⊙ take the next left turn

⊙ **reduce your speed**

There could be stationary traffic ahead, waiting to turn right. Other traffic could be emerging and it may take time to gather speed.

5.9

You are planning a long journey. Do you need to plan rest stops?

- ⊙ Yes, you should plan to stop every half an hour
- ⊙ Yes, regular stops help concentration
- ⊙ No, you will be less tired if you get there as soon as possible
- ⊙ No, only fuel stops will be needed

⊙ **Yes, regular stops help concentration**

Try to plan your journey so that you can take rest stops. It's recommended that you take a break of at least 15 minutes after every two hours of driving. This should help to maintain your concentration.

What should you do as you approach this overhead bridge?

- ⊙ Move out to the centre of the road before going through
- ⊙ Find another route, this is only for high vehicles
- ⊙ Be prepared to give way to large vehicles in the middle of the road
- ⊙ Move across to the right hand side before going through

⊙ **Be prepared to give way to large vehicles in the middle of the road**

Oncoming large vehicles may need to move to the middle of the road so that they can pass safely under the bridge. There will not be enough room for you to continue and you should be ready to stop and wait.

What advice should you give to a driver who has had a few alcoholic drinks at a party?

- ⊙ Have a strong cup of coffee and then drive home
- ⊙ Drive home carefully and slowly
- ⊙ Go home by public transport
- ⊙ Wait a short while and then drive home

⊙ **Go home by public transport**

Drinking black coffee or waiting a few hours won't make any difference. Alcohol takes time to leave the body.

A driver who has been drinking should go home by public transport or taxi. They might even be unfit to drive the following morning.

You have been taking medicine for a few days which made you feel drowsy. Today you feel better but still need to take the medicine. You should only drive

- ⊙ if your journey is necessary
- ⊙ at night on quiet roads
- ⊙ if someone goes with you
- ⊙ after checking with your doctor

⊙ **after checking with your doctor**

Take care – it's not worth taking risks. Always check with your doctor to be really sure. You may not feel drowsy now, but the medicine could have an effect on you later in the day.

5.13   *Mark one answer*

You are following a slower-moving vehicle on a narrow country road. There is a junction just ahead on the right. What should you do?

⊙ Overtake after checking your mirrors and signalling

⊙ Stay behind until you are past the junction

⊙ Accelerate quickly to pass before the junction

⊙ Slow down and prepare to overtake on the left

⊙ **Stay behind until you are past the junction**

You should never overtake as you approach a junction. If a vehicle emerged from the junction while you were overtaking, a dangerous situation could develop very quickly.

5.14   *Mark two answers*

When approaching this hazard why should you slow down?

⊙ Because of the bend

⊙ Because it's hard to see to the right

⊙ Because of approaching traffic

⊙ Because of animals crossing

⊙ Because of the level crossing

⊙ **Because of the bend**

⊙ **Because of the level crossing**

There are two hazards clearly signed in this picture. You should be preparing for the bend by slowing down and selecting the correct gear. You might also have to stop at the level crossing, so be alert and be prepared to stop if necessary.

5.15   *Mark one answer*

Some two-way roads are divided into three lanes. Why are these particularly dangerous?

⊙ Traffic in both directions can use the middle lane to overtake

⊙ Traffic can travel faster in poor weather conditions

⊙ Traffic can overtake on the left

⊙ Traffic uses the middle lane for emergencies only

⊙ **Traffic in both directions can use the middle lane to overtake**

If you intend to overtake you must consider that approaching traffic could be planning the same manoeuvre. When you have considered the situation and have decided it is safe, indicate your intentions early. This will show the approaching traffic that you intend to pull out.

You want to turn left at this junction. The view of the main road is restricted. What should you do?

⊙ Stay well back and wait to see if something comes

⊙ Build up your speed so that you can emerge quickly

⊙ Stop and apply the handbrake even if the road is clear

⊙ Approach slowly and edge out until you can see more clearly

⊙ **Approach slowly and edge out until you can see more clearly**

You should slow right down, and stop if necessary, at any junction where the view is restricted. Edge forward until you can see properly. Only then can you decide if it is safe to go.

A driver does something that upsets you. You should

⊙ try not to react

⊙ let them know how you feel

⊙ flash your headlights several times

⊙ sound your horn

⊙ **try not to react**

There are occasions when other road users make a misjudgement or a mistake. If this happens try not to let it annoy you. Don't react by showing anger. Sounding your horn, flashing your headlights or shouting won't help the situation. Good anticipation will help to prevent these incidents becoming accidents.

You start to feel tired while driving. What should you do?

⊙ Increase your speed slightly

⊙ Decrease your speed slightly

⊙ Find a less busy route

⊙ Pull over at a safe place to rest

⊙ **Pull over at a safe place to rest**

If you start to feel tired, stop at a safe place for a rest break.

Every year many fatal accidents are caused by drivers falling asleep at the wheel.

5.19

After passing your driving test, you suffer from ill health. This affects your driving. You MUST

⊙ inform your local police station

⊙ get on as best you can

⊙ not inform anyone as you hold a full licence

⊙ inform the licensing authority

⊙ **inform the licensing authority**

The licensing authority won't automatically take away your licence without investigation. For advice, contact the Driver and Vehicle Licensing Agency (or DVNI in Northern Ireland).

5.20

To avoid an accident when entering a contraflow system, you should

⊙ reduce speed in good time

⊙ switch lanes any time to make progress

⊙ choose an appropriate lane early

⊙ keep the correct separation distance

⊙ increase speed to pass through quickly

⊙ follow other motorists closely to avoid long queues

⊙ **reduce speed in good time**

⊙ **choose an appropriate lane early**

⊙ **keep the correct separation distance**

In a contraflow system you will be travelling close to oncoming traffic and sometimes in narrow lanes. You should

• obey the temporary signs governing speed limits

• get into the correct lane in good time

• keep a safe separation distance from the vehicle ahead.

5.21

You have been convicted of driving whilst unfit through drink or drugs. You will find this is likely to cause the cost of one of the following to rise considerably. Which one?

⊙ Road fund licence

⊙ Insurance premiums

⊙ Vehicle test certificate

⊙ Driving licence

⊙ **Insurance premiums**

You have shown that you are a risk to yourself and others on the road. For this reason insurance companies may charge you a higher premium.

5.22

Mark **three** answers

Driving long distances can be tiring. You can prevent this by

- stopping every so often for a walk
- opening a window for some fresh air
- ensuring plenty of refreshment breaks
- completing the journey without stopping
- eating a large meal before driving

⊙ **stopping every so often for a walk**

⊙ **opening a window for some fresh air**

⊙ **ensuring plenty of refreshment breaks**

Long-distance driving can be boring. This, coupled with a stuffy, warm vehicle, can make you feel tired. Make sure you take rest breaks to keep yourself awake and alert.

5.23

Mark **two** answers

During periods of illness your ability to drive may be impaired. You MUST

- see your doctor each time before you drive
- only take smaller doses of any medicines
- be medically fit to drive
- not drive after taking certain medicines
- take all your medicines with you when you drive

⊙ **be medically fit to drive**

⊙ **not drive after taking certain medicines**

Only drive if you are fit to do so.

Some medication can affect your concentration, your ability to stay awake and your judgement when dealing with hazards. Driving whilst taking such medication is highly dangerous.

5.24

Mark **two** answers

You feel drowsy when driving. You should

- stop and rest as soon as possible
- turn the heater up to keep you warm and comfortable
- make sure you have a good supply of fresh air
- continue with your journey but drive more slowly
- close the car windows to help you concentrate

⊙ **stop and rest as soon as possible**

⊙ **make sure you have a good supply of fresh air**

You will be putting other road users at risk if you continue to drive when drowsy. Pull over and stop in a safe place. If you are driving a long distance, think about finding some accommodation so you can get some sleep before continuing your journey.

5.25 · Mark **two** answers

You are driving along a motorway and become tired. You should

- ⊙ stop at the next service area and rest
- ⊙ leave the motorway at the next exit and rest
- ⊙ increase your speed and turn up the radio volume
- ⊙ close all your windows and set heating to warm
- ⊙ pull up on the hard shoulder and change drivers

⊙ **stop at the next service area and rest**

⊙ **leave the motorway at the next exit and rest**

If you have planned your journey properly, to include rest stops, you should arrive at your destination in good time.

5.26 · Mark **one** answer

You are taking drugs that are likely to affect your driving. What should you do?

- ⊙ Seek medical advice before driving
- ⊙ Limit your driving to essential journeys
- ⊙ Only drive if accompanied by a full licence-holder
- ⊙ Drive only for short distances

⊙ **Seek medical advice before driving**

Check with your doctor or pharmacist if you think that the drugs you're taking are likely to make you feel drowsy or impair your judgement.

5.27 · Mark **one** answer

You are about to drive home. You feel very tired and have a severe headache. You should

- ⊙ wait until you are fit and well before driving
- ⊙ drive home, but take a tablet for headaches
- ⊙ drive home if you can stay awake for the journey
- ⊙ wait for a short time, then drive home slowly

⊙ **wait until you are fit and well before driving**

All your concentration should be on your driving. Any pain you feel will distract you and you should avoid driving when drowsy. The safest course of action is to wait until you have rested and feel better.

If you are feeling tired it is best to stop as soon as you can. Until then you should

- ⊙ increase your speed to find a stopping place quickly
- ⊙ ensure a supply of fresh air
- ⊙ gently tap the steering wheel
- ⊙ keep changing speed to improve concentration

⊙ **ensure a supply of fresh air**

If you're travelling on a long journey, plan your route before you leave. This will help you to

- be decisive at intersections and junctions
- plan your rest stops
- know approximately how long the journey will take.

Make sure that the vehicle you're travelling in is well-ventilated. A warm, stuffy atmosphere can make you drowsy, which will impair your judgement and concentration.

Which THREE result from drinking alcohol?

- ⊙ Less control
- ⊙ A false sense of confidence
- ⊙ Faster reactions
- ⊙ Poor judgement of speed
- ⊙ Greater awareness of danger

⊙ **Less control**

⊙ **A false sense of confidence**

⊙ **Poor judgement of speed**

You must understand the dangers of mixing alcohol with driving. Alcohol will severely reduce your ability to drive safely. Just one drink could put you over the limit. Don't risk people's lives - don't drink and drive.

You are about to return home from holiday when you become ill. A doctor prescribes drugs which are likely to affect your driving. You should

- ⊙ drive only if someone is with you
- ⊙ avoid driving on motorways
- ⊙ not drive yourself
- ⊙ never drive at more than 30 mph

⊙ **not drive yourself**

Find another way to get home even if this proves to be very inconvenient. You must not put other road users, your passengers or yourself at risk.

5.31 Mark **one** answer

You go to a social event and need to drive a short time after. What precaution should you take?

- ⊙ Avoid drinking alcohol on an empty stomach
- ⊙ Drink plenty of coffee after drinking alcohol
- ⊙ Avoid drinking alcohol completely
- ⊙ Drink plenty of milk before drinking alcohol

⊙ **Avoid drinking alcohol completely**

This is always going to be the safest option. Just one drink could put you over the limit and dangerously impair your judgement and reactions.

5.32 Mark **one** answer

You take some cough medicine given to you by a friend. What should you do before driving?

- ⊙ Ask your friend if taking the medicine affected their driving
- ⊙ Drink some strong coffee one hour before driving
- ⊙ Check the label to see if the medicine will affect your driving
- ⊙ Drive a short distance to see if the medicine is affecting your driving

⊙ **Check the label to see if the medicine will affect your driving**

Never drive if you have taken drugs, without first checking what the side effects might be. They might affect your judgement and perception, and therefore endanger lives.

5.33 Mark **three** answers

Which THREE are likely to make you lose concentration while driving?

- ⊙ Looking at road maps
- ⊙ Listening to loud music
- ⊙ Using your windscreen washers
- ⊙ Looking in your wing mirror
- ⊙ Using a mobile phone

⊙ **Looking at road maps**

⊙ **Listening to loud music**

⊙ **Using a mobile phone**

Looking at road maps while driving is very dangerous. If you aren't sure of your route stop in a safe place and check the map. You must not allow anything to take your attention away from the road.

If you need to use a mobile phone, stop in a safe place before doing so.

5.34

Mark *one* answer

You have been involved in an argument before starting your journey. This has made you feel angry. You should

- ☉ start to drive, but open a window
- ☉ drive slower than normal and turn your radio on
- ☉ have an alcoholic drink to help you relax before driving
- ☉ calm down before you start to drive

☉ **calm down before you start to drive**

If you are feeling upset or angry you should wait until you have calmed down before setting out on a journey.

5.35

Mark *one* answer

You are driving towards this left-hand bend. What dangers should you be aware of?

- ☉ A vehicle overtaking you
- ☉ No white lines in the centre of the road
- ☉ No sign to warn you of the bend
- ☉ Pedestrians walking towards you

☉ **Pedestrians walking towards you**

Pedestrians walking on a road with no pavement should walk against the direction of the traffic.

You can't see around this bend: there may be hidden dangers. Always keep this in mind so you give yourself time to react if a hazard does arise.

5.36

Mark *one* answer

You are about to drive home. You cannot find the glasses you need to wear. You should

- ☉ drive home slowly, keeping to quiet roads
- ☉ borrow a friend's glasses and use those
- ☉ drive home at night, so that the lights will help you
- ☉ find a way of getting home without driving

☉ **find a way of getting home without driving**

Don't be tempted to drive if you've lost or forgotten your glasses. You must be able to see clearly when driving.

5.37

*Mark **one** answer*

You are invited to a pub lunch. You know that you will have to drive in the evening. What is your best course of action?

- ⊙ Avoid mixing your alcoholic drinks
- ⊙ Not drink any alcohol at all
- ⊙ Have some milk before drinking alcohol
- ⊙ Eat a hot meal with your alcoholic drinks

⊙ **Not drink any alcohol at all**

Alcohol will stay in the body for several hours and may make you unfit to drive later in the day. Drinking during the day will also affect your performance at work or study.

5.38

*Mark **three** answers*

Which THREE of these are likely effects of drinking alcohol?

- ⊙ Reduced co-ordination
- ⊙ Increased confidence
- ⊙ Poor judgement
- ⊙ Increased concentration
- ⊙ Faster reactions
- ⊙ Colour blindness

⊙ **Reduced co-ordination**

⊙ **Increased confidence**

⊙ **Poor judgement**

Alcohol can increase confidence to a point where a driver's behaviour might become 'out of character'. Someone who normally behaves sensibly suddenly takes risks and enjoys it. Never let yourself or your friends get into this situation.

5.39

*Mark **three** answers*

Drinking any amount of alcohol is likely to

- ⊙ slow down your reactions to hazards
- ⊙ increase the speed of your reactions
- ⊙ worsen your judgement of speed
- ⊙ improve your awareness of danger
- ⊙ give a false sense of confidence

⊙ **slow down your reactions to hazards**

⊙ **worsen your judgement of speed**

⊙ **give a false sense of confidence**

If you are going to drive it's always the safest option not to drink at all. Don't be tempted - it's not worth it.

What THREE things should the driver of the grey car (arrowed) be especially aware of?

- ⊙ Pedestrians stepping out between cars
- ⊙ Other cars behind the grey car
- ⊙ Doors opening on parked cars
- ⊙ The bumpy road surface
- ⊙ Cars leaving parking spaces
- ⊙ Empty parking spaces

- ⊙ **Pedestrians stepping out between cars**

- ⊙ **Doors opening on parked cars**

- ⊙ **Cars leaving parking spaces**

You need to be aware that other road users may not have seen you. Always be on the lookout for hazards that may develop suddenly and need you to take avoiding action.

Which TWO things would help to keep you alert during a long journey?

- ⊙ Finishing your journey as fast as you can
- ⊙ Keeping off the motorways and using country roads
- ⊙ Making sure that you get plenty of fresh air
- ⊙ Making regular stops for refreshments

- ⊙ **Making sure that you get plenty of fresh air**

- ⊙ **Making regular stops for refreshments**

Make sure that the vehicle you're driving is well ventilated. A warm, stuffy atmosphere will make you feel drowsy. Open a window and turn down the heating.

You find that you need glasses to read vehicle number plates at the required distance. When MUST you wear them?

- ⊙ Only in bad weather conditions
- ⊙ At all times when driving
- ⊙ Only when you think it necessary
- ⊙ Only in bad light or at night time

- ⊙ **At all times when driving**

Have your eyesight tested before you start your practical training. Then, throughout your driving life, have checks periodically to ensure that your eyes haven't deteriorated.

5.43 *Mark one answer*

You are on a motorway. You feel tired.
You should

⊙ carry on but go slowly

⊙ leave the motorway at the next exit

⊙ complete your journey as quickly
as possible

⊙ stop on the hard shoulder

⊙ **leave the motorway at
the next exit**

If you do feel tired and there's no service
station for many miles, leave the motorway
at the next exit. Find a road off the
motorway where you can pull up and
stop safely.

5.44 *Mark one answer*

Which of the following types of glasses
should NOT be worn when driving at night?

⊙ Half-moon

⊙ Round

⊙ Bi-focal

⊙ Tinted

⊙ **Tinted**

If you are driving at night or in poor visibility,
tinted lenses will reduce the efficiency of
your vision by reducing
the amount of available light reaching
your eyes.

5.45 *Mark one answer*

How does alcohol affect you?

⊙ It speeds up your reactions

⊙ It increases your awareness

⊙ It improves your co-ordination

⊙ It reduces your concentration

⊙ **It reduces your concentration**

Concentration and good judgement are
needed at all times to be a good, safe
driver. Don't put yourself or others at
risk by drinking and driving.

5.46 *Mark three answers*

What else can seriously affect your
concentration, other than alcoholic drinks?

⊙ Drugs

⊙ Tiredness

⊙ Tinted windows

⊙ Contact lenses

⊙ Loud music

⊙ **Drugs**

⊙ **Tiredness**

⊙ **Loud music**

Even a slight distraction can allow your
concentration to drift. Maintain full
concentration at all times so you stay
in full control of your vehicle.

As a driver you find that your eyesight has become very poor. Your optician says they cannot help you. The law says that you should tell

- ⊙ the licensing authority
- ⊙ your own doctor
- ⊙ the local police station
- ⊙ another optician

⊙ **the licensing authority**

This will have a serious effect on your judgement and concentration. If you cannot meet the eyesight requirements you must tell DVLA (or DVNI in Northern Ireland).

You are driving along this road. The driver on the left is reversing from a driveway. You should

- ⊙ move to the opposite side of the road
- ⊙ drive through as you have priority
- ⊙ sound your horn and be prepared to stop
- ⊙ speed up and drive through quickly

⊙ **sound your horn and be prepared to stop**

White lights at the rear of a car show that it is about to reverse. Sound your horn to warn of your presence and reduce your speed as a precaution.

This yellow sign on a vehicle indicates this is

- ⊙ a broken-down vehicle
- ⊙ a school bus
- ⊙ an ice cream van
- ⊙ a private ambulance

⊙ **a school bus**

Buses which carry children to and from school may stop at places other than scheduled bus stops. Be aware that they might pull over at any time to allow children to get on or off. This will normally be when traffic is heavy during rush hour.

5.50

If your motorway journey seems boring and you feel drowsy while driving, you should

- ⊙ open a window and drive to the next service area
- ⊙ stop on the hard shoulder for a sleep
- ⊙ speed up to arrive at your destination sooner
- ⊙ slow down and let other drivers overtake

⊙ **open a window and drive to the next service area**

Never stop on the hard shoulder to rest. If there is no service station for several miles, leave the motorway at the next exit and find somewhere safe to pull over.

5.51

You are not sure if your cough medicine will affect you. What TWO things should you do?

- ⊙ Ask your doctor
- ⊙ Check the medicine label
- ⊙ Drive if you feel alright
- ⊙ Ask a friend or relative for advice

⊙ **Ask your doctor**

⊙ **Check the medicine label**

If you're taking medicine or drugs prescribed by your doctor, check to ensure that they won't make you drowsy. If you forget to ask at the time of your visit to the surgery, check with your pharmacist.

Some over-the-counter medication can also cause drowsiness. Read the label and don't drive if you are affected.

5.52

Where would you expect to see these markers?

- ⊙ On a motorway sign
- ⊙ At the entrance to a narrow bridge
- ⊙ On a large goods vehicle
- ⊙ On a builder's skip placed on the road

⊙ **On a large goods vehicle**

⊙ **On a builder's skip placed on the road**

These markers must be fitted to vehicles over 13 metres long, large goods vehicles, and rubbish skips placed in the road. They are reflective to make them easier to see in the dark.

What is the main hazard shown in this picture?

⊙ Vehicles turning right

⊙ Vehicles doing U-turns

⊙ The cyclist crossing the road

⊙ Parked cars around the corner

⊙ **The cyclist crossing the road**

Look at the picture carefully and try to imagine you're there. The cyclist in this picture appears to be trying to cross the road. You must be able to deal with the unexpected, especially when you're approaching a hazardous junction. Look well ahead to give yourself time to deal with any hazards.

Which road user has caused a hazard?

⊙ The parked car (arrowed A)

⊙ The pedestrian waiting to cross (arrowed B)

⊙ The moving car (arrowed C)

⊙ The car turning (arrowed D)

⊙ **The parked car (arrowed A)**

The car arrowed A is parked within the area marked by zigzag lines at the pedestrian crossing. Parking here is illegal. It also

• blocks the view for pedestrians wishing to cross the road

• restricts the view of the crossing for approaching traffic.

When should you use hazard warning lights?

⊙ When you are double-parked on a two way road

⊙ When your direction indicators are not working

⊙ When warning oncoming traffic that you intend to stop

⊙ When your vehicle has broken down and is causing an obstruction

⊙ **When your vehicle has broken down and is causing an obstruction**

Hazard warning lights are an important safety feature and should be used if you have broken down and are causing an obstruction. Don't use them as an excuse to park illegally such as when using a cash machine or post box.

You may also use them on motorways to warn traffic behind you of danger ahead.

5.56   Mark **one** answer

What should the driver of the car approaching the crossing do?

⊙ Continue at the same speed

⊙ Sound the horn

⊙ Drive through quickly

⊙ Slow down and get ready to stop

⊙ **Slow down and get ready to stop**

Look well ahead to see if any hazards are developing. This will give you more time to deal with them in the correct way. The man in the picture is clearly intending to cross the road. You should be travelling at a speed that allows you to check your mirror, slow down and stop in good time. You shouldn't have to brake harshly.

5.57   Mark **one** answer

You have just been overtaken by this motorcyclist who is cutting in sharply. You should

⊙ sound the horn

⊙ brake firmly

⊙ keep a safe gap

⊙ flash your lights

⊙ **keep a safe gap**

If you need to, take your foot off the accelerator and drop back to allow a safe separation distance. Try not to react by braking sharply as you could lose control. If vehicles behind you are too close or unprepared, it could lead to an accident.

5.58   Mark **two** answers

As a provisional licence holder, you must not drive a motor car

⊙ at more than 40 mph

⊙ on your own

⊙ on the motorway

⊙ under the age of 18 years at night

⊙ with passengers in the rear seats

⊙ **on your own**

⊙ **on the motorway**

When you have passed your practical test you will be able to drive on a motorway. It is recommended that you have instruction on motorway driving before you venture out on your own. Ask your instructor about this.

What is the main hazard the driver of the red car (arrowed) should be aware of?

⊙ Glare from the sun may affect the driver's vision

⊙ The black car may stop suddenly

⊙ The bus may move out into the road

⊙ Oncoming vehicles will assume the driver is turning right

⊙ **The bus may move out into the road**

Try to anticipate the actions of the other road users around you. The driver of the red car should have made a mental note that the bus was at the bus stop. By doing this the driver would have been prepared for the bus pulling out.

As you approach a bus stop where a bus is stationary, look and see how many more passengers are waiting to board. If the last one has just got on, the bus is likely to move off.

You should give way to a bus driver who is signalling to move off from a bus stop, if you can do so safely.

Why should you be especially cautious when going past this bus?

⊙ There is traffic approaching in the distance

⊙ The driver may open the door

⊙ It may suddenly move off

⊙ People may cross the road in front of it

⊙ There are bicycles parked on the pavement

⊙ **It may suddenly move off**

⊙ **People may cross the road in front of it**

A stationary bus at a bus stop can hide pedestrians just in front of it who might be about to cross the road. Only go past at a speed that will enable you to stop safely if you need to.

5.61

What might you expect to happen in this situation?

⊙ Traffic will move into the right-hand lane

⊙ Traffic speed will increase

⊙ Traffic will move into the left-hand lane

⊙ Traffic will not need to change position

⊙ **Traffic will move into the left-hand lane**

Be courteous and allow the traffic to merge into the left-hand lane.

5.62

A driver's behaviour has upset you. It may help if you

⊙ stop and take a break

⊙ shout abusive language

⊙ gesture to them with your hand

⊙ follow their car, flashing your headlights

⊙ **stop and take a break**

Tiredness may make you more irritable than you would be normally. You might react differently to situations because of it. If you feel yourself becoming tense, take a break.

5.63

Your doctor has given you a course of medicine. Why should you ask how it will affect you?

⊙ Drugs make you a better driver by quickening your reactions

⊙ You will have to let your insurance company know about the medicine

⊙ Some types of medicine can cause your reactions to slow down

⊙ The medicine you take may affect your hearing

⊙ **Some types of medicine can cause your reactions to slow down**

Always check the label of any medication container. The contents might affect your driving. If you aren't sure, ask your doctor or pharmacist.

You are approaching this cyclist. You should

- overtake before the cyclist gets to the junction
- flash your headlights at the cyclist
- slow down and allow the cyclist to turn
- overtake the cyclist on the left-hand side

⊙ **slow down and allow the cyclist to turn**

Keep well back and allow the cyclist room to take up the correct position for the turn. Don't get too close behind or try to squeeze past.

You take the wrong route and find you are on a one-way street. You should

- reverse out of the road
- turn round in a side road
- continue to the end of the road
- reverse into a driveway

⊙ **continue to the end of the road**

Never reverse or turn your vehicle around in a one-way street. This is highly dangerous. Carry on and find another route, checking the direction signs as you drive.

If you need to check a map, first stop in a safe place.

You see this sign ahead. You should expect the road to

- go steeply uphill
- go steeply downhill
- bend sharply to the left
- bend sharply to the right

⊙ **bend sharply to the left**

Adjust your speed in good time and select the correct gear for your speed. Going too fast into the bend could cause you to lose control.

Braking late and harshly while changing direction reduces your vehicle's grip on the road and is likely to cause a skid.

5.67 *Mark one answer*

What should the driver of the red car (arrowed) do?

- Wave the pedestrians who are waiting to cross
- Wait for the pedestrian in the road to cross
- Quickly drive behind the pedestrian in the road
- Tell the pedestrian in the road she should not have crossed

⊙ **Wait for the pedestrian in the road to cross**

Some people might take longer to cross the road. They may be elderly or have a disability.

Be patient and don't hurry them by showing your impatience. They might have poor eyesight or not be able to hear traffic approaching.

If pedestrians are standing at the side of the road, don't signal or wave them to cross. Other road users may not have seen your signal and this could lead the pedestrians into a hazardous situation.

5.68 *Mark one answer*

You see this sign on the rear of a slow-moving lorry that you want to pass. It is travelling in the middle lane of a three-lane motorway. You should

- cautiously approach the lorry then pass on either side
- follow the lorry until you can leave the motorway
- wait on the hard shoulder until the lorry has stopped
- approach with care and keep to the left of the lorry

⊙ **approach with care and keep to the left of the lorry**

This sign is found on slow-moving or stationary works vehicles. If you wish to overtake, do so on the left, as indicated. Be aware that there might be workmen in the area.

You think the driver of the vehicle in front has forgotten to cancel their right indicator. You should

- ⊙ flash your lights to alert the driver
- ⊙ sound your horn before overtaking
- ⊙ overtake on the left if there is room
- ⊙ stay behind and not overtake

⊙ **stay behind and not overtake**

The driver may be unsure of the location of a junction and turn suddenly. Be cautious and don't attempt to overtake.

In areas where there are 'traffic calming' measures you should

- ⊙ travel at a reduced speed
- ⊙ always travel at the speed limit
- ⊙ position in the centre of the road
- ⊙ only slow down if pedestrians are near

⊙ **travel at a reduced speed**

Traffic calming measures such as road humps, chicanes and narrowings are intended to slow you down. Maintain a reduced speed until you reach the end of these features. They are there to protect pedestrians. Kill your speed!

You are driving along this motorway. It is raining. When following this lorry you should

- ⊙ allow at least a two-second gap
- ⊙ move left and drive on the hard shoulder
- ⊙ allow at least a four-second gap
- ⊙ be aware of spray reducing your vision
- ⊙ move right and stay in the right-hand lane

⊙ **allow at least a four-second gap**

⊙ **be aware of spray reducing your vision**

The usual two-second time gap will increase to four seconds when the roads are wet. If you stay well back you will

- be able to see past the vehicle
- be out of the spray thrown up by the lorry's tyres
- give yourself more time to stop if the need arises
- increase your chances of being seen by the lorry driver.

5.72 *Mark **two** answers*

What TWO main hazards should you be aware of when going along this street?

⊙ Glare from the sun

⊙ Car doors opening suddenly

⊙ Lack of road markings

⊙ The headlights on parked cars being switched on

⊙ Large goods vehicles

⊙ Children running out from between vehicles

⊙ **Car doors opening suddenly**

⊙ **Children running out from between vehicles**

On roads where there are many parked vehicles you should take extra care. You might not be able to see children between parked cars and they may run out into the road without looking.

People may open car doors without realising the hazard this can create. You will also need to look well down the road for oncoming traffic.

5.73 *Mark **one** answer*

What is the main hazard you should be aware of when following this cyclist?

⊙ The cyclist may move to the left and dismount

⊙ The cyclist may swerve out into the road

⊙ The contents of the cyclist's carrier may fall onto the road

⊙ The cyclist may wish to turn right at the end of the road

⊙ **The cyclist may swerve out into the road**

When following a cyclist be aware that they also have to deal with the hazards around them. They may

• wobble or swerve to avoid a pothole in the road

• see a potential hazard and change direction suddenly.

Don't follow them too closely or rev your engine impatiently.

The traffic ahead of you in the left-hand lane is slowing. You should

- ⊙ be wary of cars on your right cutting in
- ⊙ accelerate past the vehicles in the left-hand lane
- ⊙ pull up on the left-hand verge
- ⊙ move across and continue in the right-hand lane
- ⊙ slow down, keeping a safe separation distance

- ⊙ **be wary of cars on your right cutting in**

- ⊙ **slow down, keeping a safe separation distance**

Allow the traffic to merge into the nearside lane. Leave enough room so that your separation distance is not reduced drastically if a vehicle pulls in ahead of you.

Why are mirrors often slightly curved (convex)?

- ⊙ They give a wider field of vision
- ⊙ They totally cover blind spots
- ⊙ They make it easier to judge the speed of following traffic
- ⊙ They make following traffic look bigger

- ⊙ **They give a wider field of vision**

Although a convex mirror gives a wide view of the scene behind, you should be aware that it will not show you everything behind or to the side of the vehicle. Before you move off you will need to check over your shoulder to look for anything not visible in the mirrors.

A driver pulls out of a side road in front of you. You have to brake hard. You should

- ⊙ ignore the error and stay calm
- ⊙ flash your lights to show your annoyance
- ⊙ sound your horn to show your annoyance
- ⊙ overtake as soon as possible

- ⊙ **ignore the error and stay calm**

Where there are a number of side roads, be alert. Be especially careful if there are a lot of parked vehicles because they can make it more difficult for drivers emerging to see you.

Try to be tolerant if a vehicle does emerge and you have to brake quickly. Don't react aggressively.

5.77
*Mark **one** answer*

An elderly person's driving ability could be affected because they may be unable to

⊙ obtain car insurance
⊙ understand road signs
⊙ react very quickly
⊙ give signals correctly

⊙ **react very quickly**

Be tolerant of older drivers. Poor eyesight and hearing could affect the speed with which they react to a hazard and may cause them to be hesitant.

5.78
*Mark **one** answer*

You are behind this cyclist. When the traffic lights change, what should you do?

⊙ Try to move off before the cyclist
⊙ Allow the cyclist time and room
⊙ Turn right but give the cyclist room
⊙ Tap your horn and drive through first

⊙ **Allow the cyclist time and room**

Hold back and allow the cyclist to move off. In some towns, junctions have special areas marked across the front of the traffic lane. These allow cyclists to wait for the lights to change and move off ahead of other traffic.

5.79
*Mark **one** answer*

What does the solid white line at the side of the road indicate?

⊙ Traffic lights ahead
⊙ Edge of the carriageway
⊙ Footpath on the left
⊙ Cycle path

⊙ **Edge of the carriageway**

This road marking gives you information which is especially useful in bad weather when visibility is restricted.

You are driving on a road with several lanes. You see these signs above the lanes. What do they mean?

- ⊙ The two right lanes are open
- ⊙ The two left lanes are open
- ⊙ Traffic in the left lanes should stop
- ⊙ Traffic in the right lanes should stop

⊙ **The two left lanes are open**

If you see a red cross above your lane it means that there is an obstruction ahead. You will have to move into one of the lanes which is showing the green light. If all the lanes are showing a red cross, then you must stop.

You are driving on this dual carriageway. Why may you need to slow down?

- ⊙ There is a broken white line in the centre
- ⊙ There are solid white lines either side
- ⊙ There are roadworks ahead of you
- ⊙ There are no footpaths

⊙ **There are roadworks ahead of you**

Look well ahead and read any road signs as you drive. They are there to inform you of what is ahead. In this case you may need to slow right down and change direction.

Make sure you can take whatever action is necessary in plenty of time. Check your mirrors so you know what is happening around you before you change speed or direction.

Why are place names painted on the road surface?

- ⊙ To restrict the flow of traffic
- ⊙ To warn you of oncoming traffic
- ⊙ To enable you to change lanes early
- ⊙ To prevent you changing lanes

⊙ **To enable you to change lanes early**

The names of towns and cities may be painted on the road at busy junctions and complex road systems. Their purpose is to let you move into the correct lane in good time, allowing traffic to flow more freely.

5.83
Mark one answer

When the traffic lights change to green the white car should

- ⊙ wait for the cyclist to pull away
- ⊙ move off quickly and turn in front of the cyclist
- ⊙ move close up to the cyclist to beat the lights
- ⊙ sound the horn to warn the cyclist

⊙ **wait for the cyclist to pull away**

If you are waiting at traffic lights check all around you before you move away as cyclists often filter through waiting traffic. Allow the cyclist to move off safely.

5.84
Mark one answer

You intend to turn left at the traffic lights. Just before turning you should

- ⊙ check your right mirror
- ⊙ move close up to the white car
- ⊙ straddle the lanes
- ⊙ check for bicycles on your left

⊙ **check for bicycles on your left**

Check your nearside for cyclists before moving away. This is especially important if you have been in a stationary queue of traffic and are about to move off, as cyclists often try to filter past on the nearside of stationary vehicles.

5.85
Mark one answer

You are approaching crossroads. The traffic lights have failed. What should you do?

- ⊙ Brake and stop only for large vehicles
- ⊙ Brake sharply to a stop before looking
- ⊙ Be prepared to brake sharply to a stop
- ⊙ Be prepared to stop for any traffic.

⊙ **Be prepared to stop for any traffic.**

When approaching a junction where the traffic lights have failed you should proceed with caution. Treat the situation as an unmarked junction and be prepared to stop.

In heavy motorway traffic you are being followed closely by the vehicle behind. How can you lower the risk of an accident?

- ⊙ Increase your distance from the vehicle in front
- ⊙ Tap your foot on the brake pedal sharply
- ⊙ Switch on your hazard lights
- ⊙ Move onto the hard shoulder and stop

⊙ **Increase your distance from the vehicle in front**

On a busy motorway, traffic may still travel at high speeds despite the vehicles being close together. Don't follow too close to the vehicle in front. If a driver behind seems to be 'pushing' you, increase your distance from the vehicle in front by slowing down gently. This will lessen the risk of an accident involving several vehicles.

The red lights are flashing. What should you do when approaching this level crossing?

- ⊙ Go through quickly
- ⊙ Go through carefully
- ⊙ Stop before the barrier
- ⊙ Switch on hazard warning lights

⊙ **Stop before the barrier**

At level crossings the red lights flash when the barrier is down or is about to come down. You must stop, even if the barriers are not yet down.

In this picture there's a junction on the left just before the crossing, you should keep this junction clear.

When you are able to cross don't

- go onto the crossing unless the road is clear on the other side
- follow other vehicles nose to tail over it
- stop on or just past the crossing.

5.88

What does this signal from a police officer mean to oncoming traffic?

⊙ Go ahead

⊙ Stop

⊙ Turn left

⊙ Turn right

⊙ **Stop**

Police officers may need to direct traffic, for example, at a junction where the traffic lights have broken down. Check your copy of *The Highway Code* for the signals that they use.

5.89

You have just passed these warning lights. What hazard would you expect to see next?

⊙ A level crossing with no barrier

⊙ An ambulance station

⊙ A school crossing patrol

⊙ An opening bridge

⊙ **A school crossing patrol**

These lights warn that children may be crossing the road to a nearby school. Slow down so that you're ready to stop if necessary.

5.90

Hazard warning lights should be used when vehicles are

⊙ broken down and causing an obstruction

⊙ faulty and moving slowly

⊙ being towed along a road

⊙ reversing into a side road

⊙ **broken down and causing an obstruction**

Don't use hazard lights as an excuse for illegal parking. If you do use them, don't forget to switch them off when you move away. There must be a warning light on the control panel to show when the hazard lights are in operation.

You are on a dual carriageway. Ahead you see a vehicle with an amber flashing light. What will this be?

⊙ An ambulance

⊙ A fire engine

⊙ A doctor on call

⊙ A disabled person's vehicle

⊙ **A disabled person's vehicle**

An amber flashing light on a vehicle indicates that it is slow-moving.

Powered vehicles used by disabled people are limited to 8 mph. On dual carriageways they must display an amber flashing light.

For which of these may you use hazard warning lights?

⊙ When driving on a motorway to warn traffic behind of a hazard ahead

⊙ When you are double-parked on a two-way road

⊙ When your direction indicators are not working

⊙ When warning oncoming traffic that you intend to stop

⊙ **When driving on a motorway to warn traffic behind of a hazard ahead**

Hazard warning lights are an important safety feature. Use them when driving on a motorway to warn traffic behind you of danger ahead.

You should also use them if your vehicle has broken down and is causing an obstruction.

You are driving towards this level crossing. What would be the first warning of an approaching train?

⊙ Both half barriers down

⊙ A steady amber light

⊙ One half barrier down

⊙ Twin flashing red lights

⊙ **A steady amber light**

The steady amber light will be followed by twin flashing red lights that mean you must stop. An alarm will also sound to alert you to the fact that a train is approaching.

5.94 *Mark **one** answer*

While driving, you see this sign ahead. You should

⊙ stop at the sign

⊙ slow, but continue around the bend

⊙ slow to a crawl and continue

⊙ stop and look for open farm gates

⊙ **slow, but continue around the bend**

Drive around the bend at a steady speed in the correct gear. Be aware that you might have to stop for approaching trains.

5.95 *Mark **one** answer*

When may you use hazard warning lights?

⊙ To park alongside another car

⊙ To park on double yellow lines

⊙ When you are being towed

⊙ When you have broken down

⊙ **When you have broken down**

Hazard warning lights may be used to warn other road users when you

• have broken down and are causing an obstruction

• are on a motorway and want to warn the traffic behind you of a hazard ahead.

Don't use them when being towed.

5.96 *Mark **one** answer*

You are driving on a motorway. The traffic ahead is braking sharply because of an accident. How could you warn traffic behind you?

⊙ Briefly use the hazard warning lights

⊙ Switch on the hazard warning lights continuously

⊙ Briefly use the rear fog lights

⊙ Switch on the headlights continuously

⊙ **Briefly use the hazard warning lights**

The only time you are permitted to use your hazard warning lights while moving is if you are on a motorway or dual carriageway and you need to warn drivers behind you of a hazard or obstruction ahead. Only use them just long enough to ensure that your warning has been observed.

section six
VULNERABLE ROAD USERS

This ection covers:

- pedestrians
- children
- older drivers
- disabled people
- cyclists
- motorcyclists
- animals
- new drivers

6.1
*Mark **one** answer*

An injured motorcyclist is lying unconscious in the road. You should

⊙ remove the safety helmet
⊙ seek medical assistance
⊙ move the person off the road
⊙ remove the leather jacket

⊙ **seek medical assistance**

If someone has been injured, the sooner proper medical attention is given the better. Either send someone to phone for help or go yourself.

Only move an injured person if there is a risk of further danger. Never remove an injured motorcyclist's safety helmet.

6.2
*Mark **one** answer*

You are turning left into a side road. What hazards should you be especially aware of?

⊙ One way street
⊙ Pedestrians
⊙ Traffic congestion
⊙ Parked vehicles

⊙ **Pedestrians**

Make sure that you have reduced your speed and are in the correct gear for the turn. Look into the road before you turn and always give way to any pedestrians who are crossing.

6.3
*Mark **one** answer*

You have just passed your test. How can you decrease your risk of accidents on the motorway?

⊙ By keeping up with the car in front
⊙ By never going over 40 mph
⊙ By staying only in the left-hand lane
⊙ By taking further training

⊙ **By taking further training**

You're more likely to have an accident in the first year after taking your test. Lack of experience means that you might not react to hazards as quickly as a more experienced person. Further training will help you to become safer on the roads.

6.4
*Mark **one** answer*

Which age group of drivers is most likely to be involved in a road accident?

⊙ 17 - 25 year olds
⊙ 36 - 45 year olds
⊙ 46 - 55 year olds
⊙ over 55 year olds

⊙ **17 - 25 year olds**

Statistics show that if you're a driver between the ages of 17 and 25 you're more likely to be involved in a road accident than any other age group. There are several reasons contributing to this, but in most cases accidents are due to driver error.

You are turning left from a main road into a side road. People are already crossing the road into which you are turning. You should

- ⊙ continue, as it is your right of way
- ⊙ signal to them to continue crossing
- ⊙ wait and allow them to cross
- ⊙ sound your horn to warn them of your presence

⊙ **wait and allow them to cross**

Always check the road you're turning into. Approaching at the correct speed will allow you enough time to observe and react.

Give way to any pedestrians already crossing the road.

Motorcyclists will often look round over their right shoulder just before turning right. This is because

- ⊙ they need to listen for following traffic
- ⊙ motorcycles do not have mirrors
- ⊙ looking around helps them balance as they turn
- ⊙ they need to check for traffic in their blind area

⊙ **they need to check for traffic in their blind area**

If you see a motorcyclist take a quick glance over their shoulder, this could mean they are about to change direction. Recognising a clue like this helps you to be prepared and take appropriate action, making you safer on the road.

You are driving in slow-moving queues of traffic. Just before changing lane you should

- ⊙ sound the horn
- ⊙ look for motorcyclists filtering through the traffic
- ⊙ give a 'slowing down' arm signal
- ⊙ change down to first gear

⊙ **look for motorcyclists filtering through the traffic**

In this situation motorcyclists could be passing you on either side. Always check before you change lanes or change direction.

6.8
*Mark **one** answer*

You are at a road junction, turning into a minor road. There are pedestrians crossing the minor road. You should

- ⊙ stop and wave the pedestrians across
- ⊙ sound your horn to let the pedestrians know that you are there
- ⊙ give way to the pedestrians who are already crossing
- ⊙ carry on; the pedestrians should give way to you

⊙ **give way to the pedestrians who are already crossing**

Always look into the road you're turning into. If there are pedestrians crossing, give way to them but don't wave or signal to them to cross.

Signal your intention to turn as you approach.

6.9
*Mark **one** answer*

You have a collision whilst your car is moving. What is the first thing you must do?

- ⊙ Stop only if there are injured people
- ⊙ Call the emergency services
- ⊙ Stop at the scene of the accident
- ⊙ Call your insurance company

⊙ **Stop at the scene of the accident**

If you are involved in an accident which causes damage or injury to any other person, vehicle, animal or property, by law you MUST STOP. Give your name, the vehicle owner's name and address, and the vehicle's registration number to anyone who has reasonable grounds for requiring them.

6.10
*Mark **one** answer*

You intend to turn right into a side road. Just before turning you should check for motorcyclists who might be

- ⊙ overtaking on your left
- ⊙ following you closely
- ⊙ emerging from the side road
- ⊙ overtaking on your right

⊙ **overtaking on your right**

Never attempt to change direction to the right without first checking your right-hand mirror. A motorcyclist might not have seen your signal and could be hidden by the car behind you. This action should become a matter of routine.

6.11

Why should you look particularly for motorcyclists and cyclists at junctions?

- ⊙ They may want to turn into the side road
- ⊙ They may slow down to let you turn
- ⊙ They are harder to see
- ⊙ They might not see you turn

⊙ **They are harder to see**

Cyclists and motorcyclists are smaller than other vehicles and so are more difficult to see. They can easily become hidden from your view by cars parked near a junction.

6.12

You are waiting to come out of a side road. Why should you watch carefully for motorcycles?

- ⊙ Motorcycles are usually faster than cars
- ⊙ Police patrols often use motorcycles
- ⊙ Motorcycles are small and hard to see
- ⊙ Motorcycles have right of way

⊙ **Motorcycles are small and hard to see**

If you're waiting to emerge from a side road watch out for motorcycles: they're small and can be difficult to see. Be especially careful if there are parked vehicles restricting your view, there might be a motorcycle approaching.

IF YOU DON'T KNOW, DON'T GO.

6.13

You are turning left at a junction. Pedestrians have started to cross the road. You should

- ⊙ go on, giving them plenty of room
- ⊙ stop and wave at them to cross
- ⊙ blow your horn and proceed
- ⊙ give way to them

⊙ **give way to them**

If you're turning into a side road, pedestrians already crossing the road have priority and you should give way to them. Don't

- wave them across the road
- sound your horn
- flash your lights
- give any other misleading signal – other road users may misinterpret your signal and you might lead the pedestrian into a dangerous situation.

If a pedestrian is slow or indecisive be patient and wait. Don't hurry them across by revving your engine.

6.14
*Mark **three** answers*

At road junctions which of the following are most vulnerable?

⊙ Cyclists
⊙ Motorcyclists
⊙ Pedestrians
⊙ Car drivers
⊙ Lorry drivers

⊙ **Cyclists**

⊙ **Motorcyclists**

⊙ **Pedestrians**

Pedestrians and riders on two wheels can be harder to see than other road users. Make sure you keep a look-out for them, especially at junctions. Good effective observation, coupled with appropriate action, can save lives.

6.15
*Mark **one** answer*

You are turning left into a side road. Pedestrians are crossing the road near the junction. You must

⊙ wave them on
⊙ sound your horn
⊙ switch on your hazard lights
⊙ wait for them to cross

⊙ **wait for them to cross**

Check that it's clear before you turn into a junction. If there are pedestrians crossing, let them cross in their own time.

6.16
*Mark **one** answer*

You are at the front of a queue of traffic waiting to turn right into a side road. Why is it important to check your right mirror just before turning?

⊙ To look for pedestrians about to cross
⊙ To check for overtaking vehicles
⊙ To make sure the side road is clear
⊙ To check for emerging traffic

⊙ **To check for overtaking vehicles**

There could be a motorcyclist riding along the outside of the queue. Always check your mirror before turning as situations behind you can change in the time you have been waiting to turn.

You want to turn right from a junction but your view is restricted by parked vehicles. What should you do?

- ⊙ Move out quickly, but be prepared to stop
- ⊙ Sound your horn and pull out if there is no reply
- ⊙ Stop, then move slowly forward until you have a clear view
- ⊙ Stop, get out and look along the main road to check

⊙ **Stop, then move slowly forward until you have a clear view**

If you want to turn right from a junction and your view is restricted, STOP. Ease forward until you can see – there might be something approaching.

IF YOU DON'T KNOW, DON'T GO.

You want to reverse into a side road. You are not sure that the area behind your car is clear. What should you do?

- ⊙ Look through the rear window only
- ⊙ Get out and check
- ⊙ Check the mirrors only
- ⊙ Carry on, assuming it is clear

⊙ **Get out and check**

If you cannot be sure whether there is anything behind you, it is always safest to check before reversing. There may be a small child or a low obstruction close behind your car. The shape and size of your vehicle can restrict visibility.

You are about to reverse into a side road. A pedestrian wishes to cross behind you. You should

- ⊙ wave to the pedestrian to stop
- ⊙ give way to the pedestrian
- ⊙ wave to the pedestrian to cross
- ⊙ reverse before the pedestrian starts to cross

⊙ **give way to the pedestrian**

If you need to reverse into a side road try to find a place that's free from traffic and pedestrians. Look all around before and during the manoeuvre. Always stop and give way to any pedestrians who wish to cross behind you. Don't

- wave them across the road
- sound the horn
- flash your lights
- give any other misleading signal – other road users may not have seen your signal and you might lead the pedestrian into a dangerous situation.

6.20   *Mark **one** answer*

Motorcyclists are particularly vulnerable

⊙ when moving off
⊙ on dual carriageways
⊙ when approaching junctions
⊙ on motorways

⊙ **when approaching junctions**

Another road user failing to see a motorcyclist is a major cause of collisions at junctions. Wherever streams of traffic join or cross there's the potential for this type of accident to occur.

6.21   *Mark **one** answer*

You want to turn right from a main road into a side road. Just before turning you should

⊙ cancel your right-turn signal
⊙ select first gear
⊙ check for traffic overtaking on your right
⊙ stop and set the handbrake

⊙ **check for traffic overtaking on your right**

Motorcyclists often overtake queues of vehicles. Make one last check in your mirror and your blind spot to avoid turning across their path.

6.22   *Mark **one** answer*

You are driving on a main road. You intend to turn right into a side road. Just before turning you should

⊙ adjust your interior mirror
⊙ flash your headlamps
⊙ steer over to the left
⊙ check for traffic overtaking on your right

⊙ **check for traffic overtaking on your right**

A last check in the offside mirror and blind spot will allow you sight of any cyclist or motorcyclist overtaking as you wait to turn.

6.23   *Mark **one** answer*

Motorcyclists should wear bright clothing mainly because

⊙ they must do so by law
⊙ it helps keep them cool in summer
⊙ the colours are popular
⊙ drivers often do not see them

⊙ **drivers often do not see them**

Motorcycles are small vehicles and can be difficult to see. If the rider wears bright clothing it can make it easier for other road users to see them approaching, especially at junctions.

Where in particular should you look out for motorcyclists?

- In a filling station
- At a road junction
- Near a service area
- When entering a car park

⊙ **At a road junction**

Always look out for motorcyclists and cyclists, particularly at junctions. They are smaller and usually more difficult to see than other vehicles.

You see a horse rider as you approach a roundabout. They are signalling right but keeping well to the left. You should

- proceed as normal
- keep close to them
- cut in front of them
- stay well back

⊙ **stay well back**

Allow riders to enter and exit the roundabout in their own time. They may feel safer keeping to the left all the way around the roundabout. Don't drive up close behind or alongside them, as this could disturb the horses.

Where should you take particular care to look out for motorcyclists and cyclists?

- On dual carriageways
- At junctions
- At zebra crossings
- On one-way streets

⊙ **At junctions**

Motorcyclists and cyclists are often more difficult to see on the road. This is especially the case at junctions. You may not be able to see a motorcyclist approaching a junction if your view is blocked by other traffic. A motorcycle may be travelling as fast as a car, sometimes faster. Make sure that you judge speeds correctly before you emerge.

6.27
*Mark **one** answer*

In daylight, an approaching motorcyclist is using a dipped headlight. Why?

- ⊙ So that the rider can be seen more easily
- ⊙ To stop the battery overcharging
- ⊙ To improve the rider's vision
- ⊙ The rider is inviting you to proceed

⊙ **So that the rider can be seen more easily**

A motorcycle can be lost from sight behind another vehicle. The use of the headlight helps to make it more conspicuous and therefore more easily seen.

6.28
*Mark **one** answer*

Who is especially in danger of not being seen as you reverse your car?

- ⊙ Motorcyclists
- ⊙ Car drivers
- ⊙ Cyclists
- ⊙ Children

⊙ **Children**

As you look through the rear of your vehicle you may not be able to see a small child. Be aware of this before you reverse. If there are children about, get out and check if it is clear before reversing.

6.29
*Mark **one** answer*

A horse rider is in the left-hand lane approaching a roundabout. You should expect the rider to

- ⊙ go in any direction
- ⊙ turn right
- ⊙ turn left
- ⊙ go ahead

⊙ **go in any direction**

Horses and their riders will move more slowly than other road users. They might not have time to cut across heavy traffic to take up positions in the offside lane. For this reason a horse and rider may approach a roundabout in the left-hand lane, even though they're turning right.

6.30
*Mark **two** answers*

You are approaching a roundabout. There are horses just ahead of you. You should

- ⊙ be prepared to stop
- ⊙ treat them like any other vehicle
- ⊙ give them plenty of room
- ⊙ accelerate past as quickly as possible
- ⊙ sound your horn as a warning

⊙ **be prepared to stop**

⊙ **give them plenty of room**

Horse riders often keep to the outside of the roundabout even if they are turning right. Give them plenty of room and remember that they may have to cross lanes of traffic.

Which THREE should you do when passing sheep on a road?

⊙ Allow plenty of room
⊙ Go very slowly
⊙ Pass quickly but quietly
⊙ Be ready to stop
⊙ Briefly sound your horn

⊙ **Allow plenty of room**

⊙ **Go very slowly**

⊙ **Be ready to stop**

Slow down and be ready to stop if you see animals in the road ahead. Animals are easily frightened by

• noise
• vehicles passing too close to them.

Stop if signalled to do so by the person in charge.

Which THREE of the following are hazards motorcyclists present in queues of traffic?

⊙ Cutting in just in front of you
⊙ Riding in single file
⊙ Passing very close to you
⊙ Riding with their headlight on dipped beam
⊙ Filtering between the lanes

⊙ **Cutting in just in front of you**

⊙ **Passing very close to you**

⊙ **Filtering between the lanes**

Where there's more than one lane of queuing traffic, motorcyclists may use the opportunity to make progress by riding between the lanes. Be aware that they may be passing on either side. Check your mirrors before you move off.

How should you overtake horse riders?

⊙ Drive up close and overtake as soon as possible
⊙ Speed is not important but allow plenty of room
⊙ Use your horn just once to warn them
⊙ Drive slowly and leave plenty of room

⊙ **Drive slowly and leave plenty of room**

If you're driving on a country road then take extra care. Be ready for

• farm animals
• horses
• pedestrians
• farm vehicles.

Always be prepared to slow down or stop.

6.34
*Mark **one** answer*

You are reversing around a corner when you notice a pedestrian walking behind you. What should you do?

⊙ Slow down and wave the pedestrian across

⊙ Continue reversing and steer round the pedestrian

⊙ Stop and give way

⊙ Continue reversing and sound your horn

⊙ **Stop and give way**

Wait until the pedestrian has passed, then look around again before you start to reverse. Don't forget that you may not be able to see a small child directly behind your vehicle. Be aware of the possibility of hidden dangers.

6.35
*Mark **one** answer*

You are on a country road. What should you expect to see coming towards you on YOUR side of the road?

⊙ Motorcycles

⊙ Bicycles

⊙ Pedestrians

⊙ Horse riders

⊙ **Pedestrians**

On a quiet country road always be aware that there may be a hazard just around the next bend, such as a slow-moving vehicle or pedestrians. Pedestrians are advised to walk on the right-hand side of the road if there is no pavement, so they may be walking towards you on your side of the road.

6.36
*Mark **one** answer*

You notice horse riders in front. What should you do FIRST?

⊙ Pull out to the middle of the road

⊙ Slow down and be ready to stop

⊙ Accelerate around them

⊙ Signal right

⊙ **Slow down and be ready to stop**

Be particularly careful when approaching horse riders – slow down and be prepared to stop. Always pass wide and slowly and look out for signals given by horse riders.

Horses are unpredictable: always treat them as potential hazards and take great care when passing them.

You are driving past a line of parked cars. You notice a ball bouncing out into the road ahead. What should you do?

⊙ Continue driving at the same speed and sound your horn

⊙ Continue driving at the same speed and flash your headlights

⊙ Slow down and be prepared to stop for children

⊙ Stop and wave the children across to fetch their ball

⊙ **Slow down and be prepared to stop for children**

Beware of children playing in the street and running out into the road. If a ball bounces out from the pavement, slow down and stop. Don't encourage anyone to retrieve it. Other road users may not see your signal and you might lead a child into a dangerous situation.

You are driving in town. There is a bus at the bus stop on the other side of the road. Why should you be careful?

⊙ The bus may have broken down

⊙ Pedestrians may come from behind the bus

⊙ The bus may move off suddenly

⊙ The bus may remain stationary

⊙ **Pedestrians may come from behind the bus**

If you see a bus ahead watch out for pedestrians. They may not be able to see you if they're crossing behind the bus.

You are dazzled at night by a vehicle behind you. You should

⊙ set your mirror to anti-dazzle

⊙ set your mirror to dazzle the other driver

⊙ brake sharply to a stop

⊙ switch your rear lights on and off

⊙ **set your mirror to anti-dazzle**

The interior mirror of most vehicles can be set to the anti-dazzle position. You will still be able to see the lights of the traffic behind you but the dazzle will be greatly reduced.

6.40

*Mark **one** answer*

You are following a motorcyclist on an uneven road. You should

- ⊙ allow less room so you can be seen in their mirrors
- ⊙ overtake immediately
- ⊙ allow extra room in case they swerve to avoid potholes
- ⊙ allow the same room as normal because road surfaces do not affect motorcyclists

⊙ **allow extra room in case they swerve to avoid potholes**

Potholes and bumps in the road can unbalance a motorcyclist. For this reason the rider might swerve to avoid an uneven road surface. Watch out at places where this is likely to occur.

6.41

*Mark **one** answer*

You are coming up to a roundabout. A cyclist is signalling to turn right. What should you do?

- ⊙ Overtake on the right
- ⊙ Give a horn warning
- ⊙ Signal the cyclist to move across
- ⊙ Give the cyclist plenty of room

⊙ **Give the cyclist plenty of room**

If you're following a cyclist who's signalling to turn right at a roundabout leave plenty of room. Give them space and time to get into the correct lane.

6.42

*Mark **one** answer*

You are approaching this roundabout and see the cyclist signal right. Why is the cyclist keeping to the left?

- ⊙ It is a quicker route for the cyclist
- ⊙ The cyclist is going to turn left instead
- ⊙ The cyclist thinks The Highway Code does not apply to bicycles
- ⊙ The cyclist is slower and more vulnerable

⊙ **The cyclist is slower and more vulnerable**

Cycling in today's heavy traffic can be hazardous. Some cyclists may not feel happy about crossing the path of traffic to take up a position in an outside lane. Be aware of this and understand that, although in the left-hand lane, the cyclist might be turning right.

6.43

You are driving past parked cars. You notice a bicycle wheel sticking out between them. What should you do?

⊙ Accelerate past quickly and sound your horn

⊙ Slow down and wave the cyclist across

⊙ Brake sharply and flash your headlights

⊙ Slow down and be prepared to stop for a cyclist

⊙ **Slow down and be prepared to stop for a cyclist**

Scan the road as you drive. Try to anticipate hazards by being aware of the places where they are likely to occur. You'll then be able to react in good time, if necessary.

6.44

You are travelling behind a moped. You want to turn left just ahead. You should

⊙ overtake the moped before the junction

⊙ pull alongside the moped and stay level until just before the junction

⊙ sound your horn as a warning and pull in front of the moped

⊙ stay behind until the moped has passed the junction

⊙ **stay behind until the moped has passed the junction**

Passing the moped and turning into the junction could mean that you cut across the front of the rider. This might force them to slow down, stop or even lose control. Slow down and stay behind the moped until it has passed the junction and you can then turn safely.

6.45

How would you react to drivers who appear to be inexperienced?

⊙ Sound your horn to warn them of your presence

⊙ Be patient and prepare for them to react more slowly

⊙ Flash your headlights to indicate that it is safe for them to proceed

⊙ Overtake them as soon as possible

⊙ **Be patient and prepare for them to react more slowly**

Learners might not have confidence when they first start to drive. Allow them plenty of room and don't react adversely to their hesitation. We all learn from experience, but new drivers will have had less practice in dealing with all the situations that might occur.

6.46
*Mark **one** answer*

When you are overtaking a cyclist you should leave as much room as you would give to a car. What is the main reason for this?

⊙ The cyclist might change lanes

⊙ The cyclist might get off the bike

⊙ The cyclist might swerve

⊙ The cyclist might have to make a right turn

⊙ **The cyclist might swerve**

Look at the road ahead if you intend to overtake a cyclist. Check if the cyclist is likely to need to change direction for a parked vehicle or an uneven road surface. When you have a safe place to overtake leave as much room as you would for a car. Don't cut in sharply or pass too closely.

6.47
*Mark **one** answer*

You are following a cyclist. You wish to turn left just ahead. You should

⊙ overtake the cyclist before the junction

⊙ pull alongside the cyclist and stay level until after the junction

⊙ hold back until the cyclist has passed the junction

⊙ go around the cyclist on the junction

⊙ **hold back until the cyclist has passed the junction**

Make allowances for cyclists. Allow them plenty of room. Don't try to overtake and then turn left as you would have to cut in across the path of the cyclist. Be patient and stay behind them until they have passed the junction.

6.48
*Mark **one** answer*

Powered vehicles used by disabled people are small and hard to see. How do they give early warning when on a dual carriageway?

⊙ They will have a flashing red light

⊙ They will have a flashing green light

⊙ They will have a flashing blue light

⊙ They will have a flashing amber light

⊙ **They will have a flashing amber light**

Powered vehicles used by disabled people are small, low, hard to see and travel very slowly. On a dual carriageway they will have a flashing amber light to warn other road users.

6.49
*Mark **one** answer*

There is a slow-moving motorcyclist ahead of you. You are unsure what the rider is going to do. You should

- ⊙ pass on the left
- ⊙ pass on the right
- ⊙ stay behind
- ⊙ move closer

⊙ **stay behind**

If a motorcyclist is travelling slowly it may be that they are looking for a turning or entrance. Be patient and stay behind them in case they need to make a sudden change of direction.

6.50
*Mark **one** answer*

You are following two cyclists. They approach a roundabout in the left-hand lane. In which direction should you expect the cyclists to go?

- ⊙ Left
- ⊙ Right
- ⊙ Any direction
- ⊙ Straight ahead

⊙ **Any direction**

Cyclists approaching a roundabout in the left-hand lane may be turning right but may not have been able to get into the correct lane due to the heavy traffic. They may also feel safer keeping to the left all the way round the roundabout. Be aware of them and give them plenty of room.

6.51
*Mark **one** answer*

Ahead of you there is a moving vehicle with a flashing amber beacon. This means it is

- ⊙ slow moving
- ⊙ broken down
- ⊙ a doctor's car
- ⊙ a school crossing patrol

⊙ **slow moving**

As you approach the vehicle, assess the situation. Due to its slow progress you will need to judge whether it is safe to overtake.

6.52
*Mark **two** answers*

Which TWO should you allow extra room when overtaking?

- ⊙ Motorcycles
- ⊙ Tractors
- ⊙ Bicycles
- ⊙ Road-sweeping vehicles

⊙ **Motorcycles**

⊙ **Bicycles**

Don't pass riders too closely as this may cause them to lose balance. Always leave as much room as you would for a car, and don't cut in.

6.53

You are following a car driven by an elderly driver. You should

- ⊙ expect the driver to drive badly
- ⊙ flash your lights and overtake
- ⊙ be aware that the driver's reactions may not be as fast as yours
- ⊙ stay very close behind but be careful

⊙ **be aware that the driver's reactions may not be as fast as yours**

You must show consideration to other road users. The reactions of elderly drivers may be slower and they might need more time to deal with a situation. Be tolerant and don't lose patience or show your annoyance.

6.54

You are following a learner driver who stalls at a junction. You should

- ⊙ be patient as you expect them to make mistakes
- ⊙ stay very close behind and flash your headlights
- ⊙ start to rev your engine if they take too long to restart
- ⊙ immediately steer around them and drive on

⊙ **be patient as you expect them to make mistakes**

Learning is a process of practice and experience. Try to understand this and tolerate others who are at the beginning of this process.

6.55

What action would you take when elderly people are crossing the road?

- ⊙ Wave them across so they know that you have seen them
- ⊙ Be patient and allow them to cross in their own time
- ⊙ Rev the engine to let them know that you are waiting
- ⊙ Tap the horn in case they are hard of hearing

⊙ **Be patient and allow them to cross in their own time**

Be aware that elderly people might take a long time to cross the road. They might also be hard of hearing and not hear you approaching.

Don't hurry elderly people across the road by getting too close to them or revving your engine.

6.56　　Mark one answer

You should never attempt to overtake a cyclist

- ⊙ just before you turn left
- ⊙ on a left-hand bend
- ⊙ on a one-way street
- ⊙ on a dual carriageway

⊙ **just before you turn left**

If you want to turn left and there's a cyclist in front of you, hold back. Wait until the cyclist has passed the junction and then turn left behind them.

6.57　　Mark one answer

A toucan crossing is different from other crossings because

- ⊙ moped riders can use it
- ⊙ it is controlled by a traffic warden
- ⊙ it is controlled by two flashing lights
- ⊙ cyclists can use it

⊙ **cyclists can use it**

Toucan crossings are shared by pedestrians and cyclists and they are shown the green light together. Cyclists are permitted to cycle across.

The signals are push-button operated and there is no flashing amber phase.

6.58　　Mark one answer

How will a school crossing patrol signal you to stop?

- ⊙ By pointing to children on the opposite pavement
- ⊙ By displaying a red light
- ⊙ By displaying a stop sign
- ⊙ By giving you an arm signal

⊙ **By displaying a stop sign**

If a school crossing patrol steps out into the road with a stop sign you must stop. Don't

- • wave anyone across the road
- • get impatient or rev your engine.

6.59　　Mark one answer

You see a pedestrian with a white stick and red band. This means that the person is

- ⊙ physically disabled
- ⊙ deaf only
- ⊙ blind only
- ⊙ deaf and blind

⊙ **deaf and blind**

If someone is deaf as well as blind, they may be carrying a white stick with a red reflective band.

You can't see if a pedestrian is deaf. Don't assume everyone can hear you approaching.

6.60
*Mark **two** answers*

At toucan crossings

- there is no flashing amber light
- cyclists are not permitted
- there is a continuously flashing amber beacon
- pedestrians and cyclists may cross
- you only stop if someone is waiting to cross

⊙ **there is no flashing amber light**

⊙ **pedestrians and cyclists may cross**

There are some crossings where cycle routes lead the cyclists to cross at the same place as pedestrians. These are called toucan crossings. Always look out for cyclists, as they're likely to be approaching faster than pedestrians.

6.61
*Mark **one** answer*

Why should you allow extra room when overtaking a motorcyclist on a windy day?

- The rider may turn off suddenly to get out of the wind
- The rider may be blown across in front of you
- The rider may stop suddenly
- The rider may be travelling faster than normal

⊙ **The rider may be blown across in front of you**

If you're driving in high winds, be aware that the conditions might force a motorcyclist or cyclist to swerve or wobble. Take this into consideration if you're following or wish to overtake a two-wheeled vehicle.

6.62
*Mark **one** answer*

You are approaching this crossing. You should

- prepare to slow down and stop
- stop and wave the pedestrians across
- speed up and pass by quickly
- drive on unless the pedestrians step out

⊙ **prepare to slow down and stop**

Be courteous and prepare to stop. Do not wave people across as this could be dangerous if another vehicle is approaching the crossing.

6.63

Mark **one** answer

You see two elderly pedestrians about to cross the road ahead. You should

- ⊙ expect them to wait for you to pass
- ⊙ speed up to get past them quickly
- ⊙ stop and wave them across the road
- ⊙ be careful, they may misjudge your speed

⊙ **be careful, they may misjudge your speed**

Elderly people may have impaired

- hearing
- vision
- concentration
- judgement.

They may also walk slowly and so could take a long time to cross the road.

6.64

Mark **one** answer

As you approach a pelican crossing the lights change to green. Elderly people are halfway across. You should

- ⊙ wave them to cross as quickly as they can
- ⊙ rev your engine to make them hurry
- ⊙ flash your lights in case they have not heard you
- ⊙ wait because they will take longer to cross

⊙ **wait because they will take longer to cross**

Even if the lights turn to green, wait for them to clear the crossing. Allow them to cross the road in their own time and don't try to hurry them by revving your engine.

6.65

Mark **two** answers

You have stopped at a pelican crossing. A disabled person is crossing slowly in front of you. The lights have now changed to green. You should

- ⊙ allow the person to cross
- ⊙ drive in front of the person
- ⊙ drive behind the person
- ⊙ sound your horn
- ⊙ be patient
- ⊙ edge forward slowly

⊙ **allow the person to cross**

⊙ **be patient**

At a pelican crossing the green light means you may proceed as long as the crossing is clear. If someone hasn't finished crossing, be patient and wait for them.

6.66
Mark one answer

You see a pedestrian with a dog. The dog has a bright orange lead and collar. This especially warns you that the pedestrian is

⊙ elderly
⊙ dog training
⊙ colour blind
⊙ deaf

⊙ **deaf**

Take extra care as the pedestrian may not be aware of vehicles approaching.

6.67
Mark one answer

What must a driver do at a pelican crossing when the amber light is flashing?

⊙ Signal the pedestrian to cross
⊙ Always wait for the green light before proceeding
⊙ Give way to any pedestrians on the crossing
⊙ Wait for the red-and-amber light before proceeding

⊙ **Give way to any pedestrians on the crossing**

The flashing amber light allows pedestrians already on the crossing to get to the other side before a green light shows to the traffic. Be aware that some pedestrians, such as elderly people and young children, need longer to cross. Let them do this at their own pace.

6.68
Mark one answer

The road outside this school is marked with yellow zigzag lines. What do these lines mean?

⊙ You may park on the lines when dropping off schoolchildren
⊙ You may park on the lines when picking schoolchildren up
⊙ You must not wait or park your vehicle here at all
⊙ You must stay with your vehicle if you park here

⊙ **You must not wait or park your vehicle here at all**

Parking here would block the view of the school entrance and would endanger the lives of children on their way to and from school.

At night you see a pedestrian wearing reflective clothing and carrying a bright red light. What does this mean?

⊙ You are approaching roadworks

⊙ You are approaching an organised walk

⊙ You are approaching a slow-moving vehicle

⊙ You are approaching an accident blackspot

⊙ **You are approaching an organised walk**

The people involved in the walk should be keeping to the left but this can't be assumed. Pass slowly, ensuring that you have the time to do so safely. Be aware that the pedestrians have their backs to you and might not know that you're there.

The left-hand pavement is closed due to street repairs. What should you do?

⊙ Watch out for pedestrians walking in the road

⊙ Use your right-hand mirror more often

⊙ Speed up to get past the roadworks quicker

⊙ Position close to the left-hand kerb

⊙ **Watch out for pedestrians walking in the road**

Where street repairs have closed off pavements, proceed carefully and slowly as pedestrians might have to walk in the road.

These road markings must be kept clear to allow

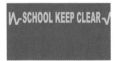

⊙ school children to be dropped off

⊙ for teachers to park

⊙ school children to be picked up

⊙ a clear view of the crossing area

⊙ **a clear view of the crossing area**

The markings are there to show that the area must be kept clear to allow an unrestricted view for

• approaching drivers and riders

• children wanting to cross the road.

6.72   *Mark **one** answer*

Yellow zigzag lines on the road outside schools mean

⊙ sound your horn to alert other road users

⊙ stop to allow children to cross

⊙ you must not wait or park on these lines

⊙ you must not drive over these lines

⊙ **you must not wait or park on these lines**

You must not stop where there are yellow zigzag markings, not even to pick up or drop off children. A vehicle parked on the zigzag lines would obstruct children's view of the road and other drivers' view of the pavement.

6.73   *Mark **one** answer*

What do these road markings outside a school mean?

⊙ You may park here if you are a teacher

⊙ Sound your horn before parking

⊙ When parking, use your hazard warning lights

⊙ You must not wait or park your vehicle here

⊙ **You must not wait or park your vehicle here**

Parking here would block people's view of the school entrance. This could endanger the lives of children on their way to and from school.

You are driving towards a zebra crossing. A person in a wheelchair is waiting to cross. What should you do?

- ⊙ Continue on your way
- ⊙ Wave to the person to cross
- ⊙ Wave to the person to wait
- ⊙ Be prepared to stop

⊙ **Be prepared to stop**

You should slow down and be prepared to stop as you would with an able-bodied person. Don't wave them across as other traffic may not stop.

You must not stop on these road markings because you may obstruct

- ⊙ children's view of the crossing area
- ⊙ teachers' access to the school
- ⊙ delivery vehicles' access to the school
- ⊙ emergency vehicles' access to the school

⊙ **children's view of the crossing area**

These markings are found on the road outside schools. DO NOT stop (even to set down or pick up children) or park on them. The markings are to make sure that drivers, riders and children have a clear view.

Which sign means that there may be people walking along the road?

⊙   ⊙

⊙   ⊙

⊙

Always check the road signs. Triangular signs are warning signs and they'll keep you informed of hazards ahead and help you to anticipate any problems. There are a number of different signs showing pedestrians. Learn the meaning of each one.

6.77   *Mark **one** answer*

What does this sign tell you?

⊙ No cycling
⊙ Cycle route ahead
⊙ Route for cycles only
⊙ End of cycle route

⊙ **Cycle route ahead**

With people's concern today for the environment, cycle routes are being created in our towns and cities. These are usually defined by road markings and signs.

Respect the presence of cyclists on the road and give them plenty of room if you need to pass.

6.78   *Mark **one** answer*

Where would you see this sign?

⊙ In the window of a car taking children to school
⊙ At the side of the road
⊙ At playground areas
⊙ On the rear of a school bus or coach

⊙ **On the rear of a school bus or coach**

Vehicles that are used to carry children to and from school will be travelling at busy times of the day. If you're following a vehicle with this sign be prepared for it to make frequent stops. It might pick up or set down passengers in places other than normal bus stops.

6.79   *Mark **one** answer*

Which sign tells you that pedestrians may be walking in the road as there is no pavement?

     ⊙

⊙   ⊙

⊙

Give pedestrians who are walking at the side of the road plenty of room when you pass them. They may turn around when they hear your engine and accidentally step into the road.

Mark **one** answer

What does this sign mean?

- No route for pedestrians and cyclists
- A route for pedestrians only
- A route for cyclists only
- A route for pedestrians and cyclists

⊙ **A route for pedestrians and cyclists**

This sign shows a shared route for pedestrians and cyclists: when it ends, the cyclists will be rejoining the main road.

Mark **one** answer

There are flashing amber lights under a school warning sign. What action should you take?

- Reduce speed until you are clear of the area
- Keep up your speed and sound the horn
- Increase your speed to clear the area quickly
- Wait at the lights until they change to green

⊙ **Reduce speed until you are clear of the area**

The flashing amber lights are switched on to warn you that children may be crossing near a school. Slow down and take extra care as you may have to stop.

Mark **one** answer

Where would you see this sign?

- Near a school crossing
- At a playground entrance
- On a school bus
- At a 'pedestrians only' area

⊙ **On a school bus**

Watch out for children crossing the road from the other side of the bus.

160

6.83

*Mark **one** answer*

What does this sign mean?

⊙ Contraflow pedal cycle lane

⊙ With-flow pedal cycle lane

⊙ Pedal cycles and buses only

⊙ No pedal cycles or buses

⊙ **With-flow pedal cycle lane**

The picture of a cycle will also usually be painted on the road, sometimes with a different colour surface. Leave these clear for cyclists and don't pass too closely when you overtake.

6.84

*Mark **one** answer*

A friend wants to help you learn to drive. They must be

⊙ over 21 and have held a full licence for at least two years

⊙ over 18 and hold an advanced driver's certificate

⊙ over 18 and have fully comprehensive insurance

⊙ over 21 and have held a full licence for at least three years

⊙ **over 21 and have held a full licence for at least three years**

Helping someone to drive is a responsible task. Before learning to drive you're advised to find a qualified Approved Driving Instructor (ADI) to teach you. This will ensure that you're taught the correct procedures from the start.

section seven
OTHER TYPES OF VEHICLE

This section covers:

- motorcycles
- lorries
- buses
- trams

7.1

*Mark **one** answer*

You are waiting to emerge left from a minor road. A large vehicle is approaching from the right. You have time to turn but you should wait. Why?

⊙ The large vehicle can easily hide an overtaking vehicle

⊙ The large vehicle can turn suddenly

⊙ The large vehicle is difficult to steer in a straight line

⊙ The large vehicle can easily hide vehicles from the left

⊙ **The large vehicle can easily hide an overtaking vehicle**

Large vehicles can hide other vehicles that are overtaking, especially motorcycles which may be filtering past queuing traffic. You need to be aware of the possibility of hidden vehicles and not assume that it is safe to emerge.

7.2

*Mark **one** answer*

You are following a long vehicle. It approaches a crossroads and signals left, but moves out to the right. You should

⊙ get closer in order to pass it quickly

⊙ stay well back and give it room

⊙ assume the signal is wrong and it is really turning right

⊙ overtake as it starts to slow down

⊙ **stay well back and give it room**

A lorry may swing out to the right as it approaches a left turn. This is to allow the rear wheels to clear the kerb as it turns. Don't try to filter through if you see a gap on the nearside.

7.3

*Mark **one** answer*

It is very windy. You are behind a motorcyclist who is overtaking a high-sided vehicle. What should you do?

⊙ Overtake the motorcyclist immediately

⊙ Keep well back

⊙ Stay level with the motorcyclist

⊙ Keep close to the motorcyclist

⊙ **Keep well back**

Motorcyclists are affected more by windy weather than other vehicles. In windy conditions, high-sided vehicles cause air turbulence. You should keep well back as the motorcyclist could be blown off course.

*Mark **one** answer*

You are following a long vehicle approaching a crossroads. The driver signals right but moves close to the left-hand kerb. What should you do?

⊙ Warn the driver of the wrong signal

⊙ Wait behind the long vehicle

⊙ Report the driver to the police

⊙ Overtake on the right-hand side

⊙ **Wait behind the long vehicle**

When a long vehicle is going to turn right it may need to keep close to the left-hand kerb. This is to prevent the rear end of the trailer cutting the corner. You need to be aware of how long vehicles behave in such situations. Don't overtake the lorry because it could turn as you're alongside. Stay behind and wait for it to turn.

*Mark **one** answer*

You are approaching a mini-roundabout. The long vehicle in front is signalling left but positioned over to the right. You should

⊙ sound your horn

⊙ overtake on the left

⊙ follow the same course as the lorry

⊙ keep well back

⊙ **keep well back**

At mini-roundabouts there isn't much room for a long vehicle to manoeuvre. It will have to swing out wide so that it can complete the turn safely. Keep well back and don't try to move up alongside it.

*Mark **one** answer*

It is very windy. You are about to overtake a motorcyclist. You should

⊙ overtake slowly

⊙ allow extra room

⊙ sound your horn

⊙ keep close as you pass

⊙ **allow extra room**

Crosswinds can blow a motorcyclist or cyclist across the lane. Passing too close could also cause a draught, unbalancing the rider.

7.7
*Mark **two** answers*

You are travelling behind a bus that pulls up at a bus stop. What should you do?

- ⊙ Accelerate past the bus sounding your horn
- ⊙ Watch carefully for pedestrians
- ⊙ Be ready to give way to the bus
- ⊙ Pull in closely behind the bus

⊙ **Watch carefully for pedestrians**

⊙ **Be ready to give way to the bus**

There might be pedestrians crossing from in front of the bus. Look out for them if you intend to pass. Consider staying back and waiting.

How many people are waiting to get on the bus? Check the queue if you can. The bus might move off straight away if there is no one waiting to get on.

If a bus is signalling to pull out, give it priority as long as it is safe to do so.

7.8
*Mark **one** answer*

You are driving along this road. What should you be prepared to do?

- ⊙ Sound your horn and continue
- ⊙ Slow down and give way
- ⊙ Report the driver to the police
- ⊙ Squeeze through the gap

⊙ **Slow down and give way**

Sometimes large vehicles may need more space than other road users. If a vehicle needs more time and space to turn be prepared to stop and wait.

7.9
*Mark **one** answer*

You keep well back while waiting to overtake a large vehicle. A car fills the gap. You should

- ⊙ sound your horn
- ⊙ drop back further
- ⊙ flash your headlights
- ⊙ start to overtake

⊙ **drop back further**

It's very frustrating when your separation distance is shortened by another vehicle. React positively, stay calm and drop further back.

What should you do as you approach this lorry?

- ⊙ Slow down and be prepared to wait
- ⊙ Make the lorry wait for you
- ⊙ Flash your lights at the lorry
- ⊙ Move to the right-hand side of the road

⊙ **Slow down and be prepared to wait**

When turning, long vehicles need much more room on the road than other vehicles. At junctions they may take up the whole of the road space, so be patient and allow them the room they need.

You are following a large articulated vehicle. It is going to turn left into a narrow road. What action should you take?

- ⊙ Move out and overtake on the right
- ⊙ Pass on the left as the vehicle moves out
- ⊙ Be prepared to stop behind
- ⊙ Overtake quickly before the lorry moves out

⊙ **Be prepared to stop behind**

Lorries are larger and longer than other vehicles and this can affect their position when approaching junctions. When turning left they may move out to the right so that they don't cut in and mount the kerb with the rear wheels.

7.12
*Mark **one** answer*

You are following a long lorry. The driver signals to turn left into a narrow road. What should you do?

⊙ Overtake on the left before the lorry reaches the junction

⊙ Overtake on the right as soon as the lorry slows down

⊙ Do not overtake unless you can see there is no oncoming traffic

⊙ Do not overtake, stay well back and be prepared to stop.

⊙ **Do not overtake, stay well back and be prepared to stop.**

When turning into narrow roads articulated and long vehicles will need more room. Initially they will need to swing out in the opposite direction to which they intend to turn. They could mask another vehicle turning out of the same junction. DON'T be tempted to overtake them or pass on the inside.

7.13
*Mark **two** answers*

You are driving in town. Ahead of you a bus is at a bus stop. Which TWO of the following should you do?

⊙ Be prepared to give way if the bus suddenly moves off

⊙ Continue at the same speed but sound your horn as a warning

⊙ Watch carefully for the sudden appearance of pedestrians

⊙ Pass the bus as quickly as you possibly can

⊙ **Be prepared to give way if the bus suddenly moves off**

⊙ **Watch carefully for the sudden appearance of pedestrians**

As you approach, look out for any signal the driver might make. If you pass the vehicle watch out for pedestrians attempting to cross the road from the other side of the bus. They will be hidden from view until the last moment.

7.14
*Mark **one** answer*

You are towing a caravan. Which is the safest type of rear-view mirror to use?

⊙ Interior wide-angle mirror
⊙ Extended-arm side mirrors
⊙ Ordinary door mirrors
⊙ Ordinary interior mirror

⊙ **Extended-arm side mirrors**

Towing a large trailer or caravan can greatly reduce your view of the road. You need to use the correct equipment to make sure you can see clearly behind and down both sides of the caravan or trailer.

7.15

Mark **one** answer

You are following a large vehicle approaching crossroads. The driver signals to turn left. What should you do?

- ☉ Overtake if you can leave plenty of room
- ☉ Overtake only if there are no oncoming vehicles
- ☉ Do not overtake until the vehicle begins to turn
- ☉ Do not overtake when at or approaching a junction

☉ **Do not overtake when at or approaching a junction**

Hold back and wait until the vehicle has turned before proceeding. Do not overtake because the vehicle turning left could hide a vehicle emerging from the same junction.

7.16

Mark **one** answer

Before overtaking a large vehicle you should keep well back. Why is this?

- ☉ To give acceleration space to overtake quickly on blind bends
- ☉ To get the best view of the road ahead
- ☉ To leave a gap in case the vehicle stops and rolls back
- ☉ To offer other drivers a safe gap if they want to overtake you

☉ **To get the best view of the road ahead**

When following a large vehicle keep well back. If you're too close you won't be able to see the road ahead and the driver of the long vehicle might not be able to see you in their mirrors.

7.17

Mark **one** answer

Why is passing a lorry more risky than passing a car?

- ☉ Lorries are longer than cars
- ☉ Lorries may suddenly pull up
- ☉ The brakes of lorries are not as good
- ☉ Lorries climb hills more slowly

☉ **Lorries are longer than cars**

Hazards to watch for include

- oncoming traffic
- junctions
- bends or dips, which could restrict your view
- any signs or road markings prohibiting overtaking.

Never begin to overtake unless you can see that it's safe to complete the manoeuvre.

7.18 — *Mark two answers*

You are driving in heavy traffic on a wet road. Spray makes it difficult to be seen. You should use your

- full beam headlights
- rear fog lights if visibility is less than 100 metres (328 feet)
- rear fog lights if visibility is more than 100 metres (328 feet)
- dipped headlights
- sidelights only

⊙ **rear fog lights if visibility is less than 100 metres (328 feet)**

⊙ **dipped headlights**

You must ensure that you can be seen by others on the road. Use your dipped headlights during the day if the visibility is bad. If you use your rear fog lights, don't forget to turn them off when the visibility improves.

7.19 — *Mark one answer*

You are about to overtake a slow-moving motorcyclist. Which one of these signs would make you take special care?

In windy weather, watch out for motorcyclists and also cyclists as they can be blown sideways into your path. When you pass them, leave plenty of room and check their position in your mirror before pulling back in.

7.20 — *Mark one answer*

Which of these is LEAST likely to be affected by crosswinds?

- Cyclists
- Motorcyclists
- High-sided vehicles
- Cars

⊙ **Cars**

Although cars are the least likely to be affected, crosswinds can take anyone by surprise, especially

- after overtaking a large vehicle
- when passing gaps between hedges or buildings
- on exposed sections of road.

When you approach a bus signalling to move off from a bus stop you should

- ⊙ get past before it moves
- ⊙ allow it to pull away, if it is safe to do so
- ⊙ flash your headlights as you approach
- ⊙ signal left and wave the bus on

⊙ **allow it to pull away, if it is safe to do so**

Give way to buses whenever you can do so safely, especially when they signal to pull away from bus stops. Look out for people who've got off the bus and may try to cross the road. Don't

- • try to accelerate past before it moves away
- • flash your lights – other road users may be misled by this signal.

As a driver why should you be more careful where trams operate?

- ⊙ Because they do not have a horn
- ⊙ Because they do not stop for cars
- ⊙ Because they do not have lights
- ⊙ Because they cannot steer to avoid you

⊙ **Because they cannot steer to avoid you**

You should take extra care when you first encounter trams. You will have to get used to dealing with a different traffic system.

Be aware that they can accelerate and travel very quickly and that they cannot change direction to avoid obstructions.

The road is wet. Why might a motorcyclist steer round drain covers on a bend?

- ⊙ To avoid puncturing the tyres on the edge of the drain covers
- ⊙ To prevent the motorcycle sliding on the metal drain covers
- ⊙ To help judge the bend using the drain covers as marker points
- ⊙ To avoid splashing pedestrians on the pavement

⊙ **To prevent the motorcycle sliding on the metal drain covers**

The actions of other drivers or riders may be due to the size or characteristics of their vehicle. If you understand this it will help you to anticipate their actions.

Motorcyclists will be checking the road ahead for uneven or slippery surfaces, especially in wet weather. They may need to move across their lane to avoid road surface hazards such as potholes and drain covers.

7.24 *Mark one answer*

You are following a large lorry on a wet road. Spray makes it difficult to see. You should

- ⊙ drop back until you can see better
- ⊙ put your headlights on full beam
- ⊙ keep close to the lorry, away from the spray
- ⊙ speed up and overtake quickly

⊙ **drop back until you can see better**

Large vehicles may throw up a lot of spray when the roads are wet. This will make it difficult for you to see ahead. Dropping back further will

- move you out of the spray and allow you to see further
- increase your separation distance. It takes longer to stop when the roads are wet and you need to allow more room.

Don't

- follow the vehicle in front too closely
- overtake, unless you can see and are sure that the way ahead is clear.

7.25 *Mark one answer*

You wish to overtake a long, slow-moving vehicle on a busy road. You should

- ⊙ follow it closely and keep moving out to see the road ahead
- ⊙ flash your headlights for the oncoming traffic to give way
- ⊙ stay behind until the driver waves you past
- ⊙ keep well back until you can see that it is clear

⊙ **keep well back until you can see that it is clear**

If you wish to overtake a long vehicle, stay well back so that you can see the road ahead. DON'T

- get up close to the vehicle – this will restrict your view of the road ahead
- get impatient – overtaking on a busy road calls for sound judgement
- take a gamble – only overtake when you can see that you can safely complete the manoeuvre.

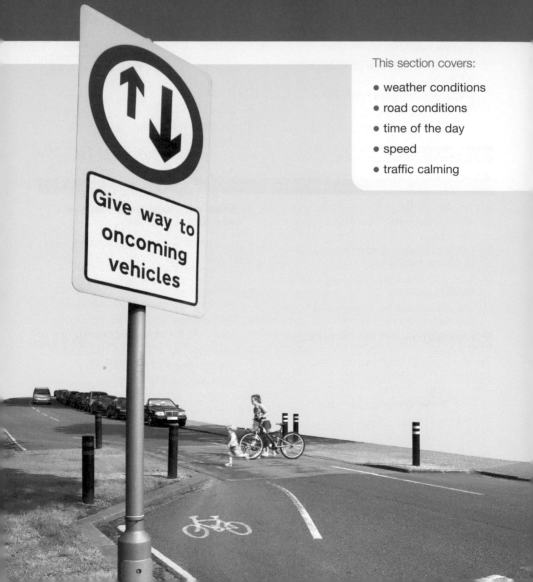

section eight
VEHICLE HANDLING

This section covers:

- weather conditions
- road conditions
- time of the day
- speed
- traffic calming

8.1

*Mark **one** answer*

Why should you test your brakes after this hazard?

- ⊙ Because you will be on a slippery road
- ⊙ Because your brakes will be soaking wet
- ⊙ Because you will have gone down a long hill
- ⊙ Because you will have just crossed a long bridge

⊙ **Because your brakes will be soaking wet**

A ford is a crossing over a stream that's shallow enough to go through. When you've gone through a ford or a deep puddle the water can affect your brakes. If they don't work properly it will help to dry them. To do this, apply a light brake pressure while moving slowly.

Don't travel at normal speeds until you are sure your brakes are working properly again.

8.2

*Mark **one** answer*

To correct a rear-wheel skid you should

- ⊙ not steer at all
- ⊙ steer away from it
- ⊙ steer into it
- ⊙ apply your handbrake

⊙ **steer into it**

Prevention is better than cure, so it's important that you take every precaution to avoid a skid from starting.

If you feel the rear wheels of your vehicle beginning to skid, try to steer in the same direction to recover control. Don't brake suddenly – this will only make the situation worse.

8.3

*Mark **one** answer*

You should switch your rear fog lights on when visibility drops below

- ⊙ your overall stopping distance
- ⊙ ten car lengths
- ⊙ 200 metres (656 feet)
- ⊙ 100 metres (328 feet)

⊙ **100 metres (328 feet)**

If visibility falls below 100 metres in fog, switching on your rear fog lights will help following road users to see you. Don't forget to turn them off once visibility improves: their brightness might be mistaken for brake lights and they could dazzle other drivers.

8.4
*Mark **three** answers*

Which THREE of the following will affect your stopping distance?

- How fast you are going
- The tyres on your vehicle
- The time of day
- The weather
- The street lighting

- ⊙ **How fast you are going**
- ⊙ **The tyres on your vehicle**
- ⊙ **The weather**

There are several factors that can affect the distance it takes to stop your vehicle.

Adjust your driving to take account of how the weather conditions could affect your tyres' grip on the road.

8.5
*Mark **two** answers*

What are TWO main reasons why coasting downhill is wrong?

- Fuel consumption will be higher
- The vehicle will pick up speed
- It puts more wear and tear on the tyres
- You have less braking and steering control
- It damages the engine

- ⊙ **The vehicle will pick up speed**
- ⊙ **You have less braking and steering control**

Coasting is when you allow the vehicle to freewheel in neutral or with the clutch pedal depressed. Doing this gives you less control over the vehicle. It's especially important not to let your vehicle coast when approaching hazards such as junctions and bends and when travelling downhill.

8.6
*Mark **two** answers*

Hills can affect the performance of your vehicle. Which TWO apply when driving up steep hills?

- Higher gears will pull better
- You will slow down sooner
- Overtaking will be easier
- The engine will work harder
- The steering will feel heavier

- ⊙ **You will slow down sooner**
- ⊙ **The engine will work harder**

The engine will need more power to pull the vehicle up the hill. When approaching a steep hill you should select a lower gear to help maintain your speed. You should do this without hesitation, so that you don't lose too much speed before engaging the lower gear.

8.7 *Mark **four** answers*

Which of the following may apply when dealing with this hazard?

Ford

⊙ It could be more difficult in winter
⊙ Use a low gear and drive slowly
⊙ Use a high gear to prevent wheelspin
⊙ Test your brakes afterwards
⊙ Always switch on fog lamps
⊙ There may be a depth gauge

⊙ **It could be more difficult in winter**

⊙ **Use a low gear and drive slowly**

⊙ **Test your brakes afterwards**

⊙ **There may be a depth gauge**

During the winter the stream is likely to flood. It is also possible that in extremely cold weather it could ice over. Assess the situation carefully before you drive through. If you drive a vehicle with low suspension you may have to find a different route.

8.8 *Mark **one** answer*

You are driving down a long steep hill. You suddenly notice your brakes are not working as well as normal. What is the usual cause of this?

⊙ The brakes overheating
⊙ Air in the brake fluid
⊙ Oil on the brakes
⊙ Badly adjusted brakes

⊙ **The brakes overheating**

This is more likely to happen on vehicles fitted with drum brakes but can apply to disc brakes as well. Using a lower gear will assist the braking and help you to keep control of your vehicle.

8.9 *Mark **one** answer*

Why is coasting wrong?

⊙ It will cause the car to skid
⊙ It will make the engine stall
⊙ The engine will run faster
⊙ There is no engine braking

⊙ **There is no engine braking**

Try to look ahead and read the road. Plan your approach to junctions and select the correct gear in good time. This will give you the control you need to deal with any hazards that occur.

You'll coast a little every time you change gear. This can't be avoided, but it should be kept to a minimum.

How can you use the engine of your vehicle to control your speed?

- ⊙ By changing to a lower gear
- ⊙ By selecting reverse gear
- ⊙ By changing to a higher gear
- ⊙ By selecting neutral

⊙ **By changing to a lower gear**

You should brake and slow down before selecting a lower gear. The gear can then be used to keep the speed low and help you control the vehicle. This is particularly helpful on long downhill stretches, where brake fade can occur if the brakes overheat.

Holding the clutch pedal down or rolling in neutral for too long while driving will

- ⊙ use more fuel
- ⊙ cause the engine to overheat
- ⊙ reduce your control
- ⊙ improve tyre wear

⊙ **reduce your control**

Holding the clutch down or staying in neutral for too long will cause your vehicle to freewheel. This is known as 'coasting' and it is dangerous as it reduces your control of the vehicle.

You will feel the effects of engine braking when you

- ⊙ only use the handbrake
- ⊙ only use neutral
- ⊙ change to a lower gear
- ⊙ change to a higher gear

⊙ **change to a lower gear**

When going downhill, prolonged use of the brakes can cause them to overheat and lose their effectiveness. Changing to a lower gear will assist your braking.

You see a vehicle coming towards you on a single-track road. You should

- ⊙ go back to the main road
- ⊙ do an emergency stop
- ⊙ stop at a passing place
- ⊙ put on your hazard warning lights

⊙ **stop at a passing place**

You must take extra care when on single track roads. You may not be able to see around bends due to high hedges or fences. Proceed with caution and expect to meet oncoming vehicles around the next bend. If you do, pull into or opposite a passing place.

8.14
*Mark **one** answer*

You are driving down a steep hill. Why could keeping the clutch down or rolling in neutral for too long be dangerous?

⊙ Fuel consumption will be higher

⊙ Your vehicle will pick up speed

⊙ It will damage the engine

⊙ It will wear tyres out more quickly

⊙ **Your vehicle will pick up speed**

Driving in neutral or with the clutch down for long periods is known as 'coasting'. There will be no engine braking and your vehicle will pick up speed on downhill slopes. Coasting can be very dangerous because it reduces steering and braking control.

8.15
*Mark **one** answer*

You are on a well-lit motorway at night. You must

⊙ use only your sidelights

⊙ always use your headlights

⊙ always use rear fog lights

⊙ use headlights only in bad weather

⊙ **always use your headlights**

If you're driving on a motorway at night or or in poor visibility, you must always use your headlights, even if the road is well-lit. The other road users in front must be able to see you in their mirrors.

8.16
*Mark **two** answers*

Which TWO of the following are correct? When overtaking at night you should

⊙ wait until a bend so that you can see the oncoming headlights

⊙ sound your horn twice before moving out

⊙ be careful because you can see less

⊙ beware of bends in the road ahead

⊙ put headlights on full beam

⊙ **be careful because you can see less**

⊙ **beware of bends in the road ahead**

Only overtake the vehicle in front if it's really necessary. At night the risks are increased due to the poor visibility.

Don't overtake if there's a possibility of

• road junctions

• bends ahead

• the brow of a bridge or hill, except on a dual carriageway

• pedestrian crossings

• double white lines ahead

• vehicles changing direction

• any other potential hazard.

You are on a motorway at night. You MUST have your headlights switched on unless

- ⊙ there are vehicles close in front of you
- ⊙ you are travelling below 50 mph
- ⊙ the motorway is lit
- ⊙ your vehicle is broken down on the hard shoulder

⊙ **your vehicle is broken down on the hard shoulder**

Always use your headlights at night on a motorway unless you have stopped on the hard shoulder.

If you break down and have to stop on the hard shoulder, switch off the headlights but leave the sidelights on so that other road users can see your vehicle.

You are on a motorway in fog. The left-hand edge of the motorway can be identified by reflective studs. What colour are they?

- ⊙ Green
- ⊙ Amber
- ⊙ Red
- ⊙ White

⊙ **Red**

Be especially careful if you're on a motorway in fog. Reflective studs are used to help you in poor visibility. Different colours are used so that you'll know which lane you are in. These are

- • red on the left-hand side of the road
- • white between lanes
- • amber on the right-hand edge of the carriageway
- • green between the carriageway and slip roads.

You are on a motorway at night with other vehicles just ahead of you. Which lights should you have on?

- ⊙ Front fog lights
- ⊙ Main beam headlights
- ⊙ Sidelights only
- ⊙ Dipped headlights

⊙ **Dipped headlights**

If you're driving behind other traffic at night on the motorway

- • leave a two-second time gap
- • dip your headlights.

Full beam will dazzle the driver ahead. Your headlights' beam should fall short of the vehicle in front.

8.20
*Mark **one** answer*

Why could keeping the clutch down or selecting neutral for long periods of time be dangerous?

⊙ Fuel spillage will occur

⊙ Engine damage may be caused

⊙ You will have less steering and braking control

⊙ It will wear tyres out more quickly

⊙ **You will have less steering and braking control**

Letting your vehicle roll or coast in neutral reduces your control over steering and braking. This can be dangerous on downhill slopes where your vehicle could pick up speed very quickly.

8.21
NI EXEMPT   *Mark **two** answers*

You are driving on a clear dry night with your rear fog lights switched on. This may

⊙ reduce glare from the road surface

⊙ make other drivers think you are braking

⊙ give a better view of the road ahead

⊙ dazzle following drivers

⊙ help your indicators to be seen more clearly

⊙ **make other drivers think you are braking**

⊙ **dazzle following drivers**

A warning light will show on the dashboard to indicate when your rear fog lights are on. You should know the meaning of all the lights on your dashboard and check them before you move off and as you drive.

8.22
*Mark **one** answer*

You are travelling at night. You are dazzled by headlights coming towards you. You should

⊙ pull down your sun visor

⊙ slow down or stop

⊙ switch on your main beam headlights

⊙ put your hand over your eyes

⊙ **slow down or stop**

If you're driving at night there will be extra hazards to deal with. Visibility may be very limited and the lights of oncoming vehicles can often dazzle you. If this happens don't

• close your eyes

• swerve

• flash your headlights. This will only distract the other driver too.

8.23

You are overtaking a car at night. You must be sure that

- ⊙ you flash your headlights before overtaking
- ⊙ you select a higher gear
- ⊙ you have switched your lights to full beam before overtaking
- ⊙ you do not dazzle other road users

⊙ **you do not dazzle other road users**

To prevent your lights from dazzling the driver of the car in front, wait until you've overtaken before switching to full beam.

8.24

In which THREE of these situations may you overtake another vehicle on the left?

- ⊙ When you are in a one-way street
- ⊙ When approaching a motorway slip road where you will be turning off
- ⊙ When the vehicle in front is signalling to turn right
- ⊙ When a slower vehicle is travelling in the right-hand lane of a dual carriageway
- ⊙ In slow-moving traffic queues when traffic in the right-hand lane is moving more slowly

⊙ **When you are in a one-way street**

⊙ **When the vehicle in front is signalling to turn right**

⊙ **In slow-moving traffic queues when traffic in the right-hand lane is moving more slowly**

At certain times of the day traffic might be heavy. If traffic is moving slowly in queues and vehicles in the right-hand lane are moving more slowly, you may overtake on the left. Don't keep changing lanes to try and beat the queue.

8.25

You are on a narrow road at night. A slower-moving vehicle ahead has been signalling right for some time. What should you do?

- ⊙ Overtake on the left
- ⊙ Flash your headlights before overtaking
- ⊙ Signal right and sound your horn
- ⊙ Wait for the signal to be cancelled before overtaking

⊙ **Wait for the signal to be cancelled before overtaking**

If the vehicle in front has been indicating right for some time but has made no attempt to turn, wait for the signal to be cancelled. The other driver may have misjudged the distance to the road junction or there might be a hidden hazard.

8.26 *Mark **one** answer*

When may you wait in a box junction?

- ⊙ When you are stationary in a queue of traffic
- ⊙ When approaching a pelican crossing
- ⊙ When approaching a zebra crossing
- ⊙ When oncoming traffic prevents you turning right

⊙ **When oncoming traffic prevents you turning right**

The purpose of this road marking is to keep the junction clear by preventing traffic from stopping in the path of crossing traffic.

You must not enter a box junction unless your exit is clear. The only exception to this is if you want to turn right but you have to wait because of oncoming traffic or other vehicles waiting to turn right.

8.27 *Mark **two** answers*

A rumble device is designed to

- ⊙ give directions
- ⊙ prevent cattle escaping
- ⊙ alert you to low tyre pressure
- ⊙ alert you to a hazard
- ⊙ encourage you to reduce speed

⊙ **alert you to a hazard**

⊙ **encourage you to reduce speed**

A rumble device usually consists of raised markings or strips across the road. It gives an audible, visual and tactile warning of a hazard. These strips are found in places where traffic has constantly ignored warning or restriction signs. They are there for a good reason. Slow down and be ready to deal with a hazard.

8.28 *Mark **one** answer*

Traffic calming measures are used to

- ⊙ stop road rage
- ⊙ help overtaking
- ⊙ slow traffic down
- ⊙ help parking

⊙ **slow traffic down**

Traffic calming measures are used to make the roads safer for vulnerable road users, such as cyclists, pedestrians and children. These can be designed as chicanes, road humps or other obstacles that encourage drivers and riders to slow down.

You see these markings on the road. Why are they there?

- To show a safe distance between vehicles
- To keep the area clear of traffic
- To make you aware of your speed
- To warn you to change direction

⊙ **To make you aware of your speed**

These lines may be painted on the road on the approach to a roundabout, village or a particular hazard. The lines are raised and painted yellow and their purpose is to make you aware of your speed. Reduce your speed in good time so that you avoid having to brake harshly over the last few metres before reaching the junction.

Which of these plates normally appear with this road sign?

- **Humps for ½ mile**
- **HumpBridge**
- **Low Bridge**
- **Soft Verge**

⊙ **Humps for ½ mile**

Road humps are used to slow down the traffic. They are found in places where there are often pedestrians, such as

- in shopping areas
- near schools
- in residential areas.

Watch out for people close to the kerb or crossing the road.

You are on a road which has speed humps. A driver in front is travelling slower than you. You should

- sound your horn
- overtake as soon as you can
- flash your headlights
- slow down and stay behind

⊙ **slow down and stay behind**

Be patient and stay behind the car in front. Normally, you should not overtake other vehicles in traffic-calmed areas because if you overtake here your speed may exceed that which is safe along that road, defeating the purpose of the traffic calming measures.

8.32
*Mark **three** answers*

Areas reserved for trams may have

- ⊙ metal studs around them
- ⊙ white line markings
- ⊙ zigzag markings
- ⊙ a different coloured surface
- ⊙ yellow hatch markings
- ⊙ a different surface texture

- ⊙ **white line markings**
- ⊙ **a different coloured surface**
- ⊙ **a different surface texture**

Trams can run on roads used by other vehicles and pedestrians. The part of the road used by the trams is known as the reserved area and this should be kept clear. It has a coloured surface and is usually edged with white road markings. It might also have different surface texture.

8.33
*Mark **one** answer*

You have to make a journey in foggy conditions. You should

- ⊙ follow other vehicles' tail lights closely
- ⊙ avoid using dipped headlights
- ⊙ leave plenty of time for your journey
- ⊙ keep two seconds behind other vehicles

- ⊙ **leave plenty of time for your journey**

If you're planning to make a journey when it's foggy, listen to the weather reports on the radio or television. Don't travel if visibility is very poor or your trip isn't necessary.

If you do travel, leave plenty of time for your journey. If someone is expecting you at the other end, let them know that you'll be taking longer than normal to arrive.

8.34
*Mark **one** answer*

You are following other vehicles in fog with your lights on. How else can you reduce the chances of being involved in an accident?

- ⊙ Keep close to the vehicle in front
- ⊙ Use your main beam instead of dipped headlights
- ⊙ Keep together with the faster vehicles
- ⊙ Reduce your speed and increase the gap

- ⊙ **Reduce your speed and increase the gap**

When you're travelling in fog, always ensure that you have your dipped headlights and/or fog lights on so that you can be seen by other road users.

Keep at a sensible speed and don't follow the vehicle in front too closely. If the road is wet and slippery you'll need to allow twice the normal stopping distance.

You are travelling in very heavy rain. Your overall stopping distance is likely to be

- doubled
- halved
- up to ten times greater
- no different

⊙ **doubled**

As well as visibility being reduced, the road will be extremely wet. This will reduce the grip the tyres have on the road and increase the distance it takes to stop. Double your separation distance.

You are driving in fog. Why should you keep well back from the vehicle in front?

- In case it changes direction suddenly
- In case its fog lights dazzle you
- In case it stops suddenly
- In case its brake lights dazzle you

⊙ **In case it stops suddenly**

If you're following another road user in fog stay well back. The driver in front won't be able to see hazards until they're close and might brake suddenly. Another reason why it is important to maintain a good separation distance in fog is that the road surface is likely to be wet and slippery.

Chains can be fitted to your wheels to help prevent

- damage to the road surface
- wear to the tyres
- skidding in deep snow
- the brakes locking

⊙ **skidding in deep snow**

Snow chains can be fitted to your tyres during snowy conditions. They can help you to move off from rest or to keep moving in deep snow. You will still need to adjust your driving according to the road conditions at the time.

Whilst driving, the fog clears and you can see more clearly. You must remember to

- switch off the fog lights
- reduce your speed
- switch off the demister
- close any open windows

⊙ **switch off the fog lights**

Bright rear fog lights might be mistaken for brake lights and could be misleading for the traffic behind.

8.39 *Mark one answer*

Why should you always reduce your speed when travelling in fog?

⊙ Because the brakes do not work as well

⊙ Because you could be dazzled by other people's fog lights

⊙ Because the engine is colder

⊙ Because it is more difficult to see events ahead

⊙ **Because it is more difficult to see events ahead**

You won't be able to see as far ahead in fog as you can on a clear day. You will need to reduce your speed so that, if a hazard looms out of the fog, you have the time and space to take avoiding action.

Travelling in fog is hazardous. If you can, try and delay your journey until it has cleared.

8.40 *Mark one answer*

Front fog lights may be used ONLY if

⊙ your headlights are not working

⊙ they are operated with rear fog lights

⊙ they were fitted by the vehicle manufacturer

⊙ visibility is seriously reduced

⊙ **visibility is seriously reduced**

It is illegal to use fog lights unless visibility is seriously reduced generally when you cannot see for more than 100 metres (328 feet). Check that they have been switched off when conditions improve.

8.41 *Mark one answer*

You are driving with your front fog lights switched on. Earlier fog has now cleared. What should you do?

⊙ Leave them on if other drivers have their lights on

⊙ Switch them off as long as visibility remains good

⊙ Flash them to warn oncoming traffic that it is foggy

⊙ Drive with them on instead of your headlights

⊙ **Switch them off as long as visibility remains good**

Switch off your fog lights if the weather improves, but be prepared to use them again if visibility reduces to less than 100 metres (328 feet).

8.42 — Mark *one* answer

You are driving on the motorway in windy conditions. When passing high-sided vehicles you should

- ⊙ increase your speed
- ⊙ be wary of a sudden gust
- ⊙ drive alongside very closely
- ⊙ expect normal conditions

⊙ **be wary of a sudden gust**

The draught caused by other vehicles could be strong enough to push you out of your lane. Keep both hands on the steering wheel to maintain full control.

8.43 — Mark *one* answer

Using rear fog lights in clear daylight will

- ⊙ be useful when towing a trailer
- ⊙ give extra protection
- ⊙ dazzle other drivers
- ⊙ make following drivers keep back

⊙ **dazzle other drivers**

Rear fog lights shine brighter than normal rear lights so that they show up in reduced visibility. When the weather is clear they could dazzle the driver behind, so switch them off.

8.44 — Mark *one* answer

On a foggy day you unavoidably have to park your car on the road. You should

- ⊙ leave your headlights on
- ⊙ leave your fog lights on
- ⊙ leave your sidelights on
- ⊙ leave your hazard lights on

⊙ **leave your sidelights on**

Ensure that your vehicle can be seen by other traffic. If possible, park your car off the road in a car park or driveway to avoid the extra risk to other road users.

8.45 — Mark *one* answer

Front fog lights may be used ONLY if

- ⊙ visibility is seriously reduced
- ⊙ they are fitted above the bumper
- ⊙ they are not as bright as the headlights
- ⊙ an audible warning device is used

⊙ **visibility is seriously reduced**

Your vehicle should have a warning light on the dashboard which illuminates when the fog lights are being used. You need to be familiar with the layout of your dashboard so you are aware if they have been switched on in error, or you have forgotten to switch them off.

8.46 *NI EXEMPT* *Mark **three** answers*

You forget to switch off your rear fog lights when the fog has cleared. This may

- ⊙ dazzle other road users
- ⊙ reduce battery life
- ⊙ cause brake lights to be less clear
- ⊙ be breaking the law
- ⊙ seriously affect engine power

- ⊙ **dazzle other road users**

- ⊙ **cause brake lights to be less clear**

- ⊙ **be breaking the law**

Don't forget to switch off your fog lights when the weather improves. You could be prosecuted for driving with them on in good visibility. The high intensity of the rear fog lights can look like brakes lights and, on a high speed road, this can cause other road users to brake unnecessarily.

8.47 *NI EXEMPT* *Mark **one** answer*

You have been driving in thick fog which has now cleared. You must switch OFF your rear fog lights because

- ⊙ they use a lot of power from the battery
- ⊙ they make your brake lights less clear
- ⊙ they will cause dazzle in your rear view mirrors
- ⊙ they may not be properly adjusted

- ⊙ **they make your brake lights less clear**

It is essential that the traffic behind is given a clear warning when you brake. In good visibility, your rear fog lights can make it hard for others to see your brake lights. Make sure you switch off your fog lights when the visibility improves.

8.48 *Mark **one** answer*

While you are driving in fog, it becomes necessary to use front fog lights. You should

- ⊙ only turn them on in heavy traffic conditions
- ⊙ remember not to use them on motorways
- ⊙ only use them on dual carriageways
- ⊙ remember to switch them off as visibility improves

- ⊙ **remember to switch them off as visibility improves**

It is an offence to have your fog lights on in conditions other than seriously reduced visibility, ie. less than 100 metres (328 feet).

You have to park on the road in fog. You should

- leave sidelights on
- leave dipped headlights and fog lights on
- leave dipped headlights on
- leave main beam headlights on

⊙ **leave sidelights on**

If you have to park your vehicle in foggy conditions it's important that it can be seen by other road users.

Try to find a place to park off the road. If this isn't possible leave it facing in the same direction as the traffic. Make sure that your lights are clean and that you leave your sidelights on.

Using front fog lights in clear daylight will

- flatten the battery
- dazzle other drivers
- improve your visibility
- increase your awareness

⊙ **dazzle other drivers**

Fog lights can be brighter than normal dipped headlights. If the weather has improved turn them off to avoid dazzling other road users.

You may use front fog lights with headlights ONLY when visibility is reduced to less than

- 100 metres (328 feet)
- 200 metres (656 feet)
- 300 metres (984 feet)
- 400 metres (1312 feet)

⊙ **100 metres (328 feet)**

It is an offence to use fog lights if the visibility is better than 100 metres (328 feet). Switch front fog lights off if the fog clears to avoid dazzling other road users, but be aware that the fog may be patchy.

You are driving on an icy road. What distance should you drive from the car in front?

- four times the normal distance
- six times the normal distance
- eight times the normal distance
- ten times the normal distance

⊙ **ten times the normal distance**

Don't travel in icy or snowy weather unless your journey is necessary.

Drive extremely carefully when roads are, or may be, icy. Stopping distances can be ten times greater than on dry roads.

8.53
*Mark **one** answer*

Front fog lights should be used

- ⊙ when visibility is reduced to 100 metres (328 feet)
- ⊙ as a warning to oncoming traffic
- ⊙ when driving during the hours of darkness
- ⊙ in any conditions and at any time

⊙ **when visibility is reduced to 100 metres (328 feet)**

When visibility is seriously reduced, switch on your fog lights if you have them fitted. It is essential not only that you can see ahead, but also that other road users are able to see you.

8.54
*Mark **one** answer*

When MUST you use dipped headlights during the day?

- ⊙ All the time
- ⊙ Along narrow streets
- ⊙ In poor visibility
- ⊙ When parking

⊙ **In poor visibility**

You MUST use dipped headlights and/or fog lights in fog when visibility is 100 metres (328 feet) or less.

You should use dipped headlights, but NOT fog lights, when visibility is reduced, such as in heavy rain.

8.55
*Mark **one** answer*

Daytime visibility is poor but not seriously reduced. You should switch on

- ⊙ headlights and fog lights
- ⊙ front fog lights
- ⊙ dipped headlights
- ⊙ rear fog lights

⊙ **dipped headlights**

Only use your fog lights when visibility is seriously reduced. Use dipped headlights in poor conditions.

8.56
*Mark **one** answer*

Front fog lights should be used ONLY when

- ⊙ travelling in very light rain
- ⊙ visibility is seriously reduced
- ⊙ daylight is fading
- ⊙ driving after midnight

⊙ **visibility is seriously reduced**

Fog lights will help others see you but remember, they must only be used if visibility is seriously reduced to less than 100 metres (328 feet).

Why are vehicles fitted with rear fog lights?

- To be seen when driving at high speed
- To use if broken down in a dangerous position
- To make them more visible in thick fog
- To warn drivers following closely to drop back

⊙ **To make them more visible in thick fog**

Rear fog lights make it easier to spot a vehicle ahead in foggy conditions.

Avoid the temptation to use other vehicles' lights as a guide though, as they will give you a false sense of security.

When snow is falling heavily you should

- only drive with your hazard lights on
- not drive unless you have a mobile phone
- only drive when your journey is short
- not drive unless it is essential

⊙ **not drive unless it is essential**

Consider if the increased risk is worth it. If the weather conditions are bad and your journey isn't essential, then stay at home.

Why is it dangerous to leave rear fog lights on when they are not needed?

- Brake lights are less clear
- Following drivers can be dazzled
- Electrical systems could be overloaded
- Direction indicators may not work properly
- The battery could fail

⊙ **Brake lights are less clear**

⊙ **Following drivers can be dazzled**

If your rear fog lights are left on when it isn't foggy, the glare they cause makes it difficult for road users behind to know whether you are braking or you have forgotten to turn off your rear fog lights. This can be a particular problem on wet roads and on motorways.

If you leave your rear fog lights on at night, road users behind you are likely to be dazzled and this could put them at risk.

8.60
*Mark **one** answer*

You have just driven out of fog. Visibility is now good. You MUST

- ⊙ switch off all your fog lights
- ⊙ keep your rear fog lights on
- ⊙ keep your front fog lights on
- ⊙ leave fog lights on in case fog returns

⊙ **switch off all your fog lights**

You must turn off your fog lights if visibility is over 100 metres (328 feet). However, be prepared for the fact that the fog may be patchy.

8.61
*Mark **one** answer*

You may drive with front fog lights switched on

- ⊙ when visibility is less than 100 metres (328 feet)
- ⊙ at any time to be noticed
- ⊙ instead of headlights on high speed roads
- ⊙ when dazzled by the lights of oncoming vehicles

⊙ **when visibility is less than 100 metres (328 feet)**

Only use front fog lights if the distance you are able to see is less than 100 metres (328 feet). Turn off your fog lights as the weather improves.

8.62
*Mark **two** answers*

You have to make a journey in fog. What are the TWO most important things you should do before you set out?

- ⊙ Top up the radiator with anti-freeze
- ⊙ Make sure that you have a warning triangle in the vehicle
- ⊙ Check that your lights are working
- ⊙ Check the battery
- ⊙ Make sure that the windows are clean

⊙ **Check that your lights are working**

⊙ **Make sure that the windows are clean**

Don't drive in fog unless you really have to. Adjust your driving to the conditions. You should always be able to pull up within the distance you can see clearly ahead.

section nine
MOTORWAY RULES

This section covers:

- speed limits
- lane discipline
- stopping
- lighting
- parking

9.1 *Mark **one** answer*

When joining a motorway you must always

- ⊙ use the hard shoulder
- ⊙ stop at the end of the acceleration lane
- ⊙ come to a stop before joining the motorway
- ⊙ give way to traffic already on the motorway

⊙ **give way to traffic already on the motorway**

You must give way to traffic already on the motorway. Don't try to force your way into the traffic stream.

You should join the motorway where there's a suitable gap in the left-hand lane. The traffic may be travelling at high speed so you should adjust your speed to fit in with the vehicles on the motorway.

9.2 *Mark **one** answer*

What is the national speed limit for cars and motorcycles in the centre lane of a three-lane motorway?

- ⊙ 40 mph
- ⊙ 50 mph
- ⊙ 60 mph
- ⊙ 70 mph

⊙ **70 mph**

Unless otherwise indicated the speed limit for the motorway applies to all the lanes.

Be on the lookout for any indication of speed limit changes due to roadworks or traffic flow control.

9.3 *NI EXEMPT* *Mark **one** answer*

You break down on a motorway. You need to call for help. Why may it be better to use an emergency roadside telephone rather than a mobile phone?

- ⊙ It connects you to a local garage
- ⊙ Using a mobile phone will distract other drivers
- ⊙ It allows easy location by the emergency services
- ⊙ Mobile phones do not work on motorways

⊙ **It allows easy location by the emergency services**

On a motorway it is best to use a roadside emergency telephone so that the emergency services are able to locate you easily. The nearest telephone is indicated by an arrow on the marker posts at the edge of the hard shoulder.

If you do use a mobile phone, the emergency services will want to know your exact location. Before you call, find out the number on the nearest marker post. This number will tell the emergency services your exact location.

The left-hand lane on a three-lane motorway is for use by

- ⊙ any vehicle
- ⊙ large vehicles only
- ⊙ emergency vehicles only
- ⊙ slow vehicles only

⊙ **any vehicle**

On a motorway all traffic should use the left-hand lane unless overtaking. Use the centre or right-hand lanes if you need to overtake.

Make sure that you move back to the left-hand lane when you've finished overtaking. Don't stay in the middle or right-hand lane if the left-hand lane is free.

Which of these IS NOT allowed to travel in the right-hand lane of a three-lane motorway?

- ⊙ A small delivery van
- ⊙ A motorcycle
- ⊙ A vehicle towing a trailer
- ⊙ A motorcycle and side-car

⊙ **A vehicle towing a trailer**

A vehicle with a trailer is restricted to 60 mph. For this reason it isn't allowed in the right-hand lane as it might hold up the faster-moving traffic that wishes to overtake in that lane.

After a breakdown you need to rejoin the main carriageway of a motorway from the hard shoulder. You should

- ⊙ move out onto the carriageway then build up your speed
- ⊙ move out onto the carriageway using your hazard lights
- ⊙ gain speed on the hard shoulder before moving out onto the carriageway
- ⊙ wait on the hard shoulder until someone flashes their headlights at you

⊙ **gain speed on the hard shoulder before moving out onto the carriageway**

Wait for a safe gap in the traffic before you move out. Indicate your intention and use the hard shoulder to gain speed but don't force your way into the traffic.

9.7
Mark **one** answer

What is the national speed limit on motorways for cars and motorcycles?

- 30 mph
- 50 mph
- 60 mph
- 70 mph

⊙ **70 mph**

Travelling at the national speed limit doesn't allow you to hog the right-hand lane. Always use the left-hand lane whenever possible. When leaving the motorway, always adjust your speed in good time to deal with

- bends or curves on the slip road
- traffic queuing at roundabouts.

9.8
Mark **two** answers

You are travelling on a motorway. You decide you need a rest. You should

- stop on the hard shoulder
- go to a service area
- park on the slip road
- park on the central reservation
- leave at the next exit

⊙ **go to a service area**

⊙ **leave at the next exit**

You must not stop on the motorway or hard shoulder except in an emergency, in a traffic queue or when signalled to do so by a police officer or traffic signals. You should plan your journey so that you have regular rest stops.

9.9
Mark **one** answer

What do these motorway signs show?

- They are countdown markers to a bridge
- They are distance markers to the next telephone
- They are countdown markers to the next exit
- They warn of a police control ahead

⊙ **They are countdown markers to the next exit**

The exit from a motorway is indicated by countdown markers. These are positioned 90 metres (100 yards) apart, the first being 270 metres (300 yards) from the start of the slip road. Move into the left-hand lane well before you reach the start of the slip road.

A crawler lane on a motorway is found

- on a steep gradient
- before a service area
- before a junction
- along the hard shoulder

⊙ **on a steep gradient**

Slow-moving, large vehicles might slow down the progress of other traffic. On a steep gradient this extra lane is provided for these slow-moving vehicles to allow the faster-moving traffic to flow more easily.

You are driving on a motorway. There are red flashing lights above every lane. You must

- pull onto the hard shoulder
- slow down and watch for further signals
- leave at the next exit
- stop and wait

⊙ **stop and wait**

Red flashing lights above every lane mean you must not go on any further. You'll also see a red cross illuminated. Stop and wait. Don't

- change lanes
- continue
- pull onto the hard shoulder (unless in an emergency).

You are joining a motorway. Why is it important to make full use of the slip road?

- Because there is space available to turn round if you need to
- To allow you direct access to the overtaking lanes
- To build up a speed similar to traffic on the motorway
- Because you can continue on the hard shoulder

⊙ **To build up a speed similar to traffic on the motorway**

Try to join the motorway without affecting the progress of the traffic already travelling on it. Always give way to traffic already on the motorway. At busy times you may have to slow down to merge into slow-moving traffic.

9.13

*Mark **one** answer*

On a motorway the amber reflective studs can be found between

⊙ the hard shoulder and the carriageway

⊙ the acceleration lane and the carriageway

⊙ the central reservation and the carriageway

⊙ each pair of the lanes

⊙ **the central reservation and the carriageway**

On motorways reflective studs are fitted into the road to help you

• in the dark

• in conditions of poor visibility.

Amber-coloured studs are on the right-hand edge of the main carriageway, next to the central reservation.

9.14

*Mark **one** answer*

When going through a contraflow system on a motorway you should

⊙ ensure that you do not exceed 30 mph

⊙ keep a good distance from the vehicle ahead

⊙ switch lanes to keep the traffic flowing

⊙ stay close to the vehicle ahead to reduce queues

⊙ **keep a good distance from the vehicle ahead**

There's likely to be a speed restriction in force. Keep to this. Don't

• switch lanes

• get too close to traffic in front of you.

Be aware there will be no permanent barrier between you and the oncoming traffic.

9.15

*Mark **one** answer*

What colour are the reflective studs between a motorway and its slip road?

⊙ Amber

⊙ White

⊙ Green

⊙ Red

⊙ **Green**

The studs between the carriageway and the hard shoulder are normally red. These change to green where there is a slip road. They will help you identify slip roads when visibility is poor or when it is dark.

What colour are the reflective studs between the lanes on a motorway?

- ⊙ Green
- ⊙ Amber
- ⊙ White
- ⊙ Red

⊙ **White**

White studs are put between the lanes on motorways. The light from your headlights is reflected back and this is especially useful in bad weather, when visibility is restricted.

You are on a three-lane motorway. There are red reflective studs on your left and white ones to your right. Where are you?

- ⊙ In the right-hand lane
- ⊙ In the middle lane
- ⊙ On the hard shoulder
- ⊙ In the left-hand lane

⊙ **In the left-hand lane**

The colours of the reflective studs on the motorway and their locations are

- red – between the hard shoulder and the carriageway
- white – lane markings
- amber – between the edge of the carriageway and the central reservation
- green – along slip road exits and entrances
- bright green/yellow – roadworks and contraflow systems.

How should you use the emergency telephone on a motorway?

- ⊙ Stay close to the carriageway
- ⊙ Face the oncoming traffic
- ⊙ Keep your back to the traffic
- ⊙ Stand on the hard shoulder

⊙ **Face the oncoming traffic**

Traffic is passing you at speed. If the draught from a large lorry catches you by surprise it could blow you off balance and even onto the carriageway. By facing the oncoming traffic you can see approaching lorries and so be prepared for their draught. You are also in a position to see other hazards approaching.

9.19
*Mark **one** answer*

On a three-lane motorway which lane should you normally use?

- ⊙ Left
- ⊙ Right
- ⊙ Centre
- ⊙ Either the right or centre

⊙ **Left**

On a three-lane motorway you should travel in the left-hand lane unless you're overtaking. This applies regardless of the speed you're travelling at.

9.20
*Mark **one** answer*

The left-hand lane of a motorway should be used for

- ⊙ breakdowns and emergencies only
- ⊙ overtaking slower traffic in the other lanes
- ⊙ slow vehicles only
- ⊙ normal driving

⊙ **normal driving**

You should keep to the left-hand lane whenever possible. Only use the other lanes for overtaking or when directed by signals. Using other lanes when the left-hand lane is empty can frustrate drivers behind you.

9.21
*Mark **three** answers*

When may you stop on a motorway?

- ⊙ If you have to read a map
- ⊙ When you are tired and need a rest
- ⊙ If red lights show above every lane
- ⊙ When told to by the police
- ⊙ If your mobile phone rings
- ⊙ In an emergency or a breakdown

⊙ **If red lights show above every lane**

⊙ **When told to by the police**

⊙ **In an emergency or a breakdown**

You may only stop on the carriageway of a motorway

- when told to do so by the police
- when flashing red lights show above every lane
- in a traffic jam
- in an emergency or breakdown.

You are towing a trailer on a motorway.
What is your maximum speed limit?

⊙ 40 mph

⊙ 50 mph

⊙ 60 mph

⊙ 70 mph

⊙ **60 mph**

Don't forget that you're towing a trailer.
If you're towing a small, light trailer it won't
reduce your vehicle's performance
by very much. However, strong winds or
buffeting from large vehicles might cause
the trailer to snake from side to side.
Be aware of your speed and don't exceed
the lower limit imposed.

You are driving on a motorway. By mistake,
you go past the exit that you wanted to
take. You should

⊙ carefully reverse on the hard shoulder

⊙ carry on to the next exit

⊙ carefully reverse in the left-hand lane

⊙ make a U-turn at the next gap
in the central reservation

⊙ **carry on to the next exit**

It is against the law to reverse, cross the
central reservation or drive against the
traffic flow on a motorway.

If you have missed your exit ask yourself
if your concentration is fading. It could be
that you need to take a rest break before
completing your journey.

You are driving on a motorway. You have
to slow down quickly due to a hazard.
You should

⊙ switch on your hazard lights

⊙ switch on your headlights

⊙ sound your horn

⊙ flash your headlights

⊙ **switch on your hazard lights**

Using your hazard lights will give the traffic
behind you an extra warning of the hazard
ahead, in addition to your brake lights.
Only use them for long enough to ensure
that your warning has been seen.

9.25 *Mark **one** answer*

You get a puncture on the motorway. You manage to get your vehicle onto the hard shoulder. You should

⊙ change the wheel yourself immediately

⊙ use the emergency telephone and call for assistance

⊙ try to wave down another vehicle for help

⊙ only change the wheel if you have a passenger to help you

⊙ **use the emergency telephone and call for assistance**

Due to the danger from passing traffic you should park as far to the left as you can and leave the vehicle by the nearside door.

Do not attempt even simple repairs. Instead walk to an emergency telephone on your side of the road and phone for assistance. While waiting for assistance to arrive wait near your car, keeping well away from the carriageway and hard shoulder.

9.26 *Mark **one** answer*

You are on a motorway. What colour are the reflective studs on the left of the carriageway?

⊙ Green

⊙ Red

⊙ White

⊙ Amber

⊙ **Red**

Red studs are placed between the edge of the carriageway and the hard shoulder. Where slip roads leave or join the motorway the studs are green.

9.27 *NI EXEMPT* *Mark **one** answer*

You are driving a car on a motorway. Unless signs show otherwise you must NOT exceed

⊙ 50 mph

⊙ 60 mph

⊙ 70 mph

⊙ 80 mph

⊙ **70 mph**

The national speed limit for a car or motorcycle on the motorway is 70 mph.

Lower speed limits may be in force, for example in roadworks, so look out for the signs. Variable speed limits operate in some areas to control very busy stretches of motorway. The speed limit may change depending on the volume of traffic.

9.28

You are driving at 70 mph on a three-lane motorway. There is no traffic ahead. Which lane should you use?

- ⊙ Any lane
- ⊙ Middle lane
- ⊙ Right lane
- ⊙ Left lane

⊙ **Left lane**

If the left-hand lane is free you should use it regardless of the speed you're travelling.

9.29

Your vehicle has broken down on a motorway. You are not able to stop on the hard shoulder. What should you do?

- ⊙ Switch on your hazard warning lights
- ⊙ Stop following traffic and ask for help
- ⊙ Attempt to repair your vehicle quickly
- ⊙ Stand behind your vehicle to warn others

⊙ **Switch on your hazard warning lights**

If you can't get your vehicle onto the hard shoulder, use your hazard warning lights to warn others. Leave your vehicle only when you can safely get clear of the carriageway.

Do not

- try to repair the vehicle
- attempt to place any warning device on the carriageway.

9.30

Why is it particularly important to carry out a check on your vehicle before making a long motorway journey?

- ⊙ You will have to do more harsh braking on motorways
- ⊙ Motorway service stations do not deal with breakdowns
- ⊙ The road surface will wear down the tyres faster
- ⊙ Continuous high speeds may increase the risk of your vehicle breaking down

⊙ **Continuous high speeds may increase the risk of your vehicle breaking down**

Before you start your journey make sure that your vehicle can cope with the demands of high-speed driving. Check your vehicle's

- oil
- water
- tyres.

Plan rest stops if you're going to be travelling a long way.

9.31 *Mark **one** answer*

You are intending to leave the motorway at the next exit. Before you reach the exit you should normally position your vehicle

- in the middle lane
- in the left-hand lane
- on the hard shoulder
- in any lane

⊙ **in the left-hand lane**

You'll see the first advance direction sign one mile from the exit. If you're travelling at 60 mph in the right-hand lane you'll only have about 50 seconds before you reach the countdown markers. There will be another sign at the half-mile point. Move in to the left-hand lane in good time. Don't cut across traffic at the last moment and don't risk missing your exit.

9.32 *Mark **one** answer*

On a motorway you may ONLY stop on the hard shoulder

- in an emergency
- if you feel tired and need to rest
- if you accidentally go past the exit that you wanted to take
- to pick up a hitchhiker

⊙ **in an emergency**

DON'T stop on the hard shoulder to

- have a rest or a picnic
- pick up hitchhikers
- answer a mobile phone
- check a road map

Never reverse along the hard shoulder if you accidentally go past the exit you wanted.

9.33 *Mark **one** answer*

The emergency telephones on a motorway are connected to the

- ambulance service
- police control
- fire brigade
- breakdown service

⊙ **police control**

The controller will ask you

- the make and colour of your vehicle
- whether you are a member of an emergency breakdown service
- the number shown on the emergency telephone casing
- whether you are travelling alone.

9.34

Mark *one* answer

You are driving on a motorway. The car ahead shows its hazard lights for a short time. This tells you that

- ⊙ the driver wants you to overtake
- ⊙ the other car is going to change lanes
- ⊙ traffic ahead is slowing or stopping suddenly
- ⊙ there is a police speed check ahead

⊙ **traffic ahead is slowing or stopping suddenly**

If the vehicle in front shows its hazard lights there may be an accident or queuing traffic ahead. Look well ahead, not just at the car in front, to help you get an earlier warning of any hazards.

9.35

Mark *one* answer

For what reason may you use the right-hand lane of a motorway?

- ⊙ For keeping out of the way of lorries
- ⊙ For driving at more than 70 mph
- ⊙ For turning right
- ⊙ For overtaking other vehicles

⊙ **For overtaking other vehicles**

The right-hand lane of the motorway is for overtaking.

Sometimes you may be directed into a right-hand lane as a result of roadworks or an accident. This will be indicated by signs or police directing the traffic.

9.36

Mark *one* answer

You have broken down on a motorway. To find the nearest emergency telephone you should always walk

- ⊙ with the traffic flow
- ⊙ facing oncoming traffic
- ⊙ in the direction shown on the marker posts
- ⊙ in the direction of the nearest exit

⊙ **in the direction shown on the marker posts**

Along the hard shoulder there are marker posts at 100-metre intervals. These will direct you to the nearest emergency telephone.

9.37 *Mark **one** answer*

As a provisional licence holder you should not drive a car

- ⊙ over 30 mph
- ⊙ at night
- ⊙ on the motorway
- ⊙ with passengers in rear seats

⊙ **on the motorway**

When you've passed your practical test ask your instructor to take you for a lesson on the motorway. You'll need to get used to the speed of traffic and how to deal with multiple lanes.

9.38 *Mark **one** answer*

You are approaching roadworks on a motorway. What should you do?

- ⊙ Speed up to clear the area quickly
- ⊙ Always use the hard shoulder
- ⊙ Obey all speed limits
- ⊙ Stay very close to the vehicle in front

⊙ **Obey all speed limits**

Accidents can often happen at roadworks. Be aware of the speed limits and reduce your speed in good time.

9.39 *Mark **four** answers*

Which FOUR of these must NOT use motorways?

- ⊙ Learner car drivers
- ⊙ Motorcycles over 50 cc
- ⊙ Double-deck buses
- ⊙ Farm tractors
- ⊙ Horse riders
- ⊙ Cyclists

⊙ **Learner car drivers**

⊙ **Farm tractors**

⊙ **Horse riders**

⊙ **Cyclists**

In addition, motorways MUST NOT be used by

- pedestrians
- motorcycles under 50 cc
- certain slow-moving vehicles, without permission
- invalid carriages weighing less than 254 kg (560 lbs).

9.40

*Mark **four** answers*

Which FOUR of these must NOT use motorways?

- Learner car drivers
- Motorcycles over 50cc
- Double-deck buses
- Farm tractors
- Learner motorcyclists
- Cyclists

- **Learner car drivers**
- **Farm tractors**
- **Learner motorcyclists**
- **Cyclists**

Learner car drivers and motorcyclists are not allowed on the motorway until they have passed their practical test.

Motorways have rules that you need to know before you venture out for the first time. When you've passed your practical test, it's a good idea to have some lessons on motorways. Check with your instructor about this.

9.41

*Mark **one** answer*

Immediately after joining a motorway you should normally

- try to overtake
- re-adjust your mirrors
- position your vehicle in the centre lane
- keep in the left-hand lane

- **keep in the left-hand lane**

Stay in the left-hand lane long enough to get used to the higher speeds of motorway traffic.

9.42

*Mark **one** answer*

You are allowed to stop on a motorway when you

- need to walk and get fresh air
- wish to pick up hitchhikers
- are told to do so by flashing red lights
- need to use a mobile telephone

- **are told to do so by flashing red lights**

You must stop if there are red lights flashing above every lane on the motorway. However, if any of the other lanes show a green arrow you may move into that lane and continue if it is safe to do so.

9.43
*Mark **one** answer*

What should you use the hard shoulder of a motorway for?

- Stopping in an emergency
- Leaving the motorway
- Stopping when you are tired
- Joining the motorway

⊙ **Stopping in an emergency**

Don't use the hard shoulder for stopping unless it is an emergency. If you want to stop for any other reason go to the next exit or service station.

9.44
*Mark **one** answer*

You are in the right-hand lane on a motorway. You see these overhead signs. This means

- move to the left and reduce your speed to 50 mph
- there are roadworks 50 metres (55 yards) ahead
- use the hard shoulder until you have passed the hazard
- leave the motorway at the next exit

⊙ **move to the left and reduce your speed to 50 mph**

You must obey this sign. There might not be any visible signs of a problem ahead. However, there might be queuing traffic or another hazard which you cannot yet see.

9.45
*Mark **one** answer*

What is the right-hand lane used for on a three-lane motorway?

- Emergency vehicles only
- Overtaking
- Vehicles towing trailers
- Coaches only

⊙ **Overtaking**

You should keep to the left and only use the right-hand lane if you're passing slower-moving traffic.

9.46

Mark **one** answer

You are travelling along the left-hand lane of a three-lane motorway. Traffic is joining from a slip road. You should

- ⊙ race the other vehicles
- ⊙ move to another lane
- ⊙ maintain a steady speed
- ⊙ switch on your hazard flashers

⊙ **move to another lane**

You should move to another lane if it is safe to do so. This can greatly assist the flow of traffic joining the motorway, especially at peak times.

9.47

Mark **one** answer

A basic rule when on motorways is

- ⊙ use the lane that has least traffic
- ⊙ keep to the left-hand lane unless overtaking
- ⊙ overtake on the side that is clearest
- ⊙ try to keep above 50 mph to prevent congestion

⊙ **keep to the left-hand lane unless overtaking**

You should normally travel in the left-hand lane unless you are overtaking a slower-moving vehicle. Once you are passed that vehicle move back into the left-hand lane as soon as it's safe to do so. Don't cut across in front of the vehicle that you're overtaking.

9.48

Mark **one** answer

On motorways you should never overtake on the left unless

- ⊙ you can see well ahead that the hard shoulder is clear
- ⊙ the traffic in the right-hand lane is signalling right
- ⊙ you warn drivers behind by signalling left
- ⊙ there is a queue of slow-moving traffic to your right that is moving more slowly than you are

⊙ **there is a queue of slow-moving traffic to your right that is moving more slowly than you are**

Only overtake on the left if traffic is moving slowly in queues and the traffic on your right is moving more slowly than the traffic in your lane.

9.49
*Mark **one** answer*

Your vehicle breaks down on the hard shoulder of a motorway. You decide to use your mobile phone to call for help. You should

⊙ stand at the rear of the vehicle while making the call

⊙ try to repair the vehicle yourself

⊙ get out of the vehicle by the right-hand door

⊙ check your location from the marker posts on the left

⊙ **check your location from the marker posts on the left**

The emergency services need to know your exact location so they can reach you as quickly as possible. Look for a number on the nearest marker post beside the hard shoulder. Give this number when you call the emergency services as it will help them to locate you. Be ready to describe where you are, for example, by reference to the last junction or service station you passed.

9.50   *NI EXEMPT*   *Mark **one** answer*

You are on a three-lane motorway towing a trailer. You may use the right-hand lane when

⊙ there are lane closures

⊙ there is slow moving traffic

⊙ you can maintain a high speed

⊙ large vehicles are in the left and centre lanes

⊙ **there are lane closures**

If you are towing a caravan or trailer you must not use the right-hand lane on a motorway with three or more lanes, except in certain circumstances, such as lane closures.

9.51
*Mark **one** answer*

You are on a motorway. There is a contraflow system ahead. What would you expect to find?

⊙ Temporary traffic lights

⊙ Lower speed limits

⊙ Wider lanes than normal

⊙ Speed humps

⊙ **Lower speed limits**

When approaching a contraflow system reduce speed in good time and obey all speed limits. You may be travelling in a narrower lane than normal with no permanent barrier between you and the oncoming traffic. Be aware that the hard shoulder may be used for traffic and the road ahead could be obstructed by slow-moving or broken down vehicles.

9.52   NI EXEMPT   Mark **one** answer

Motorway emergency telephones are usually linked to the police. In some areas they are now linked to

- ⊙ the Highways Agency Control Centre
- ⊙ the Driver Vehicle Licensing Agency
- ⊙ the Driving Standards Agency
- ⊙ the local Vehicle Registration Office

⊙ **the Highways Agency Control Centre**

In some areas motorway telephones are now linked to a Highways Agency Control Centre, instead of the police. Highways Agency Traffic Officers work in partnership with the police and assist at motorway emergencies and accidents. They are recognised by a high-visibility orange and yellow jacket and high-visibility vehicle with yellow and black chequered markings.

9.53   Mark **one** answer

What is an Emergency Refuge Area on a motorway for?

- ⊙ An area to park in when you want to use a mobile phone
- ⊙ To use in cases of emergency or breakdown
- ⊙ For an emergency recovery vehicle to park in a contra-flow system
- ⊙ To drive in when there is queuing traffic ahead

⊙ **To use in cases of emergency or breakdown**

In cases of breakdown or emergency try to get your vehicle into an Emergency Refuge Area. This is safer than just stopping on the hard shoulder as it gives you greater distance from the main carriageway. If you are able to re-join the motorway you must take extra care especially when the hard shoulder is being used as a running lane.

9.54   NI EXEMP   Mark **one** answer

Highways Agency Traffic Officers

- ⊙ will not be able to assist at a breakdown or emergency
- ⊙ are not able to stop and direct anyone on a motorway
- ⊙ will tow a broken down vehicle and it's passengers home
- ⊙ are able to stop and direct anyone on a motorway

⊙ **are able to stop and direct anyone on a motorway**

Highways Agency Traffic Officers (HATOs) do not have enforcement powers but are able to stop and direct anyone on the motorway. They work in partnership with the police at motorway incidents and provide a highly-trained and visible service. Their role is to help keep traffic moving and make your journey as safe and reliable as possible. They are recognised by an orange and yellow jacket and their vehicle has yellow and black markings.

9.55
*Mark **one** answer*

An Emergency Refuge Area is an area

- ⊙ on a motorway for use in cases of emergency or breakdown
- ⊙ for use if you think you will be involved in a road rage incident
- ⊙ on a motorway for a police patrol to park and watch traffic
- ⊙ for construction and road workers to store emergency equipment

⊙ **on a motorway for use in cases of emergency or breakdown**

Emergency Refuge Areas may be found at the side of the hard shoulder about 500 metres apart. If you break down you should use them rather than the hard shoulder if you are able to. When re-joining the motorway you must remember to take extra care especially when the hard shoulder is being used as a running lane within an Active Traffic Management area. Try to match your speed to that of traffic in the lane you are joining.

9.56
*Mark **one** answer*

You are on a motorway. A red cross is displayed above the hard shoulder. What does this mean?

- ⊙ Pull up in this lane to answer your mobile phone
- ⊙ Use this lane as a running lane
- ⊙ This lane can be used if you need a rest
- ⊙ You should not travel in this lane

⊙ **You should not travel in this lane**

Active Traffic Management schemes are being introduced on motorways. Within these areas at certain times the hard shoulder will be used as a running lane. A red cross above the hard shoulder shows that this lane should NOT be used, except for emergencies and breakdowns.

You are on a motorway in an Active Traffic Management (ATM) area. A mandatory speed limit is displayed above the hard shoulder. What does this mean?

- ⊙ You should not travel in this lane
- ⊙ The hard shoulder can be used as a running lane
- ⊙ You can park on the hard shoulder if you feel tired
- ⊙ You can pull up in this lane to answer a mobile phone

⊙ **The hard shoulder can be used as a running lane**

A mandatory speed limit sign above the hard shoulder shows that it can be used as a running lane between junctions. You must stay within the speed limit. Look out for vehicles that may have broken down and be blocking the hard shoulder.

The aim of an Active Traffic Management scheme on a motorway is to

- ⊙ prevent overtaking
- ⊙ reduce rest stops
- ⊙ prevent tailgating
- ⊙ reduce congestion

⊙ **reduce congestion**

Active Traffic Management schemes are intended to reduce congestion and make journey times more reliable. In these areas the hard shoulder may be used as a running lane to ease congestion at peak times or in the event of an incident. It may appear that you could travel faster for a short distance, but keeping traffic flow at a constant speed may improve your journey time.

9.59   *NI EXEMPT*   *Mark **one** answer*

You are in an Active Traffic Management area on a motorway. When the Actively Managed mode is operating

- ⊙ speed limits are only advisory
- ⊙ the national speed limit will apply
- ⊙ the speed limit is always 30 mph
- ⊙ all speed limit signals are set

⊙ **all speed limit signals are set**

When an Active Traffic Management (ATM) scheme is operating on a motorway you must follow the mandatory instructions shown on the gantries above each lane. This includes the hard shoulder.

9.60   *NI EXEMPT*   *Mark **one** answer*

You are travelling on a motorway. A red cross is shown above the hard shoulder and mandatory speed limits above all other lanes. This means

- ⊙ the hard shoulder can be used as a rest area if you feel tired
- ⊙ the hard shoulder is for emergency or breakdown use only
- ⊙ the hard shoulder can be used as a normal running lane
- ⊙ the hard shoulder has a speed limit of 50 mph

⊙ **the hard shoulder is for emergency or breakdown use only**

A red cross above the hard shoulder shows it is closed as a running lane and should only be used for emergencies or breakdowns. At busy times within an Active Traffic Management area the hard shoulder may be used as a running lane. This will be shown by a mandatory speed limit on the gantry above.

You are travelling on a motorway. A red cross is shown above the hard shoulder. What does this mean?

- ⊙ Use this lane as a rest area
- ⊙ Use this as a normal running lane
- ⊙ Do not use this lane to travel in
- ⊙ National speed limit applies in this lane

⊙ **Do not use this lane to travel in**

When a red cross is shown above the hard shoulder it should only be used for breakdowns or emergencies. Within Active Traffic Management (ATM) areas the hard shoulder may sometimes be used as a running lane. Speed limit signs directly above the hard shoulder will show that it's open.

You see this sign on a motorway. It means you can use

- ⊙ any lane except the hard shoulder
- ⊙ the hard shoulder only
- ⊙ the three right hand lanes only
- ⊙ all the lanes including the hard shoulder

⊙ **all the lanes including the hard shoulder**

Mandatory speed limit signs above all lanes including the hard shoulder, show that you are in an Active Traffic Management (ATM) area. In this case you can use the hard shoulder as a running lane. You must stay within the speed limit shown. Look out for any vehicles that may have broken down and be blocking the hard shoulder.

Why can it be an advantage for traffic speed to stay constant over a longer distance?

- ⊙ You will do more stop-start driving
- ⊙ You will use far more fuel
- ⊙ You will be able to use more direct routes
- ⊙ Your overall journey time will normally improve

⊙ **Your overall journey time will normally improve**

When traffic travels at a constant speed over a longer distance, journey times normally improve. You may feel that you could travel faster for short periods but this won't generally make your overall time better. Signs will show the maximum speed at which you should travel.

9.64   *NI EXEMPT*   *Mark **one** answer*

You should not normally travel on the hard shoulder of a motorway. When can you use it?

- ⊙ When taking the next exit
- ⊙ When traffic is stopped
- ⊙ When signs direct you to
- ⊙ When traffic is slow moving

⊙ **When signs direct you to**

Normally you should only use the hard shoulder for emergencies and breakdowns, and at roadworks when signs direct you to. Active Traffic Management (ATM) areas are being introduced to ease traffic congestion. In these areas the hard shoulder may be used as a running lane when speed limit signs are shown directly above.

RULES OF THE ROAD

This section covers:

- speed limits
- lane discipline
- parking
- lighting

10.1
*Mark **one** answer*

When going straight ahead at a roundabout you should

⊙ indicate left before leaving the roundabout

⊙ not indicate at any time

⊙ indicate right when approaching the roundabout

⊙ indicate left when approaching the roundabout

⊙ **indicate left before leaving the roundabout**

When you want to go straight on at a roundabout, don't signal as you approach it, but indicate left just after you pass the exit before the one you wish to take.

10.2
*Mark **one** answer*

The dual carriageway you are turning right onto has a very narrow central reservation. What should you do?

⊙ Proceed to the central reservation and wait

⊙ Wait until the road is clear in both directions

⊙ Stop in the first lane so that other vehicles give way

⊙ Emerge slightly to show your intentions

⊙ **Wait until the road is clear in both directions**

When the central reservation is narrow you should treat a dual carriageway as one road and wait until the road is clear in both directions before emerging to turn right. If you try to treat it as two separate roads and wait in the middle, you are likely to cause an obstruction and possibly an accident.

10.3
*Mark **one** answer*

You are going straight ahead at a roundabout. How should you signal?

⊙ Signal right on the approach and then left to leave the roundabout

⊙ Signal left as you leave the roundabout

⊙ Signal left on the approach to the roundabout and keep the signal on until you leave

⊙ Signal left just after you pass the exit before the one you will take

⊙ **Signal left just after you pass the exit before the one you will take**

To go straight ahead at a roundabout you should normally approach in the left-hand lane without signalling. Where there are road markings, use the lane indicated.

Ensure that you signal correctly when you are travelling around the roundabout. Other road users need to know your intentions.

Which vehicle might have to use a different course to normal at roundabouts?

⊙ Sports car

⊙ Van

⊙ Estate car

⊙ Long vehicle

⊙ **Long vehicle**

A long vehicle may have to straddle lanes either on or approaching a roundabout so that the rear wheels don't cut in over the kerb.

If you're following a long vehicle, stay well back and give it plenty of room.

Who has priority at an unmarked crossroads?

⊙ The larger vehicle

⊙ No one has priority

⊙ The faster vehicle

⊙ The smaller vehicle

⊙ **No one has priority**

Practise good observation in all directions before you emerge or make a turn. Proceed only when you're sure it's safe to do so.

What is the nearest you may park to a junction?

⊙ 10 metres (32 feet)

⊙ 12 metres (39 feet)

⊙ 15 metres (49 feet)

⊙ 20 metres (66 feet)

⊙ **10 metres (32 feet)**

Don't park within 10 metres (32 feet) of a junction (unless in an authorised parking place). This is to allow drivers emerging from, or turning into, the junction a clear view of the road they are joining. It also allows them to see hazards such as pedestrians or cyclists at the junction.

While driving, you intend to turn left into a minor road. On the approach you should

⊙ keep just left of the middle of the road

⊙ keep in the middle of the road

⊙ swing out wide just before turning

⊙ keep well to the left of the road

⊙ **keep well to the left of the road**

Don't swing out into the centre of the road in order to make the turn. This could endanger oncoming traffic and may cause other road users to misunderstand your intentions.

10.8

*Mark **one** answer*

You are intending to turn right at a crossroads. An oncoming driver is also turning right. It will normally be safer to

- ⊙ keep the other vehicle to your RIGHT and turn behind it (offside to offside)
- ⊙ keep the other vehicle to your LEFT and turn in front of it (nearside to nearside)
- ⊙ carry on and turn at the next junction instead
- ⊙ hold back and wait for the other driver to turn first

⊙ **keep the other vehicle to your RIGHT and turn behind it (offside to offside)**

At some junctions the layout may make it difficult to turn offside to offside. If this is the case, be prepared to pass nearside to nearside, but take extra care as your view ahead will be obscured by the vehicle turning in front of you.

10.9

*Mark **one** answer*

You are on a busy main road and find that you are travelling in the wrong direction. What should you do?

- ⊙ Turn into a side road on the right and reverse into the main road
- ⊙ Make a U-turn in the main road
- ⊙ Make a 'three-point' turn in the main road
- ⊙ Turn round in a side road

⊙ **Turn round in a side road**

Don't

- • turn in a busy street
- • reverse into a main road.

Find a quiet side road. Choose a place where you won't obstruct an entrance or exit. Look out for pedestrians and cyclists as well as other traffic.

10.10

*Mark **one** answer*

When you are NOT sure that it is safe to reverse your vehicle you should

- ⊙ use your horn
- ⊙ rev your engine
- ⊙ get out and check
- ⊙ reverse slowly

⊙ **get out and check**

If you can't see all around your vehicle get out and have a look. You could also ask someone reliable outside the vehicle to guide you. A small child could easily be hidden directly behind you. Don't take risks.

You must not reverse

- for longer than necessary
- for more than a car's length
- into a side road
- in a built-up area

⊙ **for longer than necessary**

You may decide to turn your vehicle around by reversing into an opening or side road. When you reverse, always look behind and all around and watch for pedestrians.

Don't reverse from a side road into a main road. You must not reverse further than is necessary.

You are waiting at a level crossing. A train has passed but the lights keep flashing. You must

- carry on waiting
- phone the signal operator
- edge over the stop line and look for trains
- park and investigate

⊙ **carry on waiting**

If the lights at a level crossing continue to flash after a train has passed, wait as there might be another train coming. Time seems to pass slowly when you're held up in a queue. Be patient and wait until the lights stop flashing.

You are driving over a level crossing. The warning lights come on and a bell rings. What should you do?

- Get everyone out of the vehicle immediately
- Stop and reverse back to clear the crossing
- Keep going and clear the crossing
- Stop immediately and use your hazard warning lights

⊙ **Keep going and clear the crossing**

Keep going – don't stop on the crossing. If the amber warning lights come on as you're approaching the crossing, you must stop unless it is unsafe to do so. Red flashing lights together with an audible signal mean you must stop.

10.14
*Mark **one** answer*

You are waiting at a level crossing. The red warning lights continue to flash after a train has passed by. What should you do?

- ⊙ Get out and investigate
- ⊙ Telephone the signal operator
- ⊙ Continue to wait
- ⊙ Drive across carefully

⊙ **Continue to wait**

At a level crossing flashing red lights mean you must stop. If the train passes but the lights keep flashing, wait. There may be another train coming.

10.15
*Mark **one** answer*

At a crossroads there are no signs or road markings. Two vehicles approach. Which has priority?

- ⊙ Neither of the vehicles
- ⊙ The vehicle travelling the fastest
- ⊙ Oncoming vehicles turning right
- ⊙ Vehicles approaching from the right

⊙ **Neither of the vehicles**

At a crossroads where there are no 'give way' signs or road markings be very careful. No vehicle has priority, even if the sizes of the roads are different.

10.16
*Mark **one** answer*

When may you drive a motor car in this bus lane?

- ⊙ Outside its hours of operation
- ⊙ To get to the front of a traffic queue
- ⊙ You may not use it at any time
- ⊙ To overtake slow-moving traffic

⊙ **Outside its hours of operation**

Some bus lanes only operate during peak hours and other vehicles may use them outside these hours. Make sure you check the sign for the hours of operation before driving in a bus lane.

*Mark **one** answer*

When may you reverse from a side road into a main road?

- ⊙ Only if both roads are clear of traffic
- ⊙ Not at any time
- ⊙ At any time
- ⊙ Only if the main road is clear of traffic

⊙ **Not at any time**

Don't reverse into a main road from a side road. The main road is likely to be busy and the traffic on it moving quickly. Cut down the risks by using a quiet side road to reverse into.

*Mark **one** answer*

You are reversing your vehicle into a side road. When would the greatest hazard to passing traffic occur?

- ⊙ After you've completed the manoeuvre
- ⊙ Just before you actually begin to manoeuvre
- ⊙ After you've entered the side road
- ⊙ When the front of your vehicle swings out

⊙ **When the front of your vehicle swings out**

Always check road and traffic conditions in all directions before reversing into a side road. Keep a good look-out throughout the manoeuvre. Act on what you see and wait if you need to.

*Mark **one** answer*

You are parked in a busy high street. What is the safest way to turn your vehicle around so you can go the opposite way?

- ⊙ Find a quiet side road to turn round in
- ⊙ Drive into a side road and reverse into the main road
- ⊙ Get someone to stop the traffic
- ⊙ Do a U-turn

⊙ **Find a quiet side road to turn round in**

Make sure you carry out the manoeuvre without causing a hazard to other vehicles. Choose a place to turn which is safe and convenient for you and for other road users.

10.20 *Mark **three** answers*

You are going along a street with parked vehicles on the left-hand side. For which THREE reasons should you keep your speed down?

- ⊙ So that oncoming traffic can see you more clearly
- ⊙ You may set off car alarms
- ⊙ Vehicles may be pulling out
- ⊙ Drivers' doors may open
- ⊙ Children may run out from between the vehicles

⊙ **Vehicles may be pulling out**

⊙ **Drivers' doors may open**

⊙ **Children may run out from between the vehicles**

Travel slowly and carefully where there are parked vehicles in a built-up area.

Beware of

- vehicles pulling out, especially bicycles and motorcycles
- pedestrians, especially children, who may run out from between cars
- drivers opening their doors.

10.21 *Mark **one** answer*

You meet an obstruction on your side of the road. You should

- ⊙ carry on, you have priority
- ⊙ give way to oncoming traffic
- ⊙ wave oncoming vehicles through
- ⊙ accelerate to get past first

⊙ **give way to oncoming traffic**

Take care if you have to pass a parked vehicle on your side of the road. Give way to oncoming traffic if there isn't enough room for you both to continue safely.

10.22 *Mark **one** answer*

You are on a road that is only wide enough for one vehicle. There is a car coming towards you. What should you do?

- ⊙ Pull into a passing place on your right
- ⊙ Force the other driver to reverse
- ⊙ Pull into a passing place if your vehicle is wider
- ⊙ Pull into a passing place on your left

⊙ **Pull into a passing place on your left**

Pull into the nearest passing place on the left if you meet another vehicle in a narrow road. If the nearest passing place is on the right, wait opposite it.

On a three-lane dual carriageway the right-hand lane can be used for

- ⊙ overtaking only, never turning right
- ⊙ overtaking or turning right
- ⊙ fast-moving traffic only
- ⊙ turning right only, never overtaking

⊙ **overtaking or turning right**

You should normally use the left-hand lane on any dual carriageway unless you are overtaking or turning right.

When overtaking on a dual carriageway, look for vehicles ahead that are turning right. They're likely to be slowing or stopped. You need to see them in good time so that you can take appropriate action.

You are approaching a busy junction. There are several lanes with road markings. At the last moment you realise that you are in the wrong lane. You should

- ⊙ continue in that lane
- ⊙ force your way across
- ⊙ stop until the area has cleared
- ⊙ use clear arm signals to cut across

⊙ **continue in that lane**

There are times where road markings can be obscured by queuing traffic, or you might be unsure which lane you need to be in.

If you realise that you're in the wrong lane, don't cut across lanes or bully other drivers to let you in. Follow the lane you're in and find somewhere safe to turn around if you need to.

You are on a two-lane dual carriageway. For which TWO of the following would you use the right-hand lane?

- ⊙ Turning right
- ⊙ Normal progress
- ⊙ Staying at the minimum allowed speed
- ⊙ Constant high speed
- ⊙ Overtaking slower traffic
- ⊙ Mending punctures

⊙ **Turning right**

⊙ **Overtaking slower traffic**

Normally you should travel in the left-hand lane and only use the right-hand lane for overtaking or turning right. Move back into the left lane as soon as it's safe but don't cut in across the path of the vehicle you've just passed.

10.26 — Mark *one* answer

You may drive over a footpath

- to overtake slow-moving traffic
- when the pavement is very wide
- if no pedestrians are near
- to get into a property

⊙ **to get into a property**

It is against the law to drive on or over a footpath, except to gain access to a property. If you need to cross a pavement, watch for pedestrians in both directions.

10.27 — Mark *one* answer

You are driving along a road that has a cycle lane. The lane is marked by a solid white line. This means that during its period of operation

- the lane may be used for parking your car
- you may drive in that lane at any time
- the lane may be used when necessary
- you must not drive in that lane

⊙ **you must not drive in that lane**

Leave the lane free for cyclists. At other times, when the lane is not in operation, you should still be aware that there may be cyclists about. Give them room and don't pass too closely.

10.28 — Mark *one* answer

A cycle lane is marked by a solid white line. You must not drive or park in it

- at any time
- during the rush hour
- if a cyclist is using it
- during its period of operation

⊙ **during its period of operation**

The cycle lanes are there for a reason. Keep them free and allow cyclists to use them.

It is illegal to drive or park in a cycle lane, marked by a solid white line, during its hours of operation. Parking in a cycle lane will obstruct cyclists and they may move into the path of traffic on the main carriageway as they ride around the obstruction. This could be hazardous for both the cyclist and other road users.

10.29

Mark one answer

Where may you overtake on a one-way street?

- Only on the left-hand side
- Overtaking is not allowed
- Only on the right-hand side
- Either on the right or the left

⊙ **Either on the right or the left**

You can overtake other traffic on either side when travelling in a one-way street. Make full use of your mirrors and ensure that it's clear all around before you attempt to overtake. Look for signs and road markings and use the most suitable lane for your destination.

10.30

Mark three answers

As a car driver, which THREE lanes are you NOT normally allowed to use?

- Crawler lane
- Bus lane
- Overtaking lane
- Acceleration lane
- Cycle lane
- Tram lane,

⊙ **Bus lane**

⊙ **Cycle lane**

⊙ **Tram lane**

Look out for signs or road markings that tell you which lane to use. Some lanes can only be used by certain road users.

Bus lanes help the traffic to flow at certain times. Some bus lanes operate 24 hours a day while others only operate at certain times. Outside these hours other drivers may use them but check the times before you do so.

Cycle lanes are there to help protect vulnerable road users.

10.31

Mark one answer

You are driving at night with full beam headlights on. A vehicle is overtaking you. You should dip your lights

- some time after the vehicle has passed you
- before the vehicle starts to pass you
- only if the other driver dips their headlights
- as soon as the vehicle passes you

⊙ **as soon as the vehicle passes you**

On full beam your lights could dazzle the driver in front. Make sure that your light beam falls short of the vehicle in front.

10.32

Mark one answer

You are in the right-hand lane of a dual carriageway. You see signs showing that the right-hand lane is closed 800 yards ahead. You should

⊙ keep in that lane until you reach the queue

⊙ move to the left immediately

⊙ wait and see which lane is moving faster

⊙ move to the left in good time

⊙ **move to the left in good time**

Keep a look-out for traffic signs. If you're directed to change lanes, do so in good time. Don't

• push your way into traffic in another lane

• leave changing lanes until the last moment.

10.33

Mark one answer

You are travelling on a well-lit road at night in a built-up area. By using dipped headlights you will be able to

⊙ see further along the road

⊙ go at a much faster speed

⊙ switch to main beam quickly

⊙ be easily seen by others

⊙ **be easily seen by others**

You may be difficult to see when you're travelling at night, even on a well lit road. If you use dipped headlights rather than sidelights other road users will see you more easily.

What is a dipped headlight?

10.34

Mark two answers

Who can use a toucan crossing?

⊙ Trains

⊙ Cyclists

⊙ Buses

⊙ Pedestrians

⊙ Trams

⊙ **Cyclists**

⊙ **Pedestrians**

Toucan crossings are similar to pelican crossings but there is no flashing amber phase. Cyclists share the crossing with pedestrians and are allowed to cycle across when the green cycle symbol is shown.

10.35

There is a tractor ahead of you. You wish to overtake but you are NOT sure if it is safe to do so. You should

- follow another overtaking vehicle through
- sound your horn to the slow vehicle to pull over
- speed through but flash your lights to oncoming traffic
- not overtake if you are in doubt

⊙ **not overtake if you are in doubt**

Never overtake if you're not sure if it's safe to do so.

Can you see far enough down the road to ensure that you can complete the manoeuvre safely?

If the answer is no, don't go.

10.36

You are driving on a road that has a cycle lane. The lane is marked by a broken white line. This means that

- you should not drive in the lane unless it is unavoidable
- you should not park in the lane unless it is unavoidable
- you can drive in the lane at any time
- the lane must be used by motorcyclists in heavy traffic

⊙ **you should not drive in the lane unless it is unavoidable**

⊙ **you should not park in the lane unless it is unavoidable**

Where signs or road markings show lanes are for cyclists only, leave them free. Do not drive or park in a cycle lane unless it is unavoidable.

10.37

Someone is waiting to cross at a zebra crossing. They are standing on the pavement. You should normally

- go on quickly before they step onto the crossing
- stop before you reach the zigzag lines and let them cross
- stop, let them cross, wait patiently
- ignore them as they are still on the pavement

⊙ **stop, let them cross, wait patiently**

By standing on the pavement, the pedestrian is showing an intention to cross. If you are looking well down the road you will give yourself enough time to slow down and stop safely. Don't forget to check your mirrors before slowing down.

10.38
*Mark **three** answers*

Which three of the following are most likely to take an unusual course at roundabouts?

- Horse riders
- Milk floats
- Delivery vans
- Long vehicles
- Estate cars
- Cyclists

⊙ **Horse riders**

⊙ **Long vehicles**

⊙ **Cyclists**

Long vehicles might have to take a slightly different position when approaching the roundabout or going around it. This is to stop the rear of the vehicle cutting in and mounting the kerb.

Horse riders and cyclists might stay in the left-hand lane although they are turning right. Be aware of this and allow them room.

10.39
*Mark **one** answer*

At toucan crossings, apart from pedestrians you should be aware of

- emergency vehicles emerging
- buses pulling out
- trams crossing in front
- cyclists riding across

⊙ **cyclists riding across**

The use of cycles is being encouraged and more toucan crossings are being installed. These crossings enable pedestrians and cyclists to cross the path of other traffic. Watch out as cyclists will approach the crossing faster than pedestrians.

10.40
*Mark **one** answer*

At a pelican crossing, what does a flashing amber light mean?

- You must not move off until the lights stop flashing
- You must give way to pedestrians still on the crossing
- You can move off, even if pedestrians are still on the crossing
- You must stop because the lights are about to change to red

⊙ **You must give way to pedestrians still on the crossing**

If there is no-one on the crossing when the amber light is flashing, you may proceed over the crossing. You don't need to wait for the green light to show.

229

10.41

*Mark **one** answer*

Where is the safest place to park your vehicle at night?

- ⊙ In a garage
- ⊙ On a busy road
- ⊙ In a quiet car park
- ⊙ Near a red route

⊙ **In a garage**

If you have a garage, use it!

Your car is less likely to be a victim of car crime if it's in your garage.

In winter the windows will be free from ice.

10.42

*Mark **one** answer*

You are towing a small caravan on a dual carriageway. You must not exceed

- ⊙ 50 mph
- ⊙ 40 mph
- ⊙ 70 mph
- ⊙ 60 mph

⊙ **60 mph**

The speed limit is reduced for vehicles towing caravans and trailers to lessen the risk of the outfit becoming unstable. Due to the increased weight and size of the vehicle and caravan combination, you should plan well ahead. Be extra-careful in windy weather, as strong winds could cause a caravan or large trailer to snake from side to side.

10.43

*Mark **one** answer*

You may only enter a box junction when

- ⊙ there are less than two vehicles in front of you
- ⊙ the traffic lights show green
- ⊙ your exit road is clear
- ⊙ you need to turn left

⊙ **your exit road is clear**

Box junctions are marked on the road to prevent the road becoming blocked. Don't enter the box unless your exit road is clear. You may only wait in the box if your exit road is clear but oncoming traffic is preventing you from completing the turn.

10.44

*Mark **one** answer*

You may wait in a yellow box junction when

⊙ oncoming traffic is preventing
  you from turning right

⊙ you are in a queue of traffic
  turning left

⊙ you are in a queue of traffic to
  go ahead

⊙ you are on a roundabout

⊙ **oncoming traffic is preventing
  you from turning right**

The purpose of this road marking is to
keep the junction clear of queuing traffic.
You may only wait in the marked area when
you're turning right and your exit lane is
clear but you can't complete the turn
because of oncoming traffic.

10.45

*Mark **one** answer*

When can you park on the left opposite
these road markings?

⊙ If the line nearest to you is broken

⊙ When there are no yellow lines

⊙ To pick up or set down passengers

⊙ During daylight hours only

⊙ **To pick up or set down
  passengers**

You must not park or stop on a road
marked with double white lines (even where
one of the lines is broken) except
to pick up or set down passengers.

10.46

*Mark **one** answer*

What is the national speed limit for cars and
motorcycles on a dual carriageway?

⊙ 30 mph

⊙ 50 mph

⊙ 60 mph

⊙ 70 mph

⊙ **70 mph**

Ensure that you know the speed limit for
the road that you're on. The speed limit on
a dual carriageway or motorway is 70 mph
for cars and motorcycles, unless there are
signs to indicate otherwise. The speed
limits for different types of vehicles are
listed in *The Highway Code*.

231

You want to turn right at a box junction. There is oncoming traffic. You should

⊙ wait in the box junction if your exit is clear

⊙ wait before the junction until it is clear of all traffic

⊙ drive on, you cannot turn right at a box junction

⊙ drive slowly into the box junction when signalled by oncoming traffic

⊙ **wait in the box junction if your exit is clear**

You can move into the box junction to wait as long as your exit is clear. The oncoming traffic will stop when the traffic lights change, allowing you to proceed.

What is the meaning of this sign?

⊙ Local speed limit applies

⊙ No waiting on the carriageway

⊙ National speed limit applies

⊙ No entry to vehicular traffic

⊙ **National speed limit applies**

This sign doesn't tell you the speed limit in figures. You should know the speed limit for the type of road that you're on. Study your copy of *The Highway Code*.

Where you see street lights but no speed limit signs the limit is usually

⊙ 30 mph

⊙ 40 mph

⊙ 50 mph

⊙ 60 mph

⊙ **30 mph**

A 30 mph limit usually applies where there are street lights but no speed limit signs.

10.50 *Mark **one** answer*

Signals are normally given by direction indicators and

- ⊙ brake lights
- ⊙ side lights
- ⊙ fog lights
- ⊙ interior lights

⊙ **brake lights**

Your brake lights will give an indication to traffic behind that you're slowing down. Good anticipation will allow you time to check your mirrors before slowing.

10.51 *Mark **one** answer*

There are no speed limit signs on the road. How is a 30 mph limit indicated?

- ⊙ By hazard warning lines
- ⊙ By street lighting
- ⊙ By pedestrian islands
- ⊙ By double or single yellow lines

⊙ **By street lighting**

There is usually a 30 mph speed limit where street lights are not more than 185 metres (600 feet) apart.

10.52 *Mark **one** answer*

What does this sign mean?

- ⊙ Minimum speed 30 mph
- ⊙ End of maximum speed
- ⊙ End of minimum speed
- ⊙ Maximum speed 30 mph

⊙ **End of minimum speed**

A red slash through this sign indicates that the restriction has ended. In this case the restriction was a minimum speed limit of 30 mph.

*Mark **one** answer*

What is the national speed limit on a single carriageway road for cars and motorcycles?

- ⊙ 70 mph
- ⊙ 60 mph
- ⊙ 50 mph
- ⊙ 30 mph

⊙ **60 mph**

Exceeding the speed limit is dangerous and can result in you receiving penalty points on your licence. It isn't worth it. You should know the speed limit for the road that you're on by observing the road signs. Different speed limits apply if you are towing a trailer.

10.54 *Mark **one** answer*

What does this sign tell you?

- ⊙ That it is a no-through road
- ⊙ End of traffic calming zone
- ⊙ Free parking zone ends
- ⊙ No waiting zone ends

⊙ **No waiting zone ends**

The blue and red circular sign on its own means that waiting restrictions are in force. This sign shows that you are leaving the controlled zone and waiting restrictions no longer apply.

10.55 *Mark **one** answer*

You are looking for somewhere to park your vehicle. The area is full EXCEPT for spaces marked 'disabled use'. You can

- ⊙ use these spaces when elsewhere is full
- ⊙ park if you stay with your vehicle
- ⊙ use these spaces, disabled or not
- ⊙ not park there unless permitted

⊙ **not park there unless permitted**

It is illegal to park in a parking space reserved for disabled users.

These spaces are provided for people with limited mobility, who may need extra space to get in and out of their vehicle.

10.56
*Mark **one** answer*

What is the meaning of this sign?

(handwritten: What is a waiting restriction?)

⊙ No entry
⊙ Waiting restrictions
⊙ National speed limit
⊙ School crossing patrol

⊙ **Waiting restrictions**

This sign indicates that there are waiting restrictions. It is normally accompanied by details of when restrictions are in force.

Details of most signs which are in common use are shown in *The Highway Code* and a more comprehensive selection is available in *Know Your Traffic Signs*.

10.57
*Mark **one** answer*

You are entering an area of roadworks. There is a temporary speed limit displayed. You should

⊙ not exceed the speed limit
⊙ obey the limit only during rush hour
⊙ ignore the displayed limit
⊙ obey the limit except at night

⊙ **not exceed the speed limit**

Where there are extra hazards such as roadworks, it's often necessary to slow traffic down by imposing a temporary speed limit. These speed limits aren't advisory – they must be adhered to.

10.58
*Mark **one** answer*

You can park on the right-hand side of a road at night

⊙ in a one-way street
⊙ with your sidelights on
⊙ more than 10 metres (32 feet) from a junction
⊙ under a lamp-post

⊙ **in a one-way street**

Red rear reflectors show up when headlights shine on them. These are useful when you are parked at night but will only reflect if you park in the same direction as the traffic flow. Normally you should park on the left, but if you're in a one-way street you may also park on the right-hand side.

In which THREE places must you NOT park?

- ⊙ Near the brow of a hill
- ⊙ At or near a bus stop
- ⊙ Where there is no pavement
- ⊙ Within 10 metres (32 feet) of a junction
- ⊙ On a 40 mph road

⊙ **Near the brow of a hill**

⊙ **At or near a bus stop**

⊙ **Within 10 metres (32 feet) of a junction**

Other traffic will have to pull out to pass you. They may have to use the other side of the road and if you park near the brow of a hill they may not be able to see oncoming traffic.

It's important not to park at or near a bus stop as this could inconvenience passengers and may put them at risk as they get on or off the bus.

Parking near a junction could restrict the view for emerging vehicles.

You want to park and you see this sign. On the days and times shown you should

Meter
ZONE

Mon - Fri
8.30 am - 6.30 pm
Saturday
8.30 am - 1.30 pm

- ⊙ park in a bay and not pay
- ⊙ park on yellow lines and pay
- ⊙ park on yellow lines and not pay
- ⊙ park in a bay and pay

⊙ **park in a bay and pay**

Parking restrictions can apply in a variety of places and situations. Make sure you know where these are by reading *The Highway Code*.

Controlled parking areas will be indicated by signs and road markings. Look at these carefully to find out where and when the restrictions apply.

Parking in the wrong place could cause an obstruction and you could be fined.

10.61
*Mark **one** answer*

You will see these markers when approaching

- ⊙ the end of a motorway
- ⊙ a concealed level crossing
- ⊙ a concealed speed limit sign
- ⊙ the end of a dual carriageway

⊙ **a concealed level crossing**

If there is a bend just before the level crossing you may not be able to see the level crossing barriers or waiting traffic. These signs give you an early warning that you may find these hazards just around the bend.

10.62
*Mark **one** answer*

A single carriageway road has this sign. What is the maximum permitted speed for a car towing a trailer?

- ⊙ 30 mph
- ⊙ 40 mph
- ⊙ 50 mph
- ⊙ 60 mph

⊙ **50 mph**

When towing trailers, speed limits are also lower on dual carriageways and motorways. On these roads vehicles towing a trailer are restricted to 60 mph.

These speed limits also apply to vehicles towing a caravan or horse box.

10.63
*Mark **one** answer*

You are on a road that has no traffic signs. There are street lights. What is the speed limit?

- ⊙ 20 mph
- ⊙ 30 mph
- ⊙ 40 mph
- ⊙ 60 mph

⊙ **30 mph**

If you aren't sure of the speed limit a good indication is the presence of street lights. If there is street lighting the speed limit will be 30 mph unless otherwise indicated.

10.64   *Mark **one** answer*

Your vehicle is parked on the road at night. When must you use sidelights?

- ⊙ Where there are continuous white lines in the middle of the road
- ⊙ Where the speed limit exceeds 30 mph
- ⊙ Where you are facing oncoming traffic
- ⊙ Where you are near a bus stop

⊙ **Where the speed limit exceeds 30 mph**

When parking at night, park in the direction of the traffic. This will enable other road users to see the reflectors on the rear of your vehicle.

You must use your sidelights when parking on a road, or in a lay-by on a road, where the speed limit is over 30 mph.

10.65   *Mark **one** answer*

What MUST you have to park in a disabled space?

- ⊙ An orange or blue badge
- ⊙ A wheelchair
- ⊙ An advanced driver certificate
- ⊙ A modified vehicle

⊙ **An orange or blue badge**

Don't park in a space reserved for disabled people unless you or your passenger are a disabled badge holder. The badge must be displayed in your vehicle in the bottom left-hand corner of the windscreen.

10.66   *Mark **one** answer*

You park overnight on a road with a 40 mph speed limit. You should park

- ⊙ facing the traffic
- ⊙ with parking lights on
- ⊙ with dipped headlights on
- ⊙ near a street light

⊙ **with parking lights on**

You must use parking lights when parking at night on a road or lay-by with a speed limit greater than 30 mph. You must also park in the direction of the traffic flow.

10.67
*Mark **two** answers*

In which TWO places should you NOT park?

- Near a school entrance
- Near a police station
- In a side road
- At a bus stop
- In a one-way street

⊙ **Near a school entrance**

⊙ **At a bus stop**

It may be tempting to park where you shouldn't while you run a quick errand. Careless parking is a selfish act and could endanger other road users.

10.68
*Mark **one** answer*

To help keep your vehicle secure at night, where should you park?

- Near a police station
- In a quiet road
- On a red route
- In a well-lit area

⊙ **In a well-lit area**

Whenever possible park in an area which will be well lit at night.

10.69
*Mark **three** answers*

You MUST stop when signalled to do so by which THREE of these?

- A police officer
- A pedestrian
- A school crossing patrol
- A bus driver
- A red traffic light

⊙ **A police officer**

⊙ **A school crossing patrol**

⊙ **A red traffic light**

Looking well ahead and 'reading' the road will help you to anticipate hazards. This will enable you to stop safely at traffic lights or if ordered to do so by an authorised person.

You may remove your seat belt when carrying out a manoeuvre that involves

⊙ reversing

⊙ a hill start

⊙ an emergency stop

⊙ driving slowly

⊙ **reversing**

Don't forget to put your seat belt back on when you've finished reversing.

You are driving on an urban clearway. You may stop only to

⊙ set down and pick up passengers

⊙ use a mobile telephone

⊙ ask for directions

⊙ load or unload goods

⊙ **set down and pick up passengers**

Urban clearways may be in built-up areas and their times of operation will be clearly signed. You should stop only for as long as is reasonable to pick up or set down passengers. You should ensure that you are not causing an obstruction for other traffic.

You are waiting at a pelican crossing. The red light changes to flashing amber. This means you must

⊙ wait for pedestrians on the crossing to clear

⊙ move off immediately without any hesitation

⊙ wait for the green light before moving off

⊙ get ready and go when the continuous amber light shows

⊙ **wait for pedestrians on the crossing to clear**

This light allows time for the pedestrians already on the crossing to get to the other side in their own time, without being rushed. Don't rev your engine or start to move off while they are still crossing.

10.73
*Mark **three** answers*

On which THREE occasions MUST you stop your vehicle?

- When in an accident where damage or injury is caused
- At a red traffic light
- When signalled to do so by a police officer
- At a junction with double broken white lines
- At a pelican crossing when the amber light is flashing and no pedestrians are crossing

- **When in an accident were damage or injury is caused**

- **At a red traffic light**

- **When signalled to do so by a police officer**

You MUST stop when signalled to do so by

- a police officer
- a traffic warden
- a school crossing patrol
- a red traffic light.

You must also stop if you are involved in accident which causes damage or injury to any other person, vehicle, animal or property.

10.74
*Mark **one** answer*

On a clearway you must not stop

- at any time
- when it is busy
- in the rush hour
- during daylight hours

- **at any time**

Clearways are in place so that traffic can flow without the obstruction of parked vehicles. Just one parked vehicle will cause an obstruction for all other traffic.

Do not stop where a clearway is in force, not even to pick up or set down passengers.

section eleven
ROAD AND TRAFFIC SIGNS

This section covers:

- road signs
- speed limits
- road markings
- regulations

11.1
*Mark **one** answer*

What shape is a STOP sign at a junction?

To make it easy to recognise, the 'stop' sign is the only sign of this shape. You must stop and make effective observation before proceeding.

11.2
*Mark **one** answer*

At a junction you see this sign partly covered by snow. What does it mean?

- ⊙ Cross roads
- ⊙ Give way
- ⊙ Stop
- ⊙ Turn right

⊙ **Stop**

The STOP sign is the only road sign that is octagonal. This is so that it can be recognised and obeyed even if it is obscured, for example by snow.

11.3
*Mark **one** answer*

What does this sign mean?

- ⊙ Turn left ahead
- ⊙ T-junction
- ⊙ No through road
- ⊙ Give way

⊙ **T-junction**

This type of sign will warn you of hazards ahead.

Make sure you look at each sign that you pass on the road, so that you do not miss any vital instructions or information.

What does this sign mean?

- ⊙ Crossroads
- ⊙ Level crossing with gate
- ⊙ Level crossing without gate
- ⊙ Ahead only

⊙ **Crossroads**

The priority through the junction is shown by the broader line. You need to be aware of the hazard posed by traffic crossing or pulling out onto a major road.

What does this sign mean?

- ⊙ Ring road
- ⊙ Mini-roundabout
- ⊙ No vehicles
- ⊙ Roundabout

⊙ **Roundabout**

As you approach a roundabout look well ahead and check all signs. Decide which exit you wish to take and move into the correct position as you approach the roundabout, signalling as required.

Which of these signs means there is a double bend ahead?

⊙ 　　⊙

⊙ 　　⊙

⊙

Triangular signs give you a warning of hazards ahead. They are there to give you time to prepare for the hazard, for example by adjusting your speed.

11.7

*Mark **one** answer*

What does this sign mean?

- ⊙ Low bridge ahead
- ⊙ Tunnel ahead
- ⊙ Ancient monument ahead
- ⊙ Accident black spot ahead

⊙ **Tunnel ahead**

When approaching a tunnel switch on your dipped headlights and reduce your speed. Be aware that your eyes might need to adjust to the sudden darkness.

11.8

*Mark **one** answer*

Which sign means 'two-way traffic crosses a one-way road'?

⊙

Traffic could be joining the road you're in from either direction. Unless you need to turn, don't change lanes as you approach the junction.

11.9

*Mark **one** answer*

Which of these signs means the end of a dual carriageway?

⊙

If you're travelling in the right-hand lane, prepare and move over into the left-hand lane as soon as it's safe to do so.

What does this sign mean?

◉ End of dual carriageway
◉ Tall bridge
◉ Road narrows
◉ End of narrow bridge

◉ **End of dual carriageway**

Don't leave moving into the left-hand lane until the last moment. Plan ahead and don't rely on other traffic letting you in.

What does this sign mean?

◉ Adverse camber
◉ Steep hill downwards
◉ Uneven road
◉ Steep hill upwards

◉ **Steep hill downwards**

This sign will give you an early warning that the road ahead will slope downhill. Prepare to alter your speed and gear. Looking at the sign from left to right will show you whether the road slopes uphill or downhill.

What does this sign mean?

◉ Uneven road surface
◉ Bridge over the road
◉ Road ahead ends
◉ Water across the road

◉ **Water across the road**

This sign is found where a shallow stream crosses the road. Heavy rainfall could increase the flow of water. If the water looks too deep or the stream has spread over a large distance, stop and find another route.

11.13
*Mark **one** answer*

What does this sign mean?

- Turn left for parking area
- No through road on the left
- No entry for traffic turning left
- Turn left for ferry terminal

⊙ **No through road on the left**

If you intend to take a left turn this sign shows you that you can't get through to another route using the left-turn junction ahead.

11.14
*Mark **one** answer*

What does this sign mean?

- T-junction
- No through road
- Telephone box ahead
- Toilet ahead

⊙ **No through road**

You will not be able to find a through route to another road. Use this road only for access.

11.15
*Mark **one** answer*

Which sign means 'no through road'?

⊙

This sign is found at the entrance to a road that can only be used for access.

At this junction there is a stop sign with a solid white line on the road surface. Why is there a stop sign here?

- ⊙ Speed on the major road is de-restricted
- ⊙ It is a busy junction
- ⊙ Visibility along the major road is restricted
- ⊙ There are hazard warning lines in the centre of the road

⊙ **Visibility along the major road is restricted**

If your view is restricted at a road junction you must stop. There may also be a 'stop' sign. Don't emerge until you're sure there's no traffic approaching.

IF YOU DON'T KNOW, DON'T GO.

You are waiting at a T-junction. A vehicle is coming from the right with the left signal flashing. What should you do?

- ⊙ Move out and accelerate hard
- ⊙ Wait until the vehicle starts to turn in
- ⊙ Pull out before the vehicle reaches the junction
- ⊙ Move out slowly

⊙ **Wait until the vehicle starts to turn in**

Other road users may give misleading signals. When you're waiting at a junction don't emerge until you're sure of their intentions.

11.18
*Mark **one** answer*

What does this sign mean?

- ⊙ Buses turning
- ⊙ Ring road
- ⊙ Mini-roundabout
- ⊙ Keep right

⊙ **Mini-roundabout**

When you see this sign, look out for any direction signs and judge whether you need to signal your intentions. Do this in good time so that other road users approaching the roundabout know what you're planning to do.

11.19
*Mark **one** answer*

What does this sign mean?

- ⊙ Two-way traffic straight ahead
- ⊙ Two-way traffic crosses a one-way road
- ⊙ Two-way traffic over a bridge
- ⊙ Two-way traffic crosses a two-way road

⊙ **Two-way traffic crosses a one-way road**

Be prepared for traffic approaching from junctions on either side of you. Try to avoid unnecessary changing of lanes just before the junction.

11.20
*Mark **one** answer*

What does this sign mean?

- ⊙ Two-way traffic ahead across a one-way road
- ⊙ Traffic approaching you has priority
- ⊙ Two-way traffic straight ahead
- ⊙ Motorway contraflow system ahead

⊙ **Two-way traffic straight ahead**

This sign may be at the end of a dual carriageway or a one-way street. It is there to warn you of oncoming traffic.

What does this sign mean?

- ⊙ Hump-back bridge
- ⊙ Traffic calming hump
- ⊙ Low bridge
- ⊙ Uneven road

⊙ **Hump-back bridge**

You will need to slow down. At humpback bridges your view ahead will be restricted and the road will often be narrow on the bridge. If the bridge is very steep be prepared to sound your horn to warn others of your approach. Going over too fast over the bridge is highly dangerous to other road users and could even cause your wheels to leave the road, with a resulting loss of control.

Which of the following signs informs you that you are coming to a 'no through road'?

⊙

This sign is found at the entrance to a road that can only be used for access.

What does this sign mean?

- ⊙ Level crossing with gate or barrier
- ⊙ Gated road ahead
- ⊙ Level crossing without gate or barrier
- ⊙ Cattle grid ahead

⊙ **Level crossing with gate or barrier**

Some crossings have gates but no attendant or signals. You should

- stop
- look both ways
- listen and make sure that there is no train approaching.

If there is a telephone, contact the signal operator to make sure that it's safe to cross.

11.24
Mark one answer

At a railway level crossing the red light signal continues to flash after a train has gone by. What should you do?

- ⊙ Phone the signal operator
- ⊙ Alert drivers behind you
- ⊙ Wait
- ⊙ Proceed with caution

⊙ **Wait**

You must always obey red flashing stop lights. If a train passes but the lights continue to flash, another train will be passing soon. Cross only when the lights go off and the barriers open.

11.25
Mark one answer

You are driving through a tunnel and you see this sign. What does it mean?

- ⊙ Direction to emergency pedestrian exit
- ⊙ Beware of pedestrians, no footpath ahead
- ⊙ No access for pedestrians
- ⊙ Beware of pedestrians crossing ahead

⊙ **Direction to emergency pedestrian exit**

If you find yourself having to evacuate a tunnel, do so as quickly as you can. Follow the signs directing you to the nearest exit point. If there are several people using the exit, don't panic but try to leave in a calm and orderly manner.

11.26
Mark one answer

What does this traffic sign mean?

- ⊙ No overtaking allowed
- ⊙ Give priority to oncoming traffic
- ⊙ Two way traffic
- ⊙ One-way traffic only

⊙ **Give priority to oncoming traffic**

Priority signs are normally shown where the road is narrow and there isn't enough room for two vehicles to pass, such as at

- a narrow bridge
- roadworks
- a width restriction.

Make sure that you know who has priority. Comply with the sign and don't force your way through. Show courtesy and consideration to other road users.

What is the meaning of this traffic sign?

- ⊙ End of two-way road
- ⊙ Give priority to vehicles coming towards you
- ⊙ You have priority over vehicles coming towards you
- ⊙ Bus lane ahead

⊙ **You have priority over vehicles coming towards you**

Don't force your way through. Show courtesy and consideration to other road users. Although you have priority, make sure oncoming traffic is going to give way before you continue.

What does this sign mean?

- ⊙ No overtaking
- ⊙ You are entering a one-way street
- ⊙ Two-way traffic ahead
- ⊙ You have priority over vehicles from the opposite direction

⊙ **You have priority over vehicles from the opposite direction**

Don't force your way through if oncoming vehicles fail to give way. If necessary, slow down and give way to avoid confrontation or an accident.

What are triangular signs for?

- ⊙ To give warnings
- ⊙ To give information
- ⊙ To give orders
- ⊙ To give directions

⊙ **To give warnings**

This type of sign will warn you of hazards ahead.

Make sure you look at each sign that you pass on the road, so that you do not miss any vital instructions or information.

11.30 — *Mark **four** answers*

Which FOUR of these would be indicated by a triangular road sign?

- ⊙ Road narrows
- ⊙ Ahead only
- ⊙ Low bridge
- ⊙ Minimum speed
- ⊙ Children crossing
- ⊙ T-junction

- ⊙ **Road narrows**
- ⊙ **Low bridge**
- ⊙ **Children crossing**
- ⊙ **T-junction**

Warning signs are there to make you aware of potential hazards on the road ahead. Act on the signs so you are prepared and can take whatever action is necessary.

11.31 — *Mark **one** answer*

What does this traffic sign mean?

- ⊙ Slippery road ahead
- ⊙ Tyres liable to punctures ahead
- ⊙ Danger ahead
- ⊙ Service area ahead

- ⊙ **Danger ahead**

This sign is there to alert you to the likelihood of danger ahead. It may be accompanied by a plate indicating the type of hazard. Be ready to reduce your speed and take avoiding action.

11.32 — *Mark **one** answer*

What does this sign mean?

- ⊙ Bus station on the right
- ⊙ Contraflow bus lane
- ⊙ With-flow bus lane
- ⊙ Give way to buses

- ⊙ **Contraflow bus lane**

There will also be markings on the road surface to indicate the bus lane. You must not use this lane for parking or overtaking.

You are about to overtake when you see this sign. You should

- overtake the other driver as quickly as possible
- move to the right to get a better view
- switch your headlights on before overtaking
- hold back until you can see clearly ahead

⊙ **hold back until you can see clearly ahead**

You won't be able to see any hazards that might be hidden in the dip. As well as oncoming traffic the dip may conceal

- cyclists
- horse riders
- parked vehicles
- pedestrians

in the road.

What does this sign mean?

- Quayside or river bank
- Steep hill downwards
- Uneven road surface
- Road liable to flooding

⊙ **Quayside or river bank**

You should be careful in these locations as the road surface is likely to be wet and slippery. There may be a steep drop to the water and there may not be a barrier along the edge of the road.

Where would you see a contraflow bus §and cycle lane?

- On a dual carriageway
- On a roundabout
- On an urban motorway
- On a one-way street

⊙ **On a one-way street**

In a contraflow lane, the traffic permitted to use it travels in the opposite direction to traffic in the other lanes on the road.

11.36 Mark **one** answer

Which sign means you have priority over oncoming vehicles?

Even though you have priority, be prepared to give way if complying with the sign is likely to cause an accident, congestion or confrontation.

11.37 Mark **one** answer

Which shape is used for a 'give way' sign?

Other warning signs are the same shape and colour, but the 'give way' sign is the only triangular one that points downwards. When you see this sign you must give way to traffic on the road which you are about to enter.

11.38 Mark **one** answer

Which of these signs means that you are entering a one-way street?

If the road has two lanes you can use either lane and overtake on either side. Use the lane that's more convenient for your destination unless road markings indicate otherwise.

Which is the sign for a ring road?

⊙

Ring roads are designed to relieve congestion in towns and city centres.

What does this sign mean?

- ⊙ The right-hand lane ahead is narrow
- ⊙ Right-hand lane for buses only
- ⊙ Right-hand lane for turning right
- ⊙ The right-hand lane is closed

⊙ **The right-hand lane is closed**

Yellow and black temporary signs may be used to inform you of roadworks or lane restrictions. Look well ahead. If you have to change lanes, do so in good time.

What does this sign mean?

- ⊙ Change to the left lane
- ⊙ Leave at the next exit
- ⊙ Contraflow system
- ⊙ One-way street

⊙ **Contraflow system**

If you use the right-hand lane in a contraflow system, you'll be travelling with no permanent barrier between you and the oncoming traffic. Observe speed limits and keep a good distance from the vehicle ahead.

11.42   *Mark **one** answer*

What does this sign mean?

⊙ Leave motorway at next exit
⊙ Lane for heavy and slow vehicles
⊙ All lorries use the hard shoulder
⊙ Rest area for lorries

⊙ **Lane for heavy and slow vehicles**

Where there's a long, steep, uphill gradient on a motorway, a crawler lane may be provided. This helps the traffic to flow by diverting the slower heavy vehicles into a dedicated lane on the left.

11.43   *Mark **one** answer*

What does this sign mean?

⊙ Direction to park-and-ride car park
⊙ No parking for buses or coaches
⊙ Directions to bus and coach park
⊙ Parking area for cars and coaches

⊙ **Direction to park-and-ride car park**

To ease the congestion in town centres, some cities and towns provide park-and-ride schemes. These allow you to park in a designated area and ride by bus into the centre.

Park-and-ride schemes are usually cheaper and easier than car parking in the town centre.

11.44   *Mark **one** answer*

What does this motorway sign mean?

⊙ Change to the lane on your left
⊙ Leave the motorway at the next exit
⊙ Change to the opposite carriageway
⊙ Pull up on the hard shoulder

⊙ **Change to the lane on your left**

On the motorway, signs sometimes show temporary warnings due to traffic or weather conditions. They may be used to indicate

• lane closures
• temporary speed limits
• weather warnings.

What does this motorway sign mean?

- Temporary minimum speed 50 mph
- No services for 50 miles
- Obstruction 50 metres (164 feet) ahead
- Temporary maximum speed 50 mph

⊙ **Temporary maximum speed 50 mph**

Look out for signs above your lane or on the central reservation. These will give you important information or warnings about the road ahead. Due to the high speeds of motorway traffic these signs may light up some distance from any hazard. Don't ignore the signs just because the road looks clear to you.

What does this sign mean?

- Through traffic to use left lane
- Right-hand lane T-junction only
- Right-hand lane closed ahead
- 11 tonne weight limit

⊙ **Right-hand lane closed ahead**

Move over as soon as you see the sign and it's safe to do so. Don't stay in a lane that is closed ahead until the last moment to beat a queue of traffic.

On a motorway this sign means

- move over onto the hard shoulder
- overtaking on the left only
- leave the motorway at the next exit
- move to the lane on your left

⊙ **move to the lane on your left**

It is important to know and obey temporary signs on the motorway: they are there for a reason. You may not be able to see the hazard straight away, as the signs give warnings well in advance due to the speed of traffic on the motorway.

11.48
*Mark **one** answer*

What does '25' mean on this motorway sign?

- The distance to the nearest town
- The route number of the road
- The number of the next junction
- The speed limit on the slip road

⊙ **The number of the next junction**

Before you set out on your journey use a road map to plan your route. When you see advance warning of your junction, make sure you get into the correct lane in plenty of time. Last-minute harsh braking and cutting across lanes at speed is extremely hazardous.

11.49
*Mark **one** answer*

What does this sign mean?

- With-flow bus and cycle lane
- Contraflow bus and cycle lane
- No buses and cycles allowed
- No waiting for buses and cycles

⊙ **With-flow bus and cycle lane**

Buses, taxis and cycles are permitted to travel in this lane in the same direction as other traffic. They will be on your left. There may be times shown on the sign to indicate when the lane is in operation.

11.50
*Mark **one** answer*

Where can you find reflective amber studs on a motorway?

- Separating the slip road from the motorway
- On the left-hand edge of the road
- On the right-hand edge of the road
- Separating the lanes

⊙ **On the right-hand edge of the road**

At night or in poor visibility reflective studs on the road help you to judge your position on the carriageway.

11.51 *Mark **one** answer*

Where on a motorway would you find green reflective studs?

- ⊙ Separating driving lanes
- ⊙ Between the hard shoulder and the carriageway
- ⊙ At slip road entrances and exits
- ⊙ Between the carriageway and the central reservation

⊙ **At slip road entrances and exits**

Knowing the colours of the reflective studs on the road will help you judge your position in foggy conditions or when visibility is poor.

11.52 *Mark **one** answer*

You are travelling along a motorway. You see this sign. You should

- ⊙ leave the motorway at the next exit
- ⊙ turn left immediately
- ⊙ change lane
- ⊙ move onto the hard shoulder

⊙ **leave the motorway at the next exit**

You'll see this sign if the motorway is closed ahead. Pull into the nearside lane as soon as it is safe to do so. Don't leave it to the last moment.

11.53 *Mark **one** answer*

What does this sign mean?

- ⊙ No motor vehicles
- ⊙ End of motorway
- ⊙ No through road
- ⊙ End of bus lane

⊙ **End of motorway**

When you leave the motorway make sure that you check your speedometer. You may be going faster than you realise. Slow down and look out for speed limit signs.

11.54   *Mark **one** answer*

What does this sign mean?

- ⊙ End of motorway
- ⊙ End of restriction
- ⊙ Lane ends ahead
- ⊙ Free recovery ends

⊙ **End of restriction**

Temporary restrictions on motorways are shown on signs which have flashing amber lights. At the end of the restriction you will see this sign without any flashing lights.

11.55   *Mark **one** answer*

You are on a motorway. You see this sign on a lorry that has stopped in the right-hand lane. You should

- ⊙ move into the right-hand lane
- ⊙ stop behind the flashing lights
- ⊙ pass the lorry on the left
- ⊙ leave the motorway at the next exit

⊙ **pass the lorry on the left**

Sometimes work is carried out on the motorway without closing the lanes. When this happens, signs are mounted on the back of lorries to warn other road users of roadworks ahead.

11.56   *Mark **one** answer*

You are on a motorway. Red flashing lights appear above your lane only. What should you do?

- ⊙ Continue in that lane and look for further information
- ⊙ Move into another lane in good time
- ⊙ Pull onto the hard shoulder
- ⊙ Stop and wait for an instruction to proceed

⊙ **Move into another lane in good time**

Flashing red lights above your lane show that your lane is closed. You should move into another lane as soon as you can do so safely.

     *Mark **one** answer*

You are driving on a motorway. There is a slow-moving vehicle ahead. On the back you see this sign. You should

- ⊙ pass on the right
- ⊙ pass on the left
- ⊙ leave at the next exit
- ⊙ drive no further

⊙ **pass on the left**

If a vehicle displaying this sign is in your lane you will have to pass it on the left. Use your mirrors and signal. When it's safe move into the lane on your left.

You should always look well ahead so that you can spot any hazards early, giving yourself time to react safely.

---

     *Mark **one** answer*

You see this signal overhead on the motorway. What does it mean?

- ⊙ Leave the motorway at the next exit
- ⊙ All vehicles use the hard shoulder
- ⊙ Sharp bend to the left ahead
- ⊙ Stop, all lanes ahead closed

⊙ **Leave the motorway at the next exit**

You will see this sign if there has been an incident ahead and the motorway is closed. You must obey the sign. Make sure that you prepare to leave as soon as you see the warning sign.

Don't pull over at the last moment or cut across other traffic.

---

     *Mark **one** answer*

Which type of vehicle does this sign apply to?

- ⊙ Wide vehicles
- ⊙ Long vehicles
- ⊙ High vehicles
- ⊙ Heavy vehicles

⊙ **High vehicles**

The triangular shapes above and below the dimensions indicate a height restriction that applies to the road ahead.

11.60
*Mark **one** answer*

What does this sign mean?

⊙ Cyclists must dismount
⊙ Cycles are not allowed
⊙ Cycle route ahead
⊙ Cycle in single file

⊙ **Cycle route ahead**

Where there's a cycle route ahead, a sign will show a bicycle in a red warning triangle. Watch out for children on bicycles and cyclists rejoining the main road.

11.61
*Mark **one** answer*

When may you NOT overtake on the left?

⊙ On a free-flowing motorway or dual carriageway
⊙ When the traffic is moving slowly in queues
⊙ On a one-way street
⊙ When the car in front is signalling to turn right

⊙ **On a free-flowing motorway or dual carriageway**

You should normally overtake on the right but there are some occasions when you may overtake on the left. These include when traffic is moving slowly in queues, or when a vehicle ahead is positioned to turn right and there's room to pass on the left.

On motorways and dual carriageways, do not overtake on the left if traffic is flowing freely.

11.62
*Mark **one** answer*

Which sign means that pedestrians may be walking along the road?

⊙   ⊙

⊙   ⊙

⊙

When you pass pedestrians in the road, leave plenty of room. You might have to use the right-hand side of the road so look well ahead, as well as in your mirrors, before pulling out. Take great care if there is a bend in the road obscuring your view ahead.

Which of these signs warn you of a pedestrian crossing?

Look well ahead and check the pavements and surrounding areas for pedestrians. Look for anyone walking towards the crossing. Check your mirrors for traffic behind in case you have to slow down or stop.

What does this sign mean?

- No footpath ahead
- Pedestrians only ahead
- Pedestrian crossing ahead
- School crossing ahead

⊙ **Pedestrian crossing ahead**

There are many signs relating to pedestrians that you need to be aware of. You will find these in *The Highway Code* and *Know Your Traffic Signs*. Some of the signs look similar but give different warnings. Make sure you know what they all mean so that you're prepared for any potential hazard.

What does this sign mean?

- School crossing patrol
- No pedestrians allowed
- Pedestrian zone – no vehicles
- Pedestrian crossing ahead

⊙ **Pedestrian crossing ahead**

Look well ahead and be ready to stop for any pedestrians crossing the road. Also check the pavements for anyone who looks like they might step into the road.

11.66
Mark *one* answer

You are approaching a zebra crossing where pedestrians are waiting. Which arm signal might you give?

A 'slowing down' signal will indicate your intentions to oncoming and following vehicles. Be aware that pedestrians might start to cross as soon as they see this signal.

11.67
Mark *one* answer

What do these zigzag lines at pedestrian crossings mean?

- ⊙ No parking at any time
- ⊙ Parking allowed only for a short time
- ⊙ Slow down to 20 mph
- ⊙ Sounding horns is not allowed

⊙ **No parking at any time**

The approach to and exit from a pedestrian crossing is marked with zigzag lines. You must not

- park on them or
- overtake the leading vehicle when approaching the crossing.

Parking here would block the view for pedestrians and the approaching traffic.

11.68
Mark *one* answer

The right-hand lane of a three-lane motorway is

- ⊙ for lorries only
- ⊙ an overtaking lane
- ⊙ the right-turn lane
- ⊙ an acceleration lane

⊙ **an overtaking lane**

You should stay in the left-hand lane of a motorway unless overtaking. The right-hand lane of a motorway is an overtaking lane and not a 'fast lane'.

After overtaking, move back to the left when it is safe to do so.

When may you cross a double solid white line in the middle of the road?

- ⊙ To pass traffic that is queuing back at a junction
- ⊙ To pass a car signalling to turn left ahead
- ⊙ To pass a road maintenance vehicle travelling at 10 mph or less
- ⊙ To pass a vehicle that is towing a trailer

⊙ **To pass a road maintenance vehicle travelling at 10 mph or less**

You may cross the solid white line to pass a stationary vehicle, pedal cycle, horse or road maintenance vehicle if they are travelling at 10 mph or less. You may also cross the solid line to enter into a side road or access a property.

What does this road marking mean?

- ⊙ Do not cross the line
- ⊙ No stopping allowed
- ⊙ You are approaching a hazard
- ⊙ No overtaking allowed

⊙ **You are approaching a hazard**

Road markings will warn you of a hazard ahead. A single broken line along the centre of the road, with long markings and short gaps, is a hazard warning line. Don't cross it unless you can see that the road is clear well ahead.

Where would you see this road marking?

- ⊙ At traffic lights
- ⊙ On road humps
- ⊙ Near a level crossing
- ⊙ At a box junction

⊙ **On road humps**

Due to the dark colour of the road, changes in level aren't easily seen. White triangles painted on the road surface give you an indication of where there are road humps.

11.72 *Mark **one** answer*

Which is a hazard warning line?

You need to know the difference between the normal centre line and a hazard warning line. If there is a hazard ahead, the markings are longer and the gaps shorter. This gives you advanced warning of an unspecified hazard ahead.

11.73 *Mark **one** answer*

You see this line across the road at the entrance to a roundabout. What does it mean?

- ⊙ Give way to traffic from the right
- ⊙ Traffic from the left has right of way
- ⊙ You have right of way
- ⊙ Stop at the line

⊙ **Give way to traffic from the right**

Slow down as you approach the roundabout checking for traffic coming from the right. If you need to stop and give way, stay behind the broken line until it is safe to emerge onto the roundabout.

11.74 *Mark **one** answer*

Where would you see these road markings?

- ⊙ At a level crossing
- ⊙ On a motorway slip road
- ⊙ At a pedestrian crossing
- ⊙ On a single-track road

⊙ **On a motorway slip road**

When driving on a motorway or slip road, you must not enter into an area marked with chevrons and bordered by a solid white line for any reason, except in an emergency.

The white line along the side of the road

- ⊙ shows the edge of the carriageway
- ⊙ shows the approach to a hazard
- ⊙ means no parking
- ⊙ means no overtaking

⊙ **shows the edge of the carriageway**

A continuous white line is used on many roads to indicate the edge of the carriageway. This can be useful when visibility is restricted. The line is discontinued at junctions, lay-bys and entrances and exits from private drives.

You see this white arrow on the road ahead. It means

- ⊙ entrance on the left
- ⊙ all vehicles turn left
- ⊙ keep left of the hatched markings
- ⊙ road bending to the left

⊙ **keep left of the hatched markings**

Don't attempt to overtake here, as there might be unseen hazards over the brow of the hill. Keep to the left.

You should NOT normally stop on these markings near schools

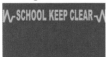

- ⊙ except when picking up children
- ⊙ under any circumstances
- ⊙ unless there is nowhere else available
- ⊙ except to set down children

⊙ **under any circumstances**

At schools you must NOT stop on yellow zigzag lines for any length of time, not even to set down or pick up children or other passengers.

11.78 *Mark **one** answer*

A white line like this along the centre of the road is a

⊙ bus lane marking

⊙ hazard warning

⊙ give way marking

⊙ lane marking

⊙ **hazard warning**

The centre of the road is usually marked by a broken white line, with lines that are shorter than the gaps. When the lines become longer than the gaps this is a hazard warning line. Look well ahead for these, especially when you are planning to overtake or turn off.

11.79 *Mark **one** answer*

What is the reason for the yellow criss-cross lines painted on the road here?

⊙ To mark out an area for trams only

⊙ To prevent queuing traffic from blocking the junction on the left

⊙ To mark the entrance lane to a car park

⊙ To warn you of the tram lines crossing the road

⊙ **To prevent queuing traffic from blocking the junction on the left**

Yellow 'box junctions' like this are often used where it's busy. Their purpose is to keep the junction clear for crossing traffic. Don't enter the painted area unless your exit is clear. The exception to this is when you are turning right and are only prevented from doing so by oncoming traffic or by other vehicles waiting to turn right.

What is the reason for the area marked in red and white along the centre of this road?

⊙ It is to separate traffic flowing in opposite directions

⊙ It marks an area to be used by overtaking motorcyclists

⊙ It is a temporary marking to warn of the roadworks

⊙ It is separating the two sides of the dual carriageway

⊙ **It is to separate traffic flowing in opposite directions**

Areas of 'hatched markings' such as these are to separate traffic streams which could be a danger to each other. They are often seen on bends or where the road becomes narrow. If the area is bordered by a solid white line, you must not enter it except in an emergency.

Where would you find these road markings?

⊙ At a railway crossing

⊙ At a junction

⊙ On a motorway

⊙ On a pedestrian crossing

⊙ **At a junction**

These markings show the direction in which the traffic should go at a mini-roundabout.

11.82   *Mark **one** answer*

This broken white line painted in the centre of the road means

- ⊙ oncoming vehicles have priority over you
- ⊙ you should give priority to oncoming vehicles
- ⊙ there is a hazard ahead of you
- ⊙ the area is a national speed limit zone

⊙ **there is a hazard ahead of you**

A long white line with short gaps means that you are approaching a hazard. If you do need to cross it, make sure that the road is clear well ahead.

11.83   *Mark **one** answer*

What is the purpose of these yellow criss-cross lines on the road?

- ⊙ To make you more aware of the traffic lights
- ⊙ To guide you into position as you turn
- ⊙ To prevent the junction becoming blocked
- ⊙ To show you where to stop when the lights change

⊙ **To prevent the junction becoming blocked**

You must not enter a box junction until your exit road or lane is clear. The exception to this is if you want to turn right and are only prevented from doing so by oncoming traffic or by other vehicles waiting to turn right.

This marking appears on the road just before a

- ⊙ 'no entry' sign
- ⊙ 'give way' sign
- ⊙ 'stop' sign
- ⊙ 'no through road' sign

⊙ **'give way' sign**

Where you see this road marking you must give way to traffic on the main road. It might not be used at junctions where there is relatively little traffic. However, if there is a double broken line across the junction the 'give way' rules still apply.

What does a sign with a brown background show?

- ⊙ Tourist directions
- ⊙ Primary roads
- ⊙ Motorway routes
- ⊙ Minor routes

⊙ **Tourist directions**

Signs with a brown background give directions to places of interest. They will often be seen on the motorway directing you along the easiest route to the attraction.

This sign means

- ⊙ tourist attraction
- ⊙ beware of trains
- ⊙ level crossing
- ⊙ beware of trams

⊙ **tourist attraction**

These signs indicate places of interest and are designed to guide you by the easiest route. They are particularly useful if you are unfamiliar with the area.

11.87 *Mark **one** answer*

Which of these signs means that the national speed limit applies?

You should know the speed limit for the road that you're travelling on and the vehicle that you're driving. The different speed limits are shown in *The Highway Code*.

11.88 *Mark **one** answer*

What is the maximum speed on a single carriageway road?

⊙ 50 mph
⊙ 60 mph
⊙ 40 mph
⊙ 70 mph

⊙ **60 mph**

If you're travelling on a dual carriageway that becomes a single carriageway road reduce your speed gradually so that you aren't exceeding the limit as you enter. There might not be a sign to remind you of the limit, so make sure you know what the speed limits are for different types of roads and vehicles.

11.89 *Mark **one** answer*

This sign is advising you to

⊙ follow the route diversion
⊙ follow the signs to the picnic area
⊙ give way to pedestrians
⊙ give way to cyclists

⊙ **follow the route diversion**

When a diversion route has been put in place, drivers are advised to follow a symbol which may be a triangle, square, circle or diamond shape on a yellow background.

Why would this temporary speed limit sign be shown?

- To warn of the end of the motorway
- To warn you of a low bridge
- To warn you of a junction ahead
- To warn of road works ahead

⊙ **To warn of road works ahead**

In the interests of road safety, temporary speed limits are imposed at all major road works. Signs like this, giving advanced warning of the speed limit, are normally placed about three quarters of a mile ahead of where the speed limit comes into force.

This traffic sign means there is

- a compulsory maximum speed limit
- an advisory maximum speed limit
- a compulsory minimum speed limit
- an advised separation distance

⊙ **a compulsory maximum speed limit**

The sign gives you an early warning of a speed restriction. If you are travelling at a higher speed, slow down in good time. You could come across queuing traffic due to roadworks or a temporary obstruction.

You approach a junction. The traffic lights are not working. A police officer gives this signal. You should

- turn left only
- turn right only
- stop level with the officer's arm
- stop at the stop line

⊙ **stop at the stop line**

If a police officer or traffic warden is directing traffic you must obey them. They will use the arm signals shown in *The Highway Code*. Learn what these mean and act accordingly.

11.93 *Mark **one** answer*

The driver of the car in front is giving this arm signal. What does it mean?

- ⊙ The driver is slowing down
- ⊙ The driver intends to turn right
- ⊙ The driver wishes to overtake
- ⊙ The driver intends to turn left

⊙ **The driver intends to turn left**

There might be an occasion where another driver uses an arm signal. This may be because the vehicle's indicators are obscured by other traffic. In order for such signals to be effective, all drivers should know the meaning of them.

Be aware that the 'left turn' signal might look similar to the 'slowing down' signal.

11.94 *Mark **one** answer*

You are signalling to turn right in busy traffic. How would you confirm your intention safely?

- ⊙ Sound the horn
- ⊙ Give an arm signal
- ⊙ Flash your headlights
- ⊙ Position over the centre line

⊙ **Give an arm signal**

In some situations you may feel your indicators cannot be seen by other road users. If you think you need to make your intention more clearly seen, give the arm signal shown in *The Highway Code*.

11.95 *Mark **one** answer*

The driver of this car is giving an arm signal. What are they about to do?

- ⊙ Turn to the right
- ⊙ Turn to the left
- ⊙ Go straight ahead
- ⊙ Let pedestrians cross

⊙ **Turn to the left**

In some situations drivers may need to give arm signals, in addition to indicators, to make their intentions clear. For arm signals to be effective, all road users should know their meaning.

*Mark **one** answer*

Which arm signal tells you that the car you are following is going to turn left?

There may be occasions when drivers need to give an arm signal in addition to an indicator. For example

- in bright sunshine
- at a complex road layout
- when stopping at a pedestrian crossing
- to confirm an indicator
- when turning right just after passing a parked vehicle.

You should understand what each arm signal means. If you give arm signals, make them clear, correct and decisive.

---

*Mark **one** answer*

How should you give an arm signal to turn left?

There may be occasions where other road users are unable to see your indicator, such as in bright sunlight or at a busy, complicated junction. In these cases a hand signal will help others to understand your intentions.

11.98
*Mark **one** answer*

Why should you make sure that your indicators are cancelled after turning?

- ⊙ To avoid flattening the battery
- ⊙ To avoid misleading other road users
- ⊙ To avoid dazzling other road users
- ⊙ To avoid damage to the indicator relay

⊙ **To avoid misleading other road users**

Leaving your indicators on could confuse other road users and may even lead to an accident.

Be aware that if you haven't taken a sharp turn your indicators may not self-cancel and you will need to turn them off manually.

11.99
*Mark **one** answer*

You are driving in busy traffic. You want to pull up on the left just after a junction on the left. When should you signal?

- ⊙ As you are passing or just after the junction
- ⊙ Just before you reach the junction
- ⊙ Well before you reach the junction
- ⊙ It would be better not to signal at all

⊙ **As you are passing or just after the junction**

You need to signal to let other drivers know your intentions. However, if you indicate too early they may think you are turning left into the junction. Correct timing of the signal is very important to avoid misleading others.

11.100
*Mark **one** answer*

You are approaching a red traffic light. The signal will change from red to

- ⊙ red and amber, then green
- ⊙ green, then amber
- ⊙ amber, then green
- ⊙ green and amber, then green

⊙ **red and amber, then green**

If you know which light is going to show next you can plan your approach accordingly. This can help prevent excessive braking or hesitation at the junction.

A red traffic light means

⊙ you should stop unless turning left

⊙ stop, if you are able to brake safely

⊙ you must stop and wait behind the stop line

⊙ proceed with caution

⊙ **you must stop and wait behind the stop line**

Learn the sequence of traffic lights.

- RED means stop and wait behind the stop line.

- RED-AND-AMBER also means stop. Don't go until the green light shows.

- GREEN means you may go if your way is clear. Don't proceed if your exit road is blocked and don't block the junction. Look out for pedestrians.

- AMBER means stop at the stop line. You may go if the amber light appears after you've crossed the stop line or you're so close to it that to pull up might cause an accident.

At traffic lights, amber on its own means

⊙ prepare to go

⊙ go if the way is clear

⊙ go if no pedestrians are crossing

⊙ stop at the stop line

⊙ **stop at the stop line**

If the lights have been on green for a while they're likely to change to red as you approach. Be ready for this so that you're able to stop in time.

11.103 · *Mark **one** answer*

You are at a junction controlled by traffic lights. When should you NOT proceed at green?

- ⊙ When pedestrians are waiting to cross
- ⊙ When your exit from the junction is blocked
- ⊙ When you think the lights may be about to change
- ⊙ When you intend to turn right

⊙ **When your exit from the junction is blocked**

As you approach the lights look into the road you wish to take. Only proceed if your exit road is clear. If the road is blocked hold back, even if you have to wait for the next green signal.

11.104 · *Mark **one** answer*

You are in the left-hand lane at traffic lights. You are waiting to turn left. At which of these traffic lights must you NOT move on?

At some junctions there may be a separate signal for different lanes. These are called 'filter' lights. They're designed to help traffic flow at major junctions. Make sure that you're in the correct lane and proceed if the way is clear and the green light shows for your lane.

What does this sign mean?

⊙ Traffic lights out of order

⊙ Amber signal out of order

⊙ Temporary traffic lights ahead

⊙ New traffic lights ahead

⊙ **Traffic lights out of order**

Where traffic lights are out of order you might see this sign. Proceed with caution as nobody has priority at the junction.

When traffic lights are out of order, who has priority?

⊙ Traffic going straight on

⊙ Traffic turning right

⊙ Nobody

⊙ Traffic turning left

⊙ **Nobody**

When traffic lights are out of order you should treat the junction as an unmarked crossroads. Be cautious as you may need to give way or stop. Keep a look out for traffic attempting to cross the junction at speed.

These flashing red lights mean STOP. In which THREE of the following places could you find them?

⊙ Pelican crossings

⊙ Lifting bridges

⊙ Zebra crossings

⊙ Level crossings

⊙ Motorway exits

⊙ Fire stations

⊙ **Lifting bridges**

⊙ **Level crossings**

⊙ **Fire stations**

You must always stop when the red lights are flashing, whether or not the way seems to be clear.

11.108 Mark **one** answer

You see this sign at a crossroads. You should

- ⊙ maintain the same speed
- ⊙ carry on with great care
- ⊙ find another route
- ⊙ telephone the police

⊙ **carry on with great care**

When traffic lights are out of order treat the junction as an unmarked crossroad.
Be very careful as no one has priority and be prepared to stop.

11.109 Mark **one** answer

A red traffic light means

- ⊙ you must stop behind the white stop line
- ⊙ you may go straight on if there is no other traffic
- ⊙ you may turn left if it is safe to do so
- ⊙ you must slow down and prepare to stop if traffic has started to cross

⊙ **you must stop behind the white stop line**

The white line is generally positioned so that pedestrians have room to cross in front of waiting traffic. Don't move off while pedestrians are crossing even if the lights change to green.

11.110 Mark **one** answer

At a junction you see this signal. It means

- ⊙ cars must stop
- ⊙ trams must stop
- ⊙ both trams and cars must stop
- ⊙ both trams and cars can continue

⊙ **trams must stop**

The white light shows that trams must stop, but the green light shows that other vehicles may go if the way is clear.

You may not live in an area where there are trams but you should still learn the signs. You never know when you may go to a town with trams.

You see this amber traffic light ahead. Which light or lights, will come on next?

- ⊙ Red alone
- ⊙ Red and amber together
- ⊙ Green and amber together
- ⊙ Green alone

⊙ **Red alone**

At junctions controlled by traffic lights you must stop behind the white line until the lights change to green. Red and amber lights showing together also mean stop.

You may proceed when the light is green unless your exit road is blocked or pedestrians are crossing in front of you.

If you're approaching traffic lights that are visible from a distance and the light has been green for some time they are likely to change. Be ready to slow down and stop.

You are approaching traffic lights. Red and amber are showing. This means

- ⊙ pass the lights if the road is clear
- ⊙ there is a fault with the lights – take care
- ⊙ wait for the green light before you cross the stop line
- ⊙ the lights are about to change to red

⊙ **wait for the green light before you cross the stop line**

Be aware that other traffic might still be clearing the junction. Make sure the way is clear before continuing.

When may you sound the horn?

- ⊙ To give you right of way
- ⊙ To attract a friend's attention
- ⊙ To warn others of your presence
- ⊙ To make slower drivers move over

⊙ **To warn others of your presence**

Don't use the horn aggressively.

You MUST NOT sound it

- between 11.30 pm and 7 am
- when you are stationary, unless a moving vehicle poses a danger.

11.114   *Mark **one** answer*

What does this sign mean?

⊙ Maximum speed limit with traffic
  calming

⊙ Minimum speed limit with traffic calming

⊙ '20 cars only' parking zone

⊙ Only 20 cars allowed at any one time

⊙ **Maximum speed limit with traffic calming**

If you're in places where there are likely to be pedestrians such as outside schools, near parks, residential areas and shopping areas, you should be extra-cautious and keep your speed down.

Many local authorities have taken measures to slow traffic down by creating traffic calming measures such as speed humps. They are there for a reason; slow down.

11.115   *Mark **one** answer*

What does this sign mean'?

⊙ New speed limit 20 mph

⊙ No vehicles over 30 tonnes

⊙ Minimum speed limit 30 mph

⊙ End of 20 mph zone

⊙ **End of 20 mph zone**

Where you see this sign the 20 mph restriction ends. Check all around for possible hazards and only increase your speed if it's safe to do so.

What does this sign mean?

- End of restricted speed area
- End of restricted parking area
- End of clearway
- End of cycle route

⊙ **End of restricted parking area**

Even though you have left the restricted area, make sure that you park where you won't endanger other road users or cause an obstruction.

What does this sign mean?

- Humpback bridge
- Humps in the road
- Entrance to tunnel
- Soft verges

⊙ **Humps in the road**

These have been put in place to slow the traffic down. They're usually found in residential areas. Slow down to an appropriate speed.

In some narrow residential streets you may find a speed limit of

- 20 mph
- 25 mph
- 35 mph
- 40 mph

⊙ **20 mph**

In some built-up areas, you may find the speed limit reduced to 20 mph. Driving at a slower speed will help give you the time and space to see and deal safely with hazards such as pedestrians and parked cars.

11.119 Mark *one* answer

What does this sign mean?

⊙ Route for trams only
⊙ Route for buses only
⊙ Parking for buses only
⊙ Parking for trams only

⊙ **Route for trams only**

Avoid blocking tram routes. Trams are fixed on their route and can't manoeuvre around other vehicles and pedestrians. Modern trams travel quickly and are quiet so you might not hear them approaching.

11.120 Mark *one* answer

What does this sign mean?

⊙ Route for trams
⊙ Give way to trams
⊙ Route for buses
⊙ Give way to buses

⊙ **Route for trams**

Take extra care when you encounter trams. Look out for road markings and signs that alert you to them. Modern trams are very quiet and you may not hear them approaching.

11.121 Mark *one* answer

What does this sign mean?

⊙ Wait at the barriers
⊙ Wait at the crossroads
⊙ Give way to trams
⊙ Give way to farm vehicles

⊙ **Give way to trams**

Obey the 'give way' signs. Trams are unable to steer around you if you misjudge when it is safe to enter the junction.

What does this sign mean?

- ⊙ No trams ahead
- ⊙ Oncoming trams
- ⊙ Trams crossing ahead
- ⊙ Trams only

⊙ **Trams crossing ahead**

This sign warns you to beware of trams. If you don't usually drive in a town where there are trams, remember to look out for them at junctions and look for tram rails, signs and signals.

What does this sign mean?

- ⊙ Waiting restrictions apply
- ⊙ Waiting permitted
- ⊙ National speed limit applies
- ⊙ Clearway (no stopping)

⊙ **Waiting restrictions apply**

There will be a plate or additional sign to tell you when the restrictions apply.

Which sign means 'no stopping'?

⊙   ⊙

⊙   ⊙

⊙

Stopping where this clearway restriction applies is likely to cause congestion. Allow the traffic to flow by obeying the signs.

11.125 Mark *one* answer

What does this sign mean?

- ⊙ Roundabout
- ⊙ Crossroads
- ⊙ No stopping
- ⊙ No entry

⊙ **No stopping**

This sign is in place to ensure a clear route for traffic. Don't stop except in an emergency.

11.126 Mark *one* answer

You see this sign ahead. It means

- ⊙ national speed limit applies
- ⊙ waiting restrictions apply
- ⊙ no stopping
- ⊙ no entry

⊙ **no stopping**

Clearways are stretches of road where you aren't allowed to stop unless in an emergency. You'll see this sign. Stopping where these restrictions apply may be dangerous and likely to cause an obstruction. Restrictions might apply for several miles and this may be indicated on the sign.

11.127 Mark *one* answer

What does this sign mean?

- ⊙ Distance to parking place ahead
- ⊙ Distance to public telephone ahead
- ⊙ Distance to public house ahead
- ⊙ Distance to passing place ahead

⊙ **Distance to parking place ahead**

If you intend to stop and rest this sign allows you time to reduce speed and pull over safely.

What does this sign mean?

⊙ Vehicles may not park on the verge or footway

⊙ Vehicles may park on the left-hand side of the road only

⊙ Vehicles may park fully on the verge or footway

⊙ Vehicles may park on the right-hand side of the road only

⊙ **Vehicles may park fully on the verge or footway**

In order to keep roads free from parked cars, there are some areas where you're allowed to park on the verge. Only do this where you see the sign. Parking on verges or footways anywhere else could lead to a fine.

What does this sign mean?

⊙ You can park on the days and times shown

⊙ No parking on the days and times shown

⊙ No parking at all from Monday to Friday

⊙ End of the urban clearway restrictions

⊙ **No parking on the days and times shown**

Urban clearways are provided to keep traffic flowing at busy times. You may stop only briefly to set down or pick up passengers. Times of operation will vary from place to place so always check the signs.

11.130 — *Mark **one** answer*

What does this sign mean?

⊙ Multi-exit roundabout
⊙ Risk of ice
⊙ Six roads converge
⊙ Place of historical interest

⊙ **Risk of ice**

It will take up to ten times longer to stop when it's icy. Where there is a risk of icy conditions you need to be aware of this and take extra care.

If you think the road may be icy don't brake or steer harshly as your tyres could lose their grip on the road.

11.131 — *Mark **one** answer*

What does this sign mean?

⊙ Crosswinds
⊙ Road noise
⊙ Airport
⊙ Adverse camber

⊙ **Crosswinds**

A warning sign with a picture of a windsock will indicate there may be strong crosswinds. This sign is often found on exposed roads.

11.132 — *Mark **one** answer*

There is a police car following you. The police officer flashes the headlights and points to the left. What should you do?

⊙ Turn left at the next junction
⊙ Pull up on the left
⊙ Stop immediately
⊙ Move over to the left

⊙ **Pull up on the left**

You must pull up on the left as soon as it's safe to do so and switch off your engine.

You must not use your horn when you are stationary

- ⊙ unless a moving vehicle may cause you danger
- ⊙ at any time whatsoever
- ⊙ unless it is used only briefly
- ⊙ except for signalling that you have just arrived

⊙ **unless a moving vehicle may cause you danger**

Only sound you horn when stationary if you think there is a risk of an accident.

Don't use it to attract someone's attention, as this causes unnecessary noise and could be misleading to other road users.

When may you use hazard warning lights when driving?

- ⊙ Instead of sounding the horn in a built-up area between 11.30 pm and 7 am
- ⊙ On a motorway or unrestricted dual carriageway, to warn of a hazard ahead
- ⊙ On rural routes, after a warning sign of animals
- ⊙ On the approach to toucan crossings where cyclists are waiting to cross

⊙ **On a motorway or unrestricted dual carriageway, to warn of a hazard ahead**

When there's queuing traffic ahead and you have to slow down and even stop, showing your hazard warning lights will alert following traffic to the hazard.

Don't forget to switch them off as the queue forms behind you.

Other drivers may sometimes flash their headlights at you. In which situation are they allowed to do this?

- ⊙ To warn of a radar speed trap ahead
- ⊙ To show that they are giving way to you
- ⊙ To warn you of their presence
- ⊙ To let you know there is a fault with your vehicle

⊙ **To warn you of their presence**

If other drivers flash their headlights this isn't a signal to show priority. The flashing of headlights has the same meaning as sounding the horn – it's a warning of their presence.

11.136
*Mark **one** answer*

You MUST obey signs giving orders. These signs are mostly in

 green rectangles
 red triangles
blue rectangles
 red circles

⊙ **red circles**

Traffic signs can be divided into three classes – those giving orders, those warning and those informing.

Warning signs are usually triangular and direction signs are generally rectangular. One noteable exeption to these classes is the eight-sided 'stop' sign.

11.137
*Mark **one** answer*

Traffic signs giving orders are generally which shape?

⊙

Road signs in the shape of a circle give orders. Those with a red circle are mostly prohibitive. The 'stop' sign is octagonal to give it greater prominence. Signs giving orders must always be obeyed.

11.138
*Mark **one** answer*

Which type of sign tells you NOT to do something?

⊙

Signs in the shape of a circle give orders. A sign with a red circle means that you aren't allowed to do something. Study *Know Your Traffic Signs* to ensure that you understand what the different traffic signs mean.

Which sign means no motor vehicles are allowed?

You would generally see this sign at the approach to a pedestrian-only zone.

Which of these signs means no motor vehicles?

If you are driving a motor vehicle or riding a motorcycle you must not travel past this sign. This area has been designated for use by pedestrians.

What does this sign mean?

⊙ No overtaking
⊙ No motor vehicles
⊙ Clearway (no stopping)
⊙ Cars and motorcycles only

⊙ **No motor vehicles**

A sign will indicate which types of vehicles are prohibited from certain roads. Make sure that you know which signs apply to the vehicle you're using.

11.142 — Mark *one* answer

What does this sign mean?

- ⊙ No parking
- ⊙ No road markings
- ⊙ No through road
- ⊙ No entry

⊙ **No entry**

'No entry' signs are used in places such as one-way streets to prevent vehicles driving against the traffic. To ignore one would be dangerous, both for yourself and other road users, as well as being against the law.

11.143 — Mark *one* answer

What does this sign mean?

- ⊙ Bend to the right
- ⊙ Road on the right closed
- ⊙ No traffic from the right
- ⊙ No right turn

⊙ **No right turn**

The 'no right turn' sign may be used to warn road users that there is a 'no entry' prohibition on a road to the right ahead.

11.144 — Mark *one* answer

Which sign means 'no entry'?

⊙

Look out for traffic signs. Disobeying or not seeing a sign could be dangerous. It may also be an offence for which you could be prosecuted.

Which sign means NO motor vehicles allowed?

This sign is used to enable pedestrians to walk free from traffic. It's often found in shopping areas.

What does this sign mean?

- ⊙ You have priority
- ⊙ No motor vehicles
- ⊙ Two-way traffic
- ⊙ No overtaking

⊙ **No overtaking**

Road signs that prohibit overtaking are placed in locations where passing the vehicle in front is dangerous. If you see this sign don't attempt to overtake. The sign is there for a reason and you must obey it.

What does this sign mean?

- ⊙ Keep in one lane
- ⊙ Give way to oncoming traffic
- ⊙ Do not overtake
- ⊙ Form two lanes

⊙ **Do not overtake**

If you're behind a slow-moving vehicle be patient. Wait until the restriction no longer applies and you can overtake safely.

11.148 — *Mark **one** answer*

Which sign means no overtaking?

This sign indicates that overtaking here is not allowed and you could face prosecution if you ignore this prohibition.

11.149 — *Mark **one** answer*

What does this sign mean?

- Service area 30 miles ahead
- Maximum speed 30 mph
- Minimum speed 30 mph
- Lay-by 30 miles ahead

Minimum speed 30 mph

This sign is shown where slow-moving vehicles would impede the flow of traffic. However, if you need to slow down to avoid a potential accident do so.

11.150 — *Mark **one** answer*

Which of these signs means turn left ahead?

Blue circles tell you what you must do and this sign gives a clear instruction. Turn left ahead.

You should be looking out for signs at all times and know what they mean.

What does this sign mean?

⊙ Give way to oncoming vehicles

⊙ Approaching traffic passes you on both sides

⊙ Turn off at the next available junction

⊙ Pass either side to get to the same destination

⊙ **Pass either side to get to the same destination**

These signs are often seen in one-way streets that have more than one lane. When you see this sign, use the route that's the most convenient and doesn't require a late change of direction.

What does a circular traffic sign with a blue background do?

⊙ Give warning of a motorway ahead

⊙ Give directions to a car park

⊙ Give motorway information

⊙ Give an instruction

⊙ **Give an instruction**

Signs with blue circles give a positive instruction. These are often found in urban areas and include signs for mini-roundabouts and directional arrows.

How will a police officer in a patrol vehicle normally get you to stop?

⊙ Flash the headlights, indicate left and point to the left

⊙ Wait until you stop, then approach you

⊙ Use the siren, overtake, cut in front and stop

⊙ Pull alongside you, use the siren and wave you to stop

⊙ **Flash the headlights, indicate left and point to the left**

You must obey signals given by the police. If a police officer in a patrol vehicle wants you to pull over they will indicate this without causing danger to you or other traffic.

11.154 *Mark **one** answer*

What does this sign mean?

- ⊙ Motorcycles only
- ⊙ No cars
- ⊙ Cars only
- ⊙ No motorcycles

⊙ **No motorcycles**

You must comply with all traffic signs and be especially aware of those signs which apply specifically to the type of vehicle you are using.

11.155 *Mark **three** answers*

At roadworks which of the following can control traffic flow?

- ⊙ A STOP–GO board
- ⊙ Flashing amber lights
- ⊙ A police officer
- ⊙ Flashing red lights
- ⊙ Temporary traffic lights

⊙ **A STOP–GO board**

⊙ **A police officer**

⊙ **Temporary traffic lights**

As you approach the warning signs you should be considering what actions you need to take. You might have to slow right down or stop. Obey any instructions you are given and don't try to beat any lights by speeding up.

11.156 *Mark **one** answer*

What MUST you do when you see this sign?

- ⊙ Stop, only if traffic is approaching
- ⊙ Stop, even if the road is clear
- ⊙ Stop, only if children are waiting to cross
- ⊙ Stop, only if a red light is showing

⊙ **Stop, even if the road is clear**

'Stop' signs are situated at junctions where visibility is restricted or there is heavy traffic. They must be obeyed: you must stop.

Take good all-round observation before moving off.

section twelve
DOCUMENTS

This section covers:

- licences
- insurance
- MOT certificate

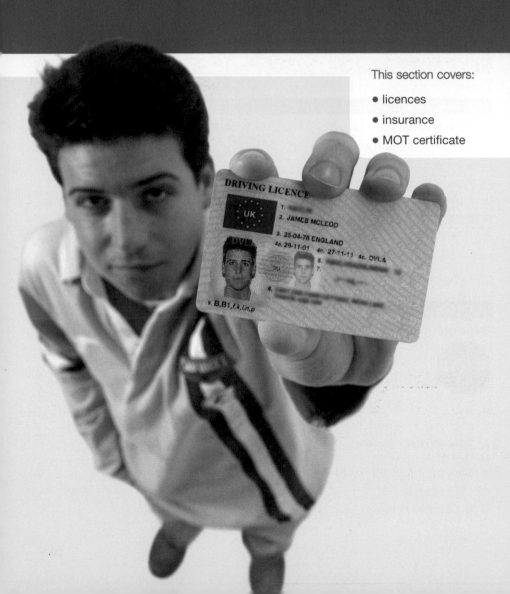

12.1
Mark one answer

An MOT certificate is normally valid for

⊙ three years after the date it was issued

⊙ 10,000 miles

⊙ one year after the date it was issued

⊙ 30,000 miles

⊙ **one year after the date it was issued**

Make a note of the date that your MOT certificate expires. Some garages remind you that your vehicle is due an MOT but not all do.

12.2
Mark one answer

A cover note is a document issued before you receive your

⊙ driving licence

⊙ insurance certificate

⊙ registration document

⊙ MOT certificate

⊙ **insurance certificate**

Sometimes an insurance company will issue a temporary insurance certificate called a cover note. It gives you the same insurance cover as your certificate but lasts for a limited period, usually one month.

12.3
Mark one answer

How old must you be to supervise a learner driver?

⊙ 18 years old

⊙ 19 years old

⊙ 20 years old

⊙ 21 years old

⊙ **21 years old**

As well as being at least 21 years old you must hold a full EC/EEA driving licence for the category of vehicle being driven and have held that licence for at least three years.

12.4
Mark two answers

Your vehicle is insured third party only. This covers

⊙ damage to your vehicle

⊙ damage to other vehicles

⊙ injury to yourself

⊙ injury to others

⊙ all damage and injury

⊙ **damage to other vehicles**

⊙ **injury to others**

This type of insurance cover is usually cheaper than comprehensive. However, it does not cover any damage to your own vehicle or property. It only covers damage and injury to others.

Before driving anyone else's motor vehicle you should make sure that

- the vehicle owner has third party insurance cover
- your own vehicle has insurance cover
- the vehicle is insured for your use
- the owner has left the insurance documents in the vehicle

- **the vehicle is insured for your use**

Driving a vehicle without insurance cover is illegal. If you cause injury to anyone or damage to property it could be very expensive and you could also be subject to a criminal prosecution.

You can arrange insurance cover with

- an insurance company
- a broker
- some motor manufacturers or dealers.

Your car needs an MOT certificate. If you drive without one this could invalidate your

- vehicle service record
- insurance
- road tax disc
- vehicle registration document

- **insurance**

If your vehicle requires an MOT certificate, it is illegal to drive it without one that is valid. As well as it being illegal, the vehicle may also be unsafe for use on the road and could endanger you, any passengers and other road users.

Without a valid MOT certificate your insurance is invalid.

To drive on the road learners MUST

- have NO penalty points on their licence
- have taken professional instruction
- have a signed, valid provisional licence
- apply for a driving test within 12 months

- **have a signed, valid provisional licence**

Before you drive on the road you must have a provisional licence, displaying your signature, in the category of vehicle that you're driving. It isn't valid without a signature.

12.8   *Mark **two** answers*

For which TWO of these must you show your motor insurance certificate?

⊙ When you are taking your driving test

⊙ When buying or selling a vehicle

⊙ When a police officer asks you for it

⊙ When you are taxing your vehicle

⊙ When having an MOT inspection

⊙ **When a police officer asks you for it**

⊙ **When you are taxing your vehicle**

When you take out motor insurance you'll be issued with a certificate. This contains details explaining who and what is insured. You'll have to produce your insurance certificate when you're paying your vehicle excise duty (road tax).

If a police officer asks for your insurance certificate and you don't have it with you, you may produce it at a police station within a specified period.

12.9   *Mark **one** answer*

What is the legal minimum insurance cover you must have to drive on public roads?

⊙ Third party, fire and theft

⊙ Comprehensive

⊙ Third party only

⊙ Personal injury cover

⊙ **Third party only**

The minimum insurance required by law is third party cover. This covers others involved in an accident but not damage to your vehicle. Basic third party insurance won't cover theft or fire damage.

Check with your insurance company for advice on the best cover for you and make sure that you read the policy carefully.

12.10   *Mark **three** answers*

You have third party insurance. What does this cover?

⊙ Damage to your own vehicle

⊙ Damage to your vehicle by fire

⊙ Injury to another person

⊙ Damage to someone's property

⊙ Damage to other vehicles

⊙ Injury to yourself

⊙ **Injury to another person**

⊙ **Damage to someone's property**

⊙ **Damage to other vehicles**

Third party insurance doesn't cover damage to your own vehicle or injury to yourself. If you have an accident and your vehicle is damaged you might have to carry out the repairs at your own expense.

12.11

Mark **three** answers

You have a duty to contact the licensing authority when

- ⊙ you go abroad on holiday
- ⊙ you change your vehicle
- ⊙ you change your name
- ⊙ your job status is changed
- ⊙ your permanent address changes
- ⊙ your job involves travelling abroad

⊙ **you change your vehicle**

⊙ **you change your name**

⊙ **your permanent address changes**

The licensing authority need to keep their records up to date. They send out a reminder when your road tax is due and need your current address to send this to.

Every vehicle in the country is registered, so it's possible to trace its history.

12.12

Mark **one** answer

Vehicle excise duty is often called 'Road Tax' or 'The Tax Disc'. You must

- ⊙ keep it with your registration document
- ⊙ display it clearly on your vehicle
- ⊙ keep it concealed safely in your vehicle
- ⊙ carry it on you at all times

⊙ **display it clearly on your vehicle**

The tax disc should be displayed at the bottom of the windscreen on the nearside (left-hand side). This allows it to be easily seen from the kerbside. It must be current, and you can't transfer the disc from vehicle to vehicle.

12.13

Mark **three** answers

You must notify the licensing authority when

- ⊙ your health affects your driving
- ⊙ your eyesight does not meet a set standard
- ⊙ you intend lending your vehicle
- ⊙ your vehicle requires an MOT certificate
- ⊙ you change your vehicle

⊙ **your health affects your driving**

⊙ **your eyesight does not meet a set standard**

⊙ **you change your vehicle**

The Driver and Vehicle Licensing Agency (DVLA) hold the records of all vehicles and drivers in Great Britain (DVLNI in Northern Ireland). They need to know of any change in circumstances so that they can keep their records up to date.

Your health might affect your ability to drive safely. Don't risk endangering your own safety or that of other road users.

12.14 *Mark **three** answers*

Which THREE pieces of information are found on a vehicle registration document?

- ⊙ Registered keeper
- ⊙ Make of the vehicle
- ⊙ Service history details
- ⊙ Date of the MOT
- ⊙ Type of insurance cover
- ⊙ Engine size

⊙ **Registered keeper**

⊙ **Make of the vehicle**

⊙ **Engine size**

Every vehicle used on the road has a registration document. This is issued by the Driver and Vehicle Licensing Agency (DVLA) or Driver and Vehicle Licensing Northern Ireland (DVLNI). The document states the vehicle's

- • date of first registration
- • registration number
- • previous keeper
- • registered keeper
- • make of vehicle
- • engine size and chassis number
- • year of manufacture
- • colour.

12.15 *NI EXEMPT* *Mark **one** answer*

The cost of your insurance may reduce if you

- ⊙ are under 25 years old
- ⊙ do not wear glasses
- ⊙ pass the driving test first time
- ⊙ take the Pass Plus scheme

⊙ **take the Pass Plus scheme**

The cost of insurance varies with your age and how long you have been driving. Usually, the younger you are the more expensive it is, especially if you are under 25 years of age.

The Pass Plus scheme provides additional training to newly qualified drivers. Pass Plus is recognised by many insurance companies and taking this extra training could give you reduced insurance premiums, as well as improving your skills and experience.

Your motor insurance policy has an excess of £100. What does this mean?

⊙ The insurance company will pay the first £100 of any claim

⊙ You will be paid £100 if you do not have an accident

⊙ Your vehicle is insured for a value of £100 if it is stolen

⊙ You will have to pay the first £100 of any claim

⊙ **You will have to pay the first £100 of any claim**

This is a method used by insurance companies to keep annual premiums down. Generally, the higher the excess you choose to pay, the lower the annual premium you will be charged.

Which THREE of the following do you need before you can drive legally?

⊙ A valid driving licence with signature

⊙ A valid tax disc displayed on your vehicle

⊙ A vehicle service record

⊙ Proper insurance cover

⊙ Breakdown cover

⊙ A vehicle handbook

⊙ **A valid driving licence with signature**

⊙ **A valid tax disc displayed on your vehicle**

⊙ **Proper insurance cover**

Make sure that you have a valid driving licence and proper insurance cover before driving any vehicle. These are legal requirements, as is displaying a valid tax disc in the vehicle.

A newly qualified driver must

⊙ display green 'L' plates

⊙ not exceed 40 mph for 12 months

⊙ be accompanied on a motorway

⊙ have valid motor insurance

⊙ **have valid motor insurance**

It is your responsibility to make sure you are properly insured for the vehicle you are driving.

12.19 Mark **one** answer

Your vehicle needs a current MOT certificate. You do not have one. Until you do have one you will not be able to renew your

- ⊙ driving licence
- ⊙ vehicle insurance
- ⊙ road tax disc
- ⊙ vehicle registration document

⊙ **road tax disc**

When you renew your road tax disc you need to produce a current, valid MOT certificate for your vehicle.

12.20 *NI EXEMPT* Mark **one** answer

A police officer asks to see your documents. You do not have them with you. You may produce them at a police station within

- ⊙ 5 days
- ⊙ 7 days
- ⊙ 14 days
- ⊙ 21 days

⊙ **7 days**

You don't have to carry the documents for your vehicle around with you. If a police officer asks to see them and you don't have them with you, you may produce them at a police station within seven days.

12.21 Mark **two** answers

You have just passed your practical test. You do not hold a full licence in another category. Within two years you get six penalty points on your licence. What will you have to do?

- ⊙ Retake only your theory test
- ⊙ Retake your theory and practical tests
- ⊙ Retake only your practical test
- ⊙ Reapply for your full licence immediately
- ⊙ Reapply for your provisional licence

⊙ **Retake your theory and practical tests**

⊙ **Reapply for your provisional licence**

If you accumulate six or more penalty points within two years of gaining your first full licence it will be revoked. The six or more points include any gained due to offences you committed before passing your test.

If this happens you may only drive as a learner until you pass both the theory and practical tests again.

Motor cars must first have an MOT test certificate when they are

⊙ one year old
⊙ three years old
⊙ five years old
⊙ seven years old

⊙ **three years old**

The vehicle you drive must be roadworthy and in good condition. If it's over three years old it must have a valid MOT test certificate.

The MOT test ensures that a vehicle meets minimum legal standards in terms of safety, components and environmental impact at the time it is tested.

When is it legal to drive a car over three years old without an MOT certificate?

⊙ Up to seven days after the old certificate has run out
⊙ When driving to an MOT centre to arrange an appointment
⊙ Just after buying a second-hand car with no MOT
⊙ When driving to an appointment at an MOT centre

⊙ **When driving to an appointment at an MOT centre**

Any car over three years old must have a valid MOT certificate before it can be used on the road. The only time a car is exempt is when it's being driven to an appointment at an MOT testing station.

Which of the following may reduce the cost of your insurance?

⊙ Having a valid MOT certificate
⊙ Taking a Pass Plus course
⊙ Driving a powerful car
⊙ Having penalty points on your licence

⊙ **Taking a Pass Plus course**

The aim of the Pass Plus course is to build up your skills and experience. It is recognised by some insurance companies, who reward people completing the scheme with cheaper insurance premiums.

12.25
*Mark **one** answer*

When you apply to renew your vehicle excise licence (tax disc) you must produce

- a valid insurance certificate
- the old tax disc
- the vehicle handbook
- a valid driving licence

⊙ **a valid insurance certificate**

Tax discs can be renewed at most post offices, your nearest vehicle registration office or by post to the licensing authority. Make sure you take all the relevant documents with your application.

12.26
*Mark **two** answers*

To supervise a learner driver you must

- have held a full licence for at least 3 years
- be at least 21 years old
- be an approved driving instructor
- hold an advanced driving certificate

⊙ **have held a full licence for at least 3 years**

⊙ **be at least 21 years old**

Don't just take someone's word that they are qualified to supervise you. The person who sits alongside you while you are learning should be a responsible adult and an experienced driver.

12.27 *NI EXEMPT*
*Mark **one** answer*

The Pass Plus scheme has been created for new drivers. What is its main purpose?

- To allow you to drive faster
- To allow you to carry passengers
- To improve your basic skills
- To let you drive on motorways

⊙ **To improve your basic skills**

New drivers are more vulnerable on the road and more likely to be involved in accidents. The Pass Plus scheme has been designed to improve your skills and help widen your driving experience.

12.28
*Mark **one** answer*

How long will a Statutory Off Road Notification (SORN) last for?

- 12 months
- 24 months
- 3 years
- 10 years

⊙ **12 months**

A SORN declaration allows you to keep a vehicle off road and untaxed for 12 months. If you want to keep your vehicle off road beyond that you must send a further SORN form to DVLA or DVLNI.

What is a Statutory Off Road Notification (SORN) declaration?

⊙ A notification to tell VOSA that a vehicle does not have a current MOT

⊙ Information kept by the police about the owner of the vehicle

⊙ A notification to tell DVLA that a vehicle is not being used on the road

⊙ Information held by insurance companies to check the vehicle is insured

⊙ **A notification to tell DVLA that a vehicle is not being used on the road**

If you want to keep a vehicle off the public road you must declare SORN. It is an offence not to do so. You then won't have to pay road tax. If you don't renew the SORN declaration or re-license the vehicle, you will incur a penalty.

A Statutory Off Road Notification (SORN) declaration is

⊙ to tell DVLA that your vehicle is being used on the road but the MOT has expired

⊙ to tell DVLA that you no longer own the vehicle

⊙ to tell DVLA that your vehicle is not being used on the road

⊙ to tell DVLA that you are buying a personal number plate

⊙ **to tell DVLA that your vehicle is not being used on the road**

This will enable you to keep a vehicle off the public road for 12 months without having to pay road tax. You must send a further SORN declaration after 12 months.

A Statutory Off Road Notification (SORN) is valid

⊙ for as long as the vehicle has an MOT

⊙ for 12 months only

⊙ only if the vehicle is more than 3 years old

⊙ provided the vehicle is insured

⊙ **for 12 months only**

If you want to keep a vehicle off the public road you must declare SORN. It is an offence not to do so. You then won't have to pay road tax for that vehicle. You will incur a penalty after 12 months if you don't renew the SORN declaration, or re-license the vehicle. If you sell the vehicle the SORN declaration ends and the new owner should declare SORN or re-license the vehicle.

12.32 — *Mark **one** answer*

A Statutory Off Road Notification (SORN) will last

- ⊙ for the life of the vehicle
- ⊙ for as long as you own the vehicle
- ⊙ for 12 months only
- ⊙ until the vehicle warranty expires

⊙ **for 12 months only**

If you are keeping a vehicle, or vehicles, off road and don't want to pay road tax you must declare SORN. You must still do this even if the vehicle is incapable of being used, for example it may be under restoration or being stored. After 12 months you must send another SORN declaration or re-license your vehicle. You will be fined if you don't do this. The SORN will end if you sell the vehicle and the new owner will be responsible immediately.

12.33 — *NI EXEMPT* — *Mark **one** answer*

What is the maximum specified fine for driving without insurance?

- ⊙ £50
- ⊙ £500
- ⊙ £1000
- ⊙ £5000

⊙ **£5000**

It is a serious offence to drive without insurance. As well as a heavy fine you may be disqualified or incur penalty points.

12.34 — *Mark **one** answer*

You claim on your insurance to have your car repaired. Your policy has an excess of £100. What does this mean?

- ⊙ The insurance company will pay the first £100 of any claim
- ⊙ You will be paid £100 if you do not claim within one year
- ⊙ Your vehicle is insured for a value of £100 if it is stolen
- ⊙ You will have to pay the first £100 of the cost of repair to your car

⊙ **You will have to pay the first £100 of the cost of repair to your car**

Having an excess on your policy will help to keep down the premium, but if you make a claim you will have to pay the excess yourself, in this case £100.

section thirteen
ACCIDENTS

This section covers:

- first aid
- warning devices
- reporting procedures
- safety regulations

13.1 *Mark **one** answer*

At the scene of an accident you should

- not put yourself at risk
- go to those casualties who are screaming
- pull everybody out of their vehicles
- leave vehicle engines switched on

⊙ **not put yourself at risk**

It's important that people at the scene of an accident do not create a further risk to themselves or other road users. If the accident has occurred on a motorway or major road, traffic will be approaching at speed. Do not put yourself at risk when trying to help casualties or warning other road users.

13.2 *Mark **four** answers*

You are the first to arrive at the scene of an accident. Which FOUR of these should you do?

- Leave as soon as another motorist arrives
- Switch off the vehicle engine(s)
- Move uninjured people away from the vehicle(s)
- Call the emergency services
- Warn other traffic

⊙ **Switch off the vehicle engine(s)**

⊙ **Move uninjured people away from the vehicle(s)**

⊙ **Call the emergency services**

⊙ **Warn other traffic**

At an accident scene you can help in practical ways, even if you don't know how to do first aid. Make sure you do not put yourself or anyone else in danger.

The safest way to warn other traffic is by switching on your hazard warning lights.

13.3 *Mark **one** answer*

You arrive at an accident. A motorcyclist is unconscious. Your FIRST priority is the casualty's

- breathing
- bleeding
- broken bones
- bruising

⊙ **breathing**

At the scene of an accident you must make sure there is no danger from further collisions or fire before attempting to give first aid to any casualties.

The first priority when dealing with an unconscious person is to make sure they can breathe. This may involve clearing their airway if they're having difficulty or you can see that there is some obstruction.

You are the first person to arrive at an accident where people are badly injured. Which THREE should you do?

- ⊙ Switch on your own hazard warning lights
- ⊙ Make sure that someone telephones for an ambulance
- ⊙ Try and get people who are injured to drink something
- ⊙ Move the people who are injured clear of their vehicles
- ⊙ Get people who are not injured clear of the scene

- ⊙ **Switch on your own hazard warning lights**
- ⊙ **Make sure that someone telephones for an ambulance**
- ⊙ **Get people who are not injured clear of the scene**

If you're the first person to arrive at the scene of an accident, the risk of further collision and fire are the first concerns.

Switching off vehicle engines will reduce the risk of fire. Your hazard warning lights will let approaching traffic know that there's a need for caution.

Make sure that the emergency services are contacted, as you can't assume this has already been done.

You arrive at the scene of an accident. It has just happened and someone is injured. Which THREE of the following should be given urgent priority?

- ⊙ Stop any severe bleeding
- ⊙ Get them a warm drink
- ⊙ Check that their breathing is OK
- ⊙ Take numbers of vehicles involved
- ⊙ Look for witnesses
- ⊙ Clear their airway and keep it open

- ⊙ **Stop any severe bleeding**
- ⊙ **Check that their breathing is OK**
- ⊙ **Clear their airway and keep it open**

Your first priority is to make sure the casualty's airway is clear and they are breathing. Then stem any bleeding using clean material.

Make sure someone calls the emergency services: they are the experts.

If you feel you are not capable of carrying out first aid, you could consider getting some training. It might save a life.

13.6 — Mark **three** answers

You arrive at a serious motorcycle accident. The motorcyclist is unconscious and bleeding. Your main priorities should be to

- try to stop the bleeding
- make a list of witnesses
- check the casualty's breathing
- take the numbers of the vehicles involved
- sweep up any loose debris
- check the casualty's airways

- ⊙ **try to stop the bleeding**
- ⊙ **check the casualty's breathing**
- ⊙ **check the casualty's airways**

At a road accident, first deal with the danger of further collisions and fire.

Injuries should be dealt with in the following order

- Airway
- Breathing
- Circulation and bleeding.

13.7 — Mark **three** answers

You arrive at the scene of an accident. It has just happened and someone is unconscious. Which of the following should be given urgent priority to help them?

- Clear the airway and keep it open
- Try to get them to drink water
- Check that they are breathing
- Look for any witnesses
- Stop any heavy bleeding
- Take the numbers of vehicles involved

- ⊙ **Clear the airway and keep it open**
- ⊙ **Check that they are breathing**
- ⊙ **Stop any heavy bleeding**

Once emergency first aid has been administered, stay with the casualty; make sure someone rings for an ambulance.

13.8 — Mark **one** answer

You arrive at the scene of a motorcycle accident. The rider is injured. When should the helmet be removed?

- Only when it is essential
- Always straight away
- Only when the motorcyclist asks
- Always, unless they are in shock

- ⊙ **Only when it is essential**

If a motorcyclist has been injured in an accident, it's important not to remove their helmet unless it is necessary to do so to keep them alive.

13.9

Mark **three** answers

At an accident someone is unconscious. Your main priorities should be to

⊙ sweep up the broken glass

⊙ take the names of witnesses

⊙ count the number of vehicles involved

⊙ check the airway is clear

⊙ make sure they are breathing

⊙ stop any heavy bleeding

⊙ **check the airway is clear**

⊙ **make sure they are breathing**

⊙ **stop any heavy bleeding**

Remember this procedure by saying ABC which stands for Airway, Breathing, Circulation.

13.10

Mark **three** answers

You have stopped at the scene of an accident to give help. Which THREE things should you do?

⊙ Keep injured people warm and comfortable

⊙ Keep injured people calm by talking to them reassuringly

⊙ Keep injured people on the move by walking them around

⊙ Give injured people a warm drink

⊙ Make sure that injured people are not left alone

⊙ **Keep injured people warm and comfortable**

⊙ **Keep injured people calm by talking to them reassuringly**

⊙ **Make sure that injured people are not left alone**

If you stop at the scene of an accident to give help and there are casualties, don't move injured people unless there is a risk of further danger. Make sure no one gives casualties anything to eat or drink.

13.11

Mark **one** answer

Which of the following should you NOT do at the scene of an accident?

⊙ Warn other traffic by switching on your hazard warning lights

⊙ Call the emergency services immediately

⊙ Offer someone a cigarette to calm them down

⊙ Ask drivers to switch off their engines

⊙ **Offer someone a cigarette to calm them down**

Keeping casualties or witnesses calm is important but never offer a cigarette because of the risk of fire.

Don't offer an injured person anything to eat or drink. They may have internal injuries or need surgery.

13.12 — Mark **three** answers

At an accident a casualty is unconscious. Which THREE of the following should you check urgently?

- Circulation
- Airway
- Shock
- Breathing
- Broken bones

⊙ **Circulation**

⊙ **Airway**

⊙ **Breathing**

An unconscious casualty may have difficulty breathing. Check that their airway is clear by tilting the head back gently and unblock it if necessary. Then make sure they are breathing.

If there is bleeding, stem the flow by placing clean material over any wounds but without pressing on any objects in the wound.

13.13 — Mark **two** answers

There has been an accident. The driver is suffering from shock. You should

- give them a drink
- reassure them
- not leave them alone
- offer them a cigarette
- ask who caused the accident

⊙ **reassure them**

⊙ **not leave them alone**

Be aware that they could have an injury that is not immediately obvious. Stay with casualties and talk to them to reassure them.

13.14 — Mark **one** answer

At an accident it is important to look after the casualty. When the area is safe, you should

- get them out of the vehicle
- give them a drink
- give them something to eat
- keep them in the vehicle

⊙ **keep them in the vehicle**

Don't move casualties who are trapped in vehicles unless they are in danger.

13.15 **13.15**   *Mark **one** answer*

You have to treat someone for shock at the scene of an accident. You should

- ⊙ reassure them constantly
- ⊙ walk them around to calm them down
- ⊙ give them something cold to drink
- ⊙ cool them down as soon as possible

⊙ **reassure them constantly**

Stay with the casualty and talk to them quietly and firmly to calm and reassure them.

Avoid moving them unnecessarily in case they are injured. Keep them warm but don't give them anything to eat or drink.

13.16   *Mark **one** answer*

You arrive at the scene of a motorcycle accident. No other vehicle is involved. The rider is unconscious, lying in the middle of the road. The first thing you should do is

- ⊙ move the rider out of the road
- ⊙ warn other traffic
- ⊙ clear the road of debris
- ⊙ give the rider reassurance

⊙ **warn other traffic**

The motorcyclist is in an extremely vulnerable position, exposed to further danger from traffic. Approaching vehicles need advance warning in order to slow right down and safely take avoiding action.

Don't put yourself or anyone else at risk. Use the hazard warning lights on your vehicle to alert other road users to the danger.

13.17   *Mark **one** answer*

At an accident a small child is not breathing. When giving mouth to mouth you should breathe

- ⊙ sharply
- ⊙ gently
- ⊙ heavily
- ⊙ rapidly

⊙ **gently**

If a young child has stopped breathing, first check that the airway is clear, then begin mouth to mouth resuscitation. Breathe very gently and continue the resuscitation procedure until they can breathe without help.

13.18
*Mark **one** answer*

When you are giving mouth to mouth you should only stop when

⊙ you think the casualty is dead
⊙ the casualty can breathe without help
⊙ the casualty has turned blue
⊙ you think the ambulance is coming

⊙ **the casualty can breathe without help**

Don't give up. Look for signs of recovery and check the casualty's pulse. Continue resuscitation until the casualty is breathing unaided.

Avoid moving them unless it's necessary for their safety.

13.19
*Mark **one** answer*

At an accident a casualty is unconscious but still breathing. You should only move them if

⊙ an ambulance is on its way
⊙ bystanders advise you to
⊙ there is further danger
⊙ bystanders will help you to

⊙ **there is further danger**

At an accident only move a casualty if they are in danger where they are. Moving a casualty unnecessarily could cause further injury.

13.20
*Mark **one** answer*

You arrive at an accident where someone is suffering from severe burns. You should

⊙ apply lotions to the injury
⊙ burst any blisters
⊙ remove anything stuck to the burns
⊙ douse the burns with cool liquid

⊙ **douse the burns with cool liquid**

Try to find fluid that is clean, cold and non-toxic. Its coolness will help take the heat out of the burn and relieve the pain. Keep the wound doused for at least ten minutes.

If blisters appear don't attempt to burst them as this could lead to infection.

13.21
*Mark **one** answer*

At an accident you suspect a casualty has back injuries. The area is safe. You should

⊙ offer them a drink
⊙ not move them
⊙ raise their legs
⊙ offer them a cigarette

⊙ **not move them**

Talk to the casualty and keep them calm. Do not attempt to move them as this could cause further injury.

Call an ambulance at the first opportunity.

You arrive at the scene of an accident. A pedestrian has a severe bleeding wound on their leg, although it is not broken. What should you do?

- Dab the wound to stop bleeding
- Keep both legs flat on the ground
- Apply firm pressure to the wound
- Raise the leg to lessen bleeding
- Fetch them a warm drink

⊙ **Apply firm pressure to the wound**

⊙ **Raise the leg to lessen bleeding**

As soon as you can, apply a pad of clean material to the wound with a bandage or a clean length of cloth. Raising the leg will lessen the flow of blood.

Avoid tying anything tightly round the leg, as any restriction to blood circulation for more than a short period of time can result in long-term injury.

You arrive at the scene of an accident. A passenger is bleeding badly from an arm wound. What should you do?

- Apply pressure over the wound and keep the arm down
- Dab the wound
- Get them a drink
- Apply pressure over the wound and raise the arm

⊙ **Apply pressure over the wound and raise the arm**

If possible, lay the casualty down. Apply firm pressure to the wound using clean material. Raising the arm above the level of the heart will also help to stem the flow of blood.

You arrive at the scene of an accident. A pedestrian is bleeding heavily from a leg wound but the leg is not broken. What should you do?

- Dab the wound to stop the bleeding
- Keep both legs flat on the ground
- Apply firm pressure to the wound
- Fetch them a warm drink

⊙ **Apply firm pressure to the wound**

Lifting and supporting the casualty's leg, so that the wound is higher than their heart, should also help reduce the flow of blood.

13.25 — Mark *one* answer

A tanker is involved in an accident. Which sign would show that the tanker is carrying dangerous goods?

⊙ LONG VEHICLE

⊙ 2YE 1089

⊙

⊙

⊙ 2YE 1089

There will be an orange label on the side and rear of the lorry. Look at this carefully and report what it says when you phone the emergency services.

Full details of hazard warning plates are given in *The Highway Code*.

13.26 — Mark **three** answers

Which of these items should you carry in your vehicle for use in the event of an accident?

⊙ Road map
⊙ Can of petrol
⊙ Jump leads
⊙ Fire extinguisher
⊙ First Aid kit
⊙ Warning triangle

⊙ **Fire extinguisher**

⊙ **First Aid kit**

⊙ **Warning triangle**

Used correctly, this equipment can provide invaluable help in the event of an accident or breakdown. It could even save a life.

13.27 — Mark *one* answer

You arrive at the scene of an accident. There has been an engine fire and someone's hands and arms have been burnt. You should NOT

⊙ douse the burn thoroughly with cool liquid
⊙ lay the casualty down
⊙ remove anything sticking to the burn
⊙ reassure them constantly

⊙ **remove anything sticking to the burn**

This could cause further damage and infection to the wound. Your first priorities are to cool the burn and check the patient for shock.

13.28

You are involved in an accident with another vehicle. Someone is injured. Your vehicle is damaged. Which FOUR of the following should you find out?

- ⊙ Whether the driver owns the other vehicle involved
- ⊙ The other driver's name, address and telephone number
- ⊙ The make and registration number of the other vehicle
- ⊙ The occupation of the other driver
- ⊙ The details of the other driver's vehicle insurance
- ⊙ Whether the other driver is licensed to drive

- ⊙ **Whether the driver owns the other vehicle involved**

- ⊙ **The other driver's name, address and telephone number**

- ⊙ **The make and registration number of the other vehicle**

- ⊙ **The details of the other driver's vehicle insurance**

Try to keep calm and don't rush. Ensure that you have all the details before you leave the accident scene.

13.29

There has been an accident. A motorcyclist is lying injured and unconscious. Why should you usually not attempt to remove their helmet?

- ⊙ Because they may not want you to
- ⊙ This could result in more serious injury
- ⊙ They will get too cold if you do this
- ⊙ Because you could scratch the helmet

- ⊙ **This could result in more serious injury**

When someone is injured, any movement which is not absolutely necessary should be avoided since it could make injuries worse. Unless it is essential, it's generally safer to leave a motorcyclists helmet in place.

13.30

After an accident, someone is unconscious in their vehicle. When should you call the emergency services?

- ⊙ Only as a last resort
- ⊙ As soon as possible
- ⊙ After you have woken them up
- ⊙ After checking for broken bones

- ⊙ **As soon as possible**

It is important to make sure that emergency services arrive on the scene as soon as possible. When a person is unconscious, they could have serious injuries that are not immediately obvious.

13.31
Mark one answer

An accident casualty has an injured arm. They can move it freely, but it is bleeding. Why should you get them to keep it in a raised position?

- ⊙ Because it will ease the pain
- ⊙ It will help them to be seen more easily
- ⊙ To stop them touching other people
- ⊙ It will help to reduce the bleeding

⊙ **It will help to reduce the bleeding**

If a casualty is bleeding heavily, raise the limb to a higher position. This will help to reduce the blood flow.

Before raising the limb you should make sure that it is not broken.

13.32
Mark one answer

An accident has just happened. An injured person is lying in a busy road. What is the FIRST thing you should do to help?

- ⊙ Treat the person for shock
- ⊙ Warn other traffic
- ⊙ Place them in the recovery position
- ⊙ Make sure the injured person is kept warm

⊙ **Warn other traffic**

You could do this by

- displaying an advance warning sign, if you have one (but not on a motorway)
- switching on hazard warning lights
- any other means that does not put you or anyone else at risk.

13.33
Mark two answers

At an accident a casualty has stopped breathing. You should

- ⊙ remove anything that is blocking the mouth
- ⊙ keep the head tilted forwards as far as possible
- ⊙ raise the legs to help with circulation
- ⊙ try to give the casualty something to drink
- ⊙ tilt the head back gently to clear the airway

⊙ **remove anything that is blocking the mouth**

⊙ **tilt the head back gently to clear the airway**

Unblocking the airway and gently tilting the head back will help the casualty to breathe. They will then be in the correct position if mouth-to-mouth resuscitation is required.

13.34

*Mark **four** answers*

You are at the scene of an accident. Someone is suffering from shock. You should

- ⊙ reassure them constantly
- ⊙ offer them a cigarette
- ⊙ keep them warm
- ⊙ avoid moving them if possible
- ⊙ avoid leaving them alone
- ⊙ give them a warm drink

- ⊙ **reassure them constantly**
- ⊙ **keep them warm**
- ⊙ **avoid moving them if possible**
- ⊙ **avoid leaving them alone**

The effects of trauma may not be immediately obvious. Prompt treatment can help to minimise the effects of shock.

- Lay the casualty down
- Loosen tight clothing
- Call an ambulance
- Check their breathing and pulse.

13.35

*Mark **three** answers*

To start mouth to mouth on a casualty you should

- ⊙ tilt their head forward
- ⊙ clear the airway
- ⊙ turn them on their side
- ⊙ tilt their head back gently
- ⊙ pinch the nostrils together
- ⊙ put their arms across their chest

- ⊙ **clear the airway**
- ⊙ **tilt their head back gently**
- ⊙ **pinch the nostrils together**

It's important to ensure that the airways are clear before you start mouth to mouth resuscitation. Gently tilt their head back and use your finger to check for and remove any obvious obstruction in the mouth.

13.36

*Mark **one** answer*

You are in an accident on a two-way road. You have a warning triangle with you. At what distance before the obstruction should you place the warning triangle?

- ⊙ 25 metres (82 feet)
- ⊙ 45 metres (147 feet)
- ⊙ 100 metres (328 feet)
- ⊙ 150 metres (492 feet)

- ⊙ **45 metres (147 feet)**

If there's a bend or hump in the road place the triangle so that approaching traffic slows down before the bend. You must give traffic enough time to react to the warning.

Use your hazard warning lights as well as a warning triangle, especially in the dark.

13.37
Mark one answer

You have an accident while driving through a tunnel. You are not injured but your vehicle cannot be driven. What should you do first?

⊙ Rely on other drivers phoning for the police

⊙ Switch off the engine and switch on hazard lights

⊙ Take the names of witnesses and other drivers

⊙ Sweep up any debris that is in the road

⊙ **Switch off the engine and switch on hazard lights**

If you are involved in an accident in a tunnel be aware of the danger this can cause to other traffic. Put on your hazard warning lights straight away and switch off your engine. Then call for help from an emergency telephone point.

13.38
Mark one answer

Before driving through a tunnel what should you do?

⊙ Switch your radio off

⊙ Remove any sunglasses

⊙ Close your sunroof

⊙ Switch on windscreen wipers

⊙ **Remove any sunglasses**

If you are wearing sunglasses you should remove them before driving into a tunnel. If you don't, your vision will be restricted, even in tunnels that appear to be well-lit.

13.39
Mark one answer

You are driving through a tunnel and the traffic is flowing normally. What should you do?

⊙ Use parking lights

⊙ Use front spot lights

⊙ Use dipped headlights

⊙ Use rear fog lights

⊙ **Use dipped headlights**

Before entering a tunnel you should switch on your dipped headlights, as this will allow you to see and be seen. In many tunnels it is a legal requirement.

Don't wear sunglasses while driving in a tunnel. You may wish to tune your radio into a local channel.

Before entering a tunnel it is good advice to

- ⊙ put on your sunglasses
- ⊙ check tyre pressures
- ⊙ change to a lower gear
- ⊙ tune your radio to a local channel

⊙ **tune your radio to a local channel**

On the approach to many tunnels a sign will indicate a local radio frequency that you can tune into. This should give a warning of any accidents or congestion in the tunnel ahead.

Accidents in tunnels can lead to many casualties. Getting an advance warning of problems could save your life and others.

You are going through a congested tunnel and have to stop. What should you do?

- ⊙ Pull up very close to the vehicle in front to save space
- ⊙ Ignore any message signs as they are never up to date
- ⊙ Keep a safe distance from the vehicle in front
- ⊙ Make a U-turn and find another route

⊙ **Keep a safe distance from the vehicle in front**

It's important to keep a safe distance from the vehicle in front at all times. This still applies in congested tunnels even if you are moving very slowly or have stopped. If the vehicle in front breaks down you may need room to manoeuvre past it.

You are driving through a tunnel. Your vehicle breaks down. What should you do?

- ⊙ Switch on hazard warning lights
- ⊙ Remain in your vehicle
- ⊙ Wait for the police to find you
- ⊙ Rely on CCTV cameras seeing you

⊙ **Switch on hazard warning lights**

If your vehicle breaks down in a tunnel it could present a danger to other traffic. First switch on your hazard warning lights and then call for help from an emergency telephone point.

Don't rely on being found by the police or being seen by a CCTV camera. The longer the vehicle stays in an exposed position, the more danger it poses to other drivers.

13.43

*Mark **one** answer*

You are going through a tunnel. What should you look out for that warns of accidents or congestion?

⊙ Hazard warning lines
⊙ Other drivers flashing their lights
⊙ Variable message signs
⊙ Areas marked with hatch markings

⊙ **Variable message signs**

Follow the instructions given by the signs or by tunnel officials.

In congested tunnels a minor accident can soon turn into a major incident with serious or even fatal results.

13.44

*Mark **one** answer*

You are going through a tunnel. What systems are provided to warn of any accidents or congestion?

⊙ Double white centre lines
⊙ Variable message signs
⊙ Chevron 'distance markers'
⊙ Rumble strips

⊙ **Variable message signs**

Take notice of any instructions given on variable message signs or by tunnel officials. They will warn you of any accidents or congestion ahead and advise on what action to take.

13.45

*Mark **one** answer*

Your vehicle has broken down on an automatic railway level crossing. What should you do FIRST?

⊙ Get everyone out of the vehicle and clear of the crossing
⊙ Phone the signal operator so that trains can be stopped
⊙ Walk along the track to give warning to any approaching trains
⊙ Try to push the vehicle clear of the crossing as soon as possible

⊙ **Get everyone out of the vehicle and clear of the crossing**

Ensure that everyone is well clear of the crossing. In the event of an accident, debris could be scattered over some distance in various directions.

13.46

Mark *one* answer

Your vehicle breaks down in a tunnel. What should you do?

- ⊙ Stay in your vehicle and wait for the police
- ⊙ Stand in the lane behind your vehicle to warn others
- ⊙ Stand in front of your vehicle to warn oncoming drivers
- ⊙ Switch on hazard lights then go and call for help immediately

⊙ **Switch on hazard lights then go and call for help immediately**

A broken-down vehicle in a tunnel can cause serious congestion and danger to other road users. If your vehicle breaks down, get help without delay. Switch on your hazard warning lights, then go to an emergency telephone point to call for help.

13.47

Mark *one* answer

Your vehicle has a puncture on a motorway. What should you do?

- ⊙ Drive slowly to the next service area to get assistance
- ⊙ Pull up on the hard shoulder. Change the wheel as quickly as possible
- ⊙ Pull up on the hard shoulder. Use the emergency phone to get assistance
- ⊙ Switch on your hazard lights. Stop in your lane

⊙ **Pull up on the hard shoulder. Use the emergency phone to get assistance**

Pull up on the hard shoulder and make your way to the nearest emergency telephone to call for assistance.

Do not attempt to repair your vehicle while it is on the hard shoulder because of the risk posed by traffic passing at high speeds.

13.48

Mark *one* answer

When driving through a tunnel you should

- ⊙ Look out for variable message signs
- ⊙ Use your air conditioning system
- ⊙ Switch on your rear fog lights
- ⊙ Always use your windscreen wipers

⊙ **Look out for variable message signs**

A minor incident in a tunnel can quickly turn into a major disaster. Variable message signs are provided to warn of any incidents or congestion. Follow their advice.

13.49 *Mark **one** answer*

You have stalled in the middle of a level crossing and cannot restart the engine. The warning bell starts to ring. You should

- ⊙ get out and clear of the crossing
- ⊙ run down the track to warn the signal operator
- ⊙ carry on trying to restart the engine
- ⊙ push the vehicle clear of the crossing

⊙ **get out and clear of the crossing**

Try to stay calm, especially if you have passengers on board. If you can't restart your engine before the warning bells ring, leave the vehicle and get yourself and any passengers well clear of the crossing.

13.50 *Mark **one** answer*

While driving, a warning light on your vehicle's instrument panel comes on. You should

- ⊙ continue if the engine sounds all right
- ⊙ hope that it is just a temporary electrical fault
- ⊙ deal with the problem when there is more time
- ⊙ check out the problem quickly and safely

⊙ **check out the problem quickly and safely**

Make sure you know what the different warning lights mean. An illuminated warning light could mean that your car is unsafe to drive. Don't take risks. If you aren't sure about the problem, get a qualified mechanic to check it.

13.51 *Mark **two** answers*

What TWO safeguards could you take against fire risk to your vehicle?

- ⊙ Keep water levels above maximum
- ⊙ Carry a fire extinguisher
- ⊙ Avoid driving with a full tank of petrol
- ⊙ Use unleaded petrol
- ⊙ Check out any strong smell of petrol
- ⊙ Use low octane fuel

⊙ **Carry a fire extinguisher**

⊙ **Check out any strong smell of petrol**

The fuel in your vehicle can be a dangerous fire hazard. Never

- use a naked flame near the vehicle if you can smell fuel
- smoke when refuelling your vehicle.

Your engine catches fire. What should you do first?

- ⊙ Lift the bonnet and disconnect the battery
- ⊙ Lift the bonnet and warn other traffic
- ⊙ Call a breakdown service
- ⊙ Call the fire brigade

⊙ **Call the fire brigade**

If you suspect a fire in the engine compartment you should pull up as safely and as quickly as possible. DO NOT open the bonnet as this will fuel the fire further.

Get any passengers out of the vehicle and dial 999 immediately to contact the fire brigade.

You see a car on the hard shoulder of a motorway with a HELP pennant displayed. This means the driver is most likely to be

- ⊙ a disabled person
- ⊙ first aid trained
- ⊙ a foreign visitor
- ⊙ a rescue patrol person

⊙ **a disabled person**

If a disabled driver's vehicle breaks down and they are unable to walk to an emergency phone, they are advised to stay in their car and switch on the hazard warning lights. They may also display a 'Help' pennant in their vehicle.

You are on a motorway. A large box falls onto the road from a lorry. The lorry does not stop. You should

- ⊙ go to the next emergency telephone and inform the police
- ⊙ catch up with the lorry and try to get the driver's attention
- ⊙ stop close to the box until the police arrive
- ⊙ pull over to the hard shoulder, then remove the box

⊙ **go to the next emergency telephone and inform the police**

Lorry drivers are sometimes unaware of objects falling from their vehicles. If you see something fall off a lorry onto the motorway, watch to see if the driver pulls over. If they don't stop, do not attempt to retrieve it yourself. You should

- pull over onto the hard shoulder near an emergency telephone
- report the hazard to the police.

13.55 — *Mark* **three** *answers*

You break down on a level crossing. The lights have not yet begun to flash. Which THREE things should you do?

- ⊙ Telephone the signal operator
- ⊙ Leave your vehicle and get everyone clear
- ⊙ Walk down the track and signal the next train
- ⊙ Move the vehicle if a signal operator tells you to
- ⊙ Tell drivers behind what has happened

⊙ **Telephone the signal operator**

⊙ **Leave your vehicle and get everyone clear**

⊙ **Move the vehicle if a signal operator tells you to**

If your vehicle breaks down on a level crossing, your first priority is to get everyone out of the vehicle and clear of the crossing. Then use the railway telephone, if there is one, to tell the signal operator. If you have time before the train arrives, move the vehicle clear of crossing, but only do this if alarm signals are not on.

13.56 — *Mark* **two** *answers*

You are on a motorway. When can you use hazard warning lights?

- ⊙ When a vehicle is following too closely
- ⊙ When you slow down quickly because of danger ahead
- ⊙ When you are towing another vehicle
- ⊙ When driving on the hard shoulder
- ⊙ When you have broken down on the hard shoulder

⊙ **When you slow down quickly because of danger ahead**

⊙ **When you have broken down on the hard shoulder**

Hazard warning lights will warn the traffic travelling behind you that there is a hazard ahead.

13.57 — Mark three answers

You have broken down on a motorway. When you use the emergency telephone you will be asked

- ⊙ for the number on the telephone that you are using
- ⊙ for your driving licence details
- ⊙ for the name of your vehicle insurance company
- ⊙ for details of yourself and your vehicle
- ⊙ whether you belong to a motoring organisation

- ⊙ **for the number on the telephone that you are using**
- ⊙ **for details of yourself and your vehicle**
- ⊙ **whether you belong to a motoring organisation**

Have these details ready before you use the emergency telephone and be sure to give the correct information.

For your own safety always face the traffic when you speak on a roadside telephone.

13.58 — Mark one answer

You are on the motorway. Luggage falls from your vehicle. What should you do?

- ⊙ Stop at the next emergency telephone and contact the police
- ⊙ Stop on the motorway and put on hazard lights while you pick it up
- ⊙ Walk back up the motorway to pick it up
- ⊙ Pull up on the hard shoulder and wave traffic down

- ⊙ **Stop at the next emergency telephone and contact the police**

If any object falls onto the motorway carriageway from your vehicle pull over onto the hard shoulder near an emergency telephone and phone for assistance. Don't

- stop on the carriageway
- attempt to retrieve anything.

13.59 — Mark one answer

On the motorway, the hard shoulder should be used

- ⊙ to answer a mobile phone
- ⊙ when an emergency arises
- ⊙ for a short rest when tired
- ⊙ to check a road atlas

- ⊙ **when an emergency arises**

Pull onto the hard shoulder and use the emergency telephone to report your problem. The telephone connects you to police control and lets them know your exact location. They will inform the appropriate emergency services for you.

Never cross the carriageway to use the telephone on the other side.

13.60
*Mark **two** answers*

Your tyre bursts while you are driving. Which TWO things should you do?

- Pull on the handbrake
- Brake as quickly as possible
- Pull up slowly at the side of the road
- Hold the steering wheel firmly to keep control
- Continue on at a normal speed

⊙ **Pull up slowly at the side of the road**

⊙ **Hold the steering wheel firmly to keep control**

A tyre bursting can lead to a loss of control, especially if you're travelling at high speed. Using the correct procedure should help you to stop the vehicle safely.

13.61
*Mark **two** answers*

Which TWO things should you do when a front tyre bursts?

- Apply the handbrake to stop the vehicle
- Brake firmly and quickly
- Let the vehicle roll to a stop
- Hold the steering wheel lightly
- Grip the steering wheel firmly

⊙ **Let the vehicle roll to a stop**

⊙ **Grip the steering wheel firmly**

Try not to react by applying the brakes harshly. This could lead to further loss of steering control. Indicate your intention to pull up at the side of the road and roll to a stop.

13.62
*Mark **two** answers*

For which TWO should you use hazard warning lights?

- When you slow down quickly on a motorway because of a hazard ahead
- When you have broken down
- When you wish to stop on double yellow lines
- When you need to park on the pavement

⊙ **When you slow down quickly on a motorway because of a hazard ahead**

⊙ **When you have broken down**

Hazard warning lights are fitted to all modern cars and some motorcycles. They should only be used to warn other road users of a hazard ahead.

13.63
*Mark **one** answer*

When are you allowed to use hazard warning lights?

- ⊙ When stopped and temporarily obstructing traffic
- ⊙ When travelling during darkness without headlights
- ⊙ When parked for shopping on double yellow lines
- ⊙ When travelling slowly because you are lost

⊙ **When stopped and temporarily obstructing traffic**

You must not use hazard warning lights when moving, except when slowing suddenly on a motorway or unrestricted dual carriageway to warn the traffic behind.

Never use hazard warning lights to excuse dangerous or illegal parking.

13.64
*Mark **one** answer*

You have broken down on a two-way road. You have a warning triangle. You should place the warning triangle at least how far from your vehicle?

- ⊙ 5 metres (16 feet)
- ⊙ 25 metres (82 feet)
- ⊙ 45 metres (147 feet)
- ⊙ 100 metres (328 feet)

⊙ **45 metres (147 feet)**

Carry an advance warning triangle in your vehicle. They fold flat and don't take up much room. Use it to warn other road users if your vehicle has broken down or there's been an accident.

Place your warning triangle at least 45 metres (147 feet) from your vehicle on the same side of the road.

You may need to place it further back if the vehicle is hidden by, for example, a bend, hill or dip in the road.

13.65
*Mark **three** answers*

The police may ask you to produce which three of these documents following an accident?

- ⊙ Vehicle registration document
- ⊙ Driving licence
- ⊙ Theory test certificate
- ⊙ Insurance certificate
- ⊙ MOT test certificate
- ⊙ Road tax disc

⊙ **Driving licence**

⊙ **Insurance certificate**

⊙ **MOT test certificate**

You must stop if you have been involved in a collision which results in any injury or damage.

13.66 — *Mark **one** answer*

You have broken down on a two-way road. You have a warning triangle. It should be displayed

- ⊙ on the roof of your vehicle
- ⊙ at least 150 metres (492 feet) behind your vehicle
- ⊙ at least 45 metres (147 feet) behind your vehicle
- ⊙ just behind your vehicle

⊙ **at least 45 metres (147 feet) behind your vehicle**

If you need to display a warning triangle make sure that it can be clearly seen by other road users.

Place it on the same side of the road as the broken down vehicle and away from any obstruction that would make it hard to see.

13.67 — N.I Exempt — *Mark **one** answer*

You lose control of your car and damage a garden wall. No one is around. What must you do?

- ⊙ Report the accident to the police within 24 hours
- ⊙ Go back to tell the house owner the next day
- ⊙ Report the accident to your insurance company when you get home
- ⊙ Find someone in the area to tell them about it immediately

⊙ **Report the accident to the police within 24 hours**

If the property owner is not available at the time, you must inform the police of the accident. This should be done as soon as possible and within 24 hours.

section fourteen
VEHICLE LOADING

This section covers:

- stability
- towing regulations

14.1
*Mark **two** answers*

You are towing a small trailer on a busy three-lane motorway. All the lanes are open. You must

⊙ not exceed 60 mph

⊙ not overtake

⊙ have a stabiliser fitted

⊙ use only the left and centre lanes

⊙ **not exceed 60 mph**

⊙ **use only the left and centre lanes**

You should be aware of the motorway regulations for vehicles towing trailers. These state that a vehicle towing a trailer must not

• use the right-hand lane of a three-lane motorway unless directed to do so, for example, at roadworks or due to a lane closure

• exceed 60 mph.

14.2
*Mark **one** answer*

Any load that is carried on a roof rack MUST be

⊙ securely fastened when driving

⊙ carried only when strictly necessary

⊙ as light as possible

⊙ covered with plastic sheeting

⊙ **securely fastened when driving**

The safest way to carry items on the roof is in a specially designed roof box. This will help to keep your luggage secure and dry, and also has less wind resistance than loads carried on a roof rack.

14.3
*Mark **one** answer*

If a trailer swerves or snakes when you are towing it you should

⊙ ease off the accelerator and reduce your speed

⊙ let go of the steering wheel and let it correct itself

⊙ brake hard and hold the pedal down

⊙ increase your speed as quickly as possible

⊙ **ease off the accelerator and reduce your speed**

Strong winds or buffeting from large vehicles can cause a trailer or caravan to snake or swerve. If this happens, ease off the accelerator. Don't

• brake harshly

• steer sharply

• increase your speed.

14.4

Mark **one** answer

How can you stop a caravan snaking from side to side?

- ⊙ Turn the steering wheel slowly to each side
- ⊙ Accelerate to increase your speed
- ⊙ Stop as quickly as you can
- ⊙ Slow down very gradually

⊙ **Slow down very gradually**

Keep calm and don't brake harshly or you could lose control completely.

14.5

Mark **two** answers

On which TWO occasions might you inflate your tyres to more than the recommended normal pressure?

- ⊙ When the roads are slippery
- ⊙ When driving fast for a long distance
- ⊙ When the tyre tread is worn below 2mm
- ⊙ When carrying a heavy load
- ⊙ When the weather is cold
- ⊙ When the vehicle is fitted with anti-lock brakes

⊙ **When driving fast for a long distance**

⊙ **When carrying a heavy load**

Check the vehicle handbook; this should give you guidance on the correct tyre pressures for your vehicle.

If you are carrying a heavy load in the rear of your vehicle, you may need to adjust the headlight aim as well as the tyre pressures.

14.6

Mark **one** answer

A heavy load on your roof rack will

- ⊙ improve the road holding
- ⊙ reduce the stopping distance
- ⊙ make the steering lighter
- ⊙ reduce stability

⊙ **reduce stability**

A heavy load on your roof rack will reduce the stability of the vehicle because it moves the centre of gravity away from that designed by the manufacturer. Be aware of this when you negotiate bends and corners.

If you change direction at speed, your vehicle and/or load could become unstable and you could lose control.

14.7
*Mark **one** answer*

You are towing a caravan along a motorway. The caravan begins to swerve from side to side. What should you do?

⊙ Ease off the accelerator slowly
⊙ Steer sharply from side to side
⊙ Do an emergency stop
⊙ Speed up very quickly

⊙ **Ease off the accelerator slowly**

Try not to brake or steer heavily as this will only make matters worse and you could lose control altogether. Keep calm and regain control by easing off the accelerator.

14.8
*Mark **two** answers*

Overloading your vehicle can seriously affect the

⊙ gearbox
⊙ steering
⊙ handling
⊙ battery life
⊙ journey time

⊙ **steering**

⊙ **handling**

Any load will have an effect on the handling of your vehicle and this becomes worse as you increase the load. Any change in the centre of gravity or weight the vehicle is carrying will affect its braking and handling on bends.

You need to be aware of this when carrying passengers, heavy loads, fitting a roof rack or towing a trailer.

14.9
Mark one answer

Who is responsible for making sure that a vehicle is not overloaded?

⊙ The driver of the vehicle
⊙ The owner of the items being carried
⊙ The person who loaded the vehicle
⊙ The licensing authority

⊙ **The driver of the vehicle**

Your vehicle must not be overloaded. Carrying heavy loads will affect control and handling characteristics. If your vehicle is overloaded and it causes an accident you'll be responsible.

Which of these is a suitable restraint for a child under three years?

⊙ A child seat
⊙ An adult holding a child
⊙ An adult seat belt
⊙ A lap belt

⊙ **A child seat**

The driver is responsible for ensuring that children under three wear suitable child restraints. If the child is in the front seat a restraint must be used. If the child is in the rear seat, a restraint must be used if available. Suitable forms of restraint include a harness or baby carrier. Any harness or booster seat used should be appropriate to the child's size and weight.

A child under three years is being carried in your vehicle. They should be secured in a restraint. Which of these is suitable?

⊙ An adult holding a child
⊙ A lap belt
⊙ A baby carrier
⊙ An adult seat belt

⊙ **A baby carrier**

If a child of 14 or under is a passenger in your car, you as the driver are responsible for them wearing a suitable restraint.

For a child under three years old, a harness or child seat would also be suitable restraints. These should be appropriate to the child's size and weight.

You are planning to tow a caravan. Which of these will mostly help to aid the vehicle handling?

⊙ A jockey wheel fitted to the towbar
⊙ Power steering fitted to the towing vehicle
⊙ Anti-lock brakes fitted to the towing vehicle
⊙ A stabiliser fitted to the towbar

⊙ **A stabiliser fitted to the towbar**

Towing a caravan or trailer affects the way the towing vehicle handles. It is highly recommended that you take a caravan manoeuvring course. These are provided by various organisations for anyone wishing to tow a trailer.

14.13

Mark one answer

Are passengers allowed to ride in a caravan that is being towed?

- ⊙ Yes, if they are over fourteen
- ⊙ No, not at any time
- ⊙ Only if all the seats in the towing vehicle are full
- ⊙ Only if a stabiliser is fitted

⊙ **No, not at any time**

Riding in a towed caravan is highly dangerous. The safety of the entire unit is dependent on the stability of the trailer. Moving passengers would make the caravan unstable and could cause loss of control.

14.14

Mark one answer

A trailer must stay securely hitched up to the towing vehicle. What additional safety device can be fitted to the trailer braking system?

- ⊙ Stabiliser
- ⊙ Jockey wheel
- ⊙ Corner steadies
- ⊙ Breakaway cable

⊙ **Breakaway cable**

In the event of a towbar failure the cable activates the trailer brakes, then snaps. This allows the towing vehicle to get free of the trailer and out of danger.

THE
HIGHWAY
CODE

REVISED 2004

THE HIGHWAY CODE

7.5T

local

www.highwaycode.gov.uk

i

For
pedestrians
cyclists
motorcyclists
and drivers

30

REDUCE
SPEED

Contents

Introduction

The Highway Code is essential reading for everyone. Its rules apply to all road users: pedestrians, horse riders and cyclists, as well as motorcyclists and drivers.

Many of the rules in the Code are legal requirements, and if you disobey these rules you are committing a criminal offence. You may be fined, given penalty points on your licence or be disqualified from driving. In the most serious cases you may be sent to prison. Such rules are identified by the use of the words **MUST/MUST NOT**. In addition, the rule includes an abbreviated reference to the legislation which creates the offence. An explanation of the abbreviations is on page 405.

Although failure to comply with the other rules of the Code will not, in itself, cause a person to be prosecuted, The Highway Code may be used in evidence in any court proceedings under the Traffic Acts to establish liability.

Knowing and applying the rules contained in The Highway Code could significantly reduce road accident casualties. Cutting the number of deaths and injuries that occur on our roads every day is a responsibility we all share. The Highway Code can help us discharge that responsibility.

Rules for pedestrians

General guidance

1. Pavements or footpaths should be used if provided. Where possible, avoid walking next to the kerb with your back to the traffic. If you have to step into the road, look both ways first.

2. If there is no pavement or footpath, walk on the right-hand side of the road so that you can see oncoming traffic. You should take extra care and
- be prepared to walk in single file, especially on narrow roads or in poor light
- keep close to the side of the road.

It may be safer to cross the road well before a sharp right-hand bend (so that oncoming traffic has a better chance of seeing you). Cross back after the bend.

Rule 3: Be seen in the dark; wear something reflective

3. Help other road users to see you. Wear or carry something light coloured, bright or fluorescent in poor daylight conditions. When it is dark, use reflective materials (e.g. armbands, sashes, waistcoats and jackets), which can be seen, by drivers using headlights, up to three times as far away as non-reflective materials.

4. Young children should not be out alone on the pavement or road (see Rule 7). When taking children out, walk between them and the traffic and hold their hands firmly. Strap very young children into push-chairs or use reins.

5. Organised walks. Groups of people should use a path if available; if one is not, they should keep to the left. Look-outs should be positioned at the front and back of the group, and they should wear fluorescent clothes in daylight and reflective clothes in the dark.

At night, the look-out in front should carry a white light and the one at the back a red light. People on the outside of large groups should also carry lights and wear reflective clothing.

6. Motorways. You **MUST NOT** walk on motorways or slip roads except in an emergency (see Rule 249).
Laws RTRA sect 17, MT(E&W)R 1982 as amended & MT(S)R regs 2 &13

Crossing the road

7. The Green Cross Code.
The advice given below on crossing the road is for all pedestrians. Children should be taught the Code and should not be allowed out alone until they can understand and use it properly. The age when they can do this is different for each child.

Many children cannot judge how fast vehicles are going or how far away they are. Children learn by example, so parents and carers should always use the Code in full when out with their children. They are responsible for deciding at what age children can use it safely by themselves.

a. First find a safe place to cross.
It is safer to cross using a subway, a footbridge, an island, a zebra, pelican, toucan or puffin crossing, or where there is a crossing point controlled by a police officer, a school crossing patrol or a traffic warden. Where there is a crossing nearby, use it. Otherwise choose a place where you can see clearly in all directions. Try to avoid crossing between parked cars (see Rule 14) and on blind bends and brows of hills. Move to a space where drivers can see you clearly.

b. Stop just before you get to the kerb, where you can see if anything is coming. Do not get too close to the traffic. If there is no pavement, keep back from the edge of the road but make sure you can still see approaching traffic.

c. Look all around for traffic and listen. Traffic could come from any direction. Listen as well, because you can sometimes hear traffic before you see it.

d. If traffic is coming, let it pass.
Look all around again and listen. Do not cross until there is a safe gap in the traffic and you are certain that there is plenty of time. Remember, even if traffic is a long way off, it may be approaching very quickly.

e. When it is safe, go straight across the road – do not run. Keep looking and listening for traffic while you cross, in case there is any traffic you did not see, or in case other traffic appears suddenly.

8. At a junction. When crossing the road, look out for traffic turning into the road, especially from behind you.

9. Pedestrian Safety Barriers. Where there are barriers, cross the road only at the gaps provided for pedestrians. Do not climb over the barriers or walk between them and the road.

10. Tactile paving. Small raised studs which can be felt underfoot may be used to advise blind or partially sighted people that they are approaching a crossing point with a dropped kerb.

11. One-way streets. Check which way the traffic is moving. Do not cross until it is safe to do so without stopping. Bus and cycle lanes may operate in the opposite direction to the rest of the traffic.

12. Bus and cycle lanes. Take care when crossing these lanes as traffic may be moving faster than in the other lanes, or against the flow of traffic.

13. Routes shared with cyclists. Cycle tracks may run alongside footpaths, with a dividing line segregating the two. Keep to the section for pedestrians. Take extra care where cyclists and pedestrians share the same path without separation (see Rule 48).

14. Parked vehicles. If you have to cross between parked vehicles, use the outside edges of the vehicles as if they were the kerb. Stop there and make sure you can see all around and that the traffic can see you. Never cross the road in front of, or behind, any vehicle with its engine running, especially a large vehicle, as the driver may not be able to see you.

15. Reversing vehicles. Never cross behind a vehicle which is reversing, showing white reversing lights or sounding a warning.

16. Moving vehicles. You **MUST NOT** get on to or hold on to a moving vehicle.
Law RTA 1988 sect 26

17. At night. Wear something reflective to make it easier for others to see you (see Rule 3). If there is no pedestrian crossing nearby, cross the road near a street light so that traffic can see you more easily.

Crossings

18. At all crossings. When using any type of crossing you should
- always check that the traffic has stopped before you start to cross or push a pram onto a crossing
- always cross between the studs or over the zebra markings. Do not cross at the side of the crossing or on the zig-zag lines, as it can be dangerous.

You **MUST NOT** loiter on zebra, pelican or puffin crossings.
Laws ZPPPCRGD reg 19 & RTRA sect 25(5)

19. Zebra crossings. Give traffic plenty of time to see you and to stop before you start to cross. Vehicles will need more time when the road is slippery. Remember that traffic does not have to stop until someone has moved onto the crossing.

Wait until traffic has stopped from both directions or the road is clear before crossing. Keep looking both ways, and listening, in case a driver or rider has not seen you and attempts to overtake a vehicle that has stopped.

20. Where there is an island in the middle of a zebra crossing, wait on the island and follow Rule 19 before you cross the second half of the road – it is a separate crossing.

21. At traffic lights. There may be special signals for pedestrians. You should only start to cross the road when the green figure shows.

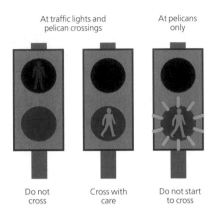

At traffic lights and pelican crossings | At pelicans only

Do not cross | Cross with care | Do not start to cross

Rule 21-24: Pedestrian signals at traffic lights and pelican crossings

If you have started to cross the road and the green figure goes out, you should still have time to reach the other side, but do not delay. If no pedestrian signals have been provided, watch carefully and do not cross until the traffic lights are red and the traffic has stopped. Keep looking and check for traffic that may be turning the corner. Remember that traffic lights may let traffic move in some lanes while traffic in other lanes has stopped.

22. Pelican crossings. These are signal-controlled crossings operated by pedestrians. Push the control button to activate the traffic signals. When the red figure shows, do not cross. When a steady green figure shows, check the traffic has stopped then cross with care.

When the green figure begins to flash you should not start to cross. If you have already started you should have time to finish crossing safely.

23. At some pelican crossings there is a bleeping sound to indicate to blind or partially-sighted people when the steady green figure is showing, and there may be a tactile signal to help deafblind people.

24. When the road is congested, traffic on your side of the road may be forced to stop even though their lights are green. Traffic may still be moving on the other side of the road, so press the button and wait for the signal to cross.

25. Puffin and toucan crossings. These differ from pelican crossings as there is no flashing green figure phase. On puffin crossings the red and green figures are above the control box on your side of the road. Press the button and wait for the green figure to show. On toucan crossings cyclists are permitted to ride across the road (see Rule 65).

26. 'Staggered' pelican or puffin crossings. When the crossings on each side of the central refuge are not in line they are two separate crossings. On reaching the central island press the button again and wait for a steady green figure.

27. Crossings controlled by an authorised person. Do not cross the road unless you are signalled to do so by a police officer, traffic warden or school crossing patrol. Always cross in front of them.

28. Where there are no controlled crossing points available it is advisable to cross where there is an island in the middle of the road. Use the Green Cross Code to cross to the island and then stop and use it again to cross the second half of the road.

Situations needing extra care

29. Emergency vehicles. If an ambulance, fire engine, police or other emergency vehicle approaches using flashing blue lights, headlights and/or sirens, keep off the road.

30. Buses. Get on or off a bus only when it has stopped to allow you to do so. Watch out for cyclists when you are getting off. Never cross the road directly behind or in front of a bus; wait until it has moved off and you can see clearly in both directions.

31. Tramways. These may run through pedestrian areas. Their path will be marked out by shallow kerbs, changes in the paving or other road surface, white lines or yellow dots. Cross at designated crossings where provided. Flashing amber lights may warn you that a tram is approaching. Elsewhere look both ways along the track before crossing. Do not walk along the track. Trams move quickly and silently and cannot steer to avoid you.

32. Railway level crossings. Do not cross if the red lights show, an alarm is sounding or the barriers are being lowered. The tone of the alarm will change if another train is approaching. If there are no lights, alarms or barriers, stop, look both ways and listen before crossing.

33. Street and pavement repairs. A pavement may be closed temporarily because it is not safe to use. Take extra care if you are directed to walk in or to cross the road.

Rules about animals

Horseriders

34. Safety equipment. Children under the age of 14 **MUST** wear a helmet which complies with the Regulations. It **MUST** be fastened securely. Other riders should also follow this advice.
Law H(PHYR)R

35. Other clothing. You should wear
- boots or shoes with hard soles and heels
- light-coloured or fluorescent clothing in daylight
- reflective clothing if you have to ride at night or in poor visibility.

36. At night. It is safer not to ride on the road at night or in poor visibility, but if you do, make sure your horse has reflective bands above the fetlock joints. Carry a light which shows white to the front and red to the rear.

Riding

37. Before you take a horse on to a road, you should

- ensure all tack fits well and is in good condition
- make sure you can control the horse. Always ride with other, less nervous horses if you think that your horse will be nervous of traffic. Never ride a horse without a saddle or bridle.

38. Before riding off or turning, look behind you to make sure it is safe, then give a clear arm signal.

39. When riding on the road you should

- keep to the left
- keep both hands on the reins unless you are signalling
- keep both feet in the stirrups
- not carry another person
- not carry anything which might affect your balance or get tangled up with the reins
- keep a horse you are leading to your left
- move in the direction of the traffic flow in a one-way street
- never ride more than two abreast, and ride in single file where the road narrows or on the approach to a bend.

40. You **MUST NOT** take a horse on to a footpath, pavement or cycle track. Use a bridleway where possible.
Laws HA 1835 sect 72 & R(S)A sect 129(5)

41. Avoid roundabouts wherever possible. If you use them you should

- keep to the left and watch out for vehicles crossing your path to leave or join the roundabout
- signal right when riding across exits to show you are not leaving
- signal left just before you leave the roundabout.

Other animals

42. Dogs. Do not let a dog out on the road on its own. Keep it on a short lead when walking on the pavement, road or path shared with cyclists.

43. When in a vehicle make sure dogs or other animals are suitably restrained so they cannot distract you while you are driving or injure you if you stop quickly.

44. Animals being herded. These should be kept under control at all times. You should, if possible, send another person along the road in front to warn other road users, especially at a bend or the brow of a hill. It is safer not to move animals after dark, but if you do, then wear reflective clothing and ensure that lights are carried (white at the front and red at the rear of the herd).

Rules for cyclists

These rules are in addition to those in the following sections, which apply to all vehicles (except the motorway section on page 381). See also page 402 on choosing and maintaining your bicycle.

45. Clothing. You should wear
- a cycle helmet which conforms to current regulations
- appropriate clothes for cycling. Avoid clothes which may get tangled in the chain, or in a wheel or may obscure your lights
- light-coloured or fluorescent clothing which helps other road users to see you in daylight and poor light
- reflective clothing and/or accessories (belt, arm or ankle bands) in the dark.

Rule 45: Help yourself to be seen

46. At night your cycle **MUST** have front and rear lights lit. It **MUST** also be fitted with a red rear reflector (and amber pedal reflectors, if manufactured after 1/10/85). White front reflectors and spoke reflectors will also help you to be seen.
Law RVLR regs 18 & 24

When cycling

47. Use cycle routes when practicable. They can make your journey safer.

48. Cycle Tracks. These are normally located away from the road, but may occasionally be found alongside footpaths or pavements. Cyclists and pedestrians may be segregated or they may share the same space (unsegregated). When using segregated tracks you **MUST** keep to the side intended for cyclists. Take care when passing pedestrians, especially children, elderly or disabled people, and allow them plenty of room. Always be prepared to slow down and stop if necessary.
Law HA 1835 sect 72

49. Cycle Lanes. These are marked by a white line (which may be broken) along the carriageway (see Rule 119). Keep within the lane wherever possible.

50. You **MUST** obey all traffic signs and traffic light signals.
Laws RTA 1988 sect 36, TSRGD reg 10(1)

51. You should
- keep both hands on the handlebars except when signalling or changing gear
- keep both feet on the pedals
- not ride more than two abreast
- ride in single file on narrow or busy roads
- not ride close behind another vehicle

- not carry anything which will affect your balance or may get tangled up with your wheels or chain
- be considerate of other road users, particularly blind and partially sighted pedestrians. Let them know you are there when necessary, for example by ringing your bell.

52. You should

- look all around before moving away from the kerb, turning or manoeuvring, to make sure it is safe to do so. Give a clear signal to show other road users what you intend to do (see page 391)
- look well ahead for obstructions in the road, such as drains, pot-holes and parked vehicles so that you do not have to swerve suddenly to avoid them. Leave plenty of room when passing parked vehicles and watch out for doors being opened into your path
- take extra care near road humps, narrowings and other traffic calming features.

53. You **MUST NOT**

- carry a passenger unless your cycle has been built or adapted to carry one
- hold on to a moving vehicle or trailer
- ride in a dangerous, careless or inconsiderate manner
- ride when under the influence of drink or drugs.

Law RTA 1988 sects 24, 26, 28, 29 & 30 as amended by RTA 1991

54. You **MUST NOT** cycle on a pavement. Do not leave your cycle where it would endanger or obstruct road users or pedestrians, for example, lying on the pavement. Use cycle parking facilities where provided.
Laws HA 1835 sect 72 & R(S)A sect 129

55. You **MUST NOT** cross the stop line when the traffic lights are red. Some junctions have an advanced stop line to enable you to position yourself ahead of other traffic (see Rule 154).
Laws RTA 1988 sect 36, TSRGD regs 10 & 36(1)

56. Bus Lanes. These may be used by cyclists only if the signs include a cycle symbol. Watch out for people getting on or off a bus. Be very careful when overtaking a bus or leaving a bus lane as you will be entering a busier traffic flow.

Road junctions

57. On the left. When approaching a junction on the left, watch out for vehicles turning in front of you, out of or into the side road. Do not ride on the inside of vehicles signalling or slowing down to turn left.

58. Pay particular attention to long vehicles which need a lot of room to manoeuvre at corners. They may have to move over to the right before turning left. Wait until they have completed the manoeuvre because the rear wheels come very close to the kerb while turning. Do not be tempted to ride in the space between them and the kerb.

59. On the right. If you are turning right, check the traffic to ensure it is safe, then signal and move to the centre of the road. Wait until there is a safe gap in the oncoming traffic before completing the turn. It may be safer to wait on the left until there is a safe gap or to dismount and push your cycle across the road.

60. Dual carriageways. Remember that traffic on most dual carriageways moves quickly. When crossing wait for a safe gap and cross each carriageway in turn. Take extra care when crossing slip roads.

Roundabouts

61. Full details about the correct procedure at roundabouts are contained in Rules 160–166. Roundabouts can be hazardous and should be approached with care.

62. You may feel safer either keeping to the left on the roundabout or dismounting and walking your cycle round on the pavement or verge. If you decide to keep to the left you should
- be aware that drivers may not easily see you
- take extra care when cycling across exits and you may need to signal right to show you are not leaving the roundabout
- watch out for vehicles crossing your path to leave or join the roundabout.

63. Give plenty of room to long vehicles on the roundabout as they need more space to manoeuvre. Do not ride in the space they need to get round the roundabout. It may be safer to wait until they have cleared the roundabout.

Crossing the road

64. Do not ride across a pelican, puffin or zebra crossing. Dismount and wheel your cycle across.

65. Toucan crossings. These are light-controlled crossings which allow cyclists and pedestrians to cross at the same time. They are push button operated. Pedestrians and cyclists will see the green signal together. Cyclists are permitted to ride across.

66. Cycle-only crossings. Cycle tracks on opposite sides of the road may be linked by signalled crossings. You may ride across but you **MUST NOT** cross until the green cycle symbol is showing.
Law TSRGD reg 36(1)

Rules for motorcyclists

These Rules are in addition to those in the following sections which apply to all vehicles. For motorcycle licence requirements see page 402.

General

67. On all journeys, the rider and pillion passenger on a motorcycle, scooter or moped **MUST** wear a protective helmet. Helmets **MUST** comply with the Regulations and they **MUST** be fastened securely. It is also advisable to wear eye protectors, which **MUST** comply with the Regulations. Consider wearing ear protection. Strong boots, gloves and suitable clothing may help to protect you if you fall off.
Laws RTA 1988 sects 16 &17 & MC(PH)R as amended reg 4, & RTA sect 18 & MC(EP)R as amended reg 4

68. You **MUST NOT** carry more than one pillion passenger and he/she **MUST** sit astride the machine on a proper seat and should keep both feet on the footrests.
Law RTA 1988 sect 23

Rule 69-70: Make sure you can be seen

69. Daylight riding. Make yourself as visible as possible from the side as well as the front and rear. You could wear a white or brightly coloured helmet. Wear fluorescent clothing or strips. Dipped headlights, even in good daylight, may also make you more conspicuous.

70. Riding in the dark. Wear reflective clothing or strips to improve your chances of being seen in the dark. These reflect light from the headlamps of other vehicles making you more visible from a long distance. See Rules 93–96 for lighting requirements.

71. Manoeuvring. You should be aware of what is behind and to the sides before manoeuvring. Look behind you; use mirrors if they are fitted. When overtaking traffic queues look out for pedestrians crossing between vehicles and vehicles emerging from junctions.
Remember:
Observation - Signal - Manoeuvre.

Rules for drivers & motorcyclists

72. Vehicle condition. You **MUST** ensure your vehicle and trailer complies with the full requirements of the Road Vehicles (Construction and Use) Regulations and Road Vehicles Lighting Regulations. (See page 405).

73. Before setting off. You should ensure that
- you have planned your route and allowed sufficient time
- clothing and footwear do not prevent you using the controls in the correct manner

- you know where all the controls are and how to use them before you need them. All vehicles are different; do not wait until it is too late to find out
- your mirrors and seat are adjusted correctly to ensure comfort, full control and maximum vision
- head restraints are properly adjusted to reduce the risk of neck injuries in the event of an accident

- you have sufficient fuel before commencing your journey, especially if it includes motorway driving. It can be dangerous to lose power when driving in traffic.

74. Vehicle towing and loading.

As a driver

- you **MUST NOT** tow more than your licence permits you to
- you **MUST NOT** overload your vehicle or trailer. You should not tow a weight greater than that recommended by the manufacturer of your vehicle
- you **MUST** secure your load and it **MUST NOT** stick out dangerously
- you should properly distribute the weight in your caravan or trailer with heavy items mainly over the axle(s) and ensure a

downward load on the tow ball. Manufacturer's recommended weight and tow ball load should not be exceeded. This should avoid the possibility of swerving or snaking and going out of control. If this does happen, ease off the accelerator and reduce speed gently to regain control.

Law CUR reg 100, MV(DL)R reg 43

Seat belts

75. You **MUST** wear a seat belt if one is available, unless you are exempt. Those exempt from the requirement include the holders of medical exemption certificates and people making local deliveries in a vehicle designed for the purpose.

Laws RTA 1988 sects 14 & 15, MV(WSB)R & MV(WSBCFS)R

Seat belt requirements

This table summarises the main legal requirements for wearing seat belts

	FRONT SEAT (all vehicles)	REAR SEAT (cars and small minibuses*)	WHOSE RESPONSIBILITY
DRIVER	**MUST** be worn if fitted		**DRIVER**
CHILD under 3 years of age	Appropriate child restraint **MUST** be worn	Appropriate child restraint **MUST** be worn if available	**DRIVER**
CHILD aged 3 to 11 and under 1.5 metres (about 5 feet) in height	Appropriate child restraint **MUST** be worn if available. If not, an adult seat belt **MUST** be worn	Appropriate child restraint **MUST** be worn if available If not, an adult seat belt **MUST** be worn if available.	**DRIVER**
CHILD aged 12 or 13 or younger child 1.5 metres or more in height	Adult seat belt **MUST** be worn if available.	Adult seat belt **MUST** be worn if available	**DRIVER**
PASSENGER over the age of 14	**MUST** be worn if available	**MUST** be worn if available	**PASSENGER**

* Minibuses with an unladen weight of 2540kg or less

76. The driver **MUST** ensure that all children under 14 years of age wear seat belts or sit in an approved child restraint. This should be a baby seat, child seat, booster seat or booster cushion appropriate to the child's weight and size, fitted to the manufacturer's instructions.
Laws RTA 1988 sects 14 & 15, MV(WSB)R & MV(WSBCFS)R

Rule 76: Make sure children wear the correct restraint

77. You **MUST** wear seatbelts in minibuses with an unladen weight of 2540 kg or less. You should wear them in large minibuses and coaches where available.
Laws RTA 1988 sects 14 & 15, MV(WSB)R & MV(WSBCFS)R

78. Children in cars. Drivers who are carrying children in cars should ensure that
- children do not sit behind the rear seats in an estate car or hatchback, unless a special child seat has been fitted
- the child safety door locks, where fitted, are used when children are in the car
- children are kept under control
- a rear-facing baby seat is NEVER fitted into a seat protected by an airbag.

Fitness to drive
79. Make sure that you are fit to drive.
You **MUST** report to the Driver and Vehicle Licensing Agency (DVLA) any health condition likely to affect your driving.
Law RTA 1988 sect 94

80. Driving when you are tired greatly increases your accident risk. To minimise this risk
- make sure you are fit to drive. Do not undertake a long journey (longer than an hour) if you feel tired
- avoid undertaking long journeys between midnight and 6am, when natural alertness is at a minimum
- plan your journey to take sufficient breaks. A minimum break of at least 15 minutes after every two hours of driving is recommended
- if you feel at all sleepy, stop in a safe place. Do not stop on the hard shoulder of a motorway
- the most effective ways to counter sleepiness are to take a short nap (up to 15 minutes) or drink, for example, two cups of strong coffee. Fresh air, exercise or turning up the radio may help for a short time, but are *not* as effective.

81. Vision. You **MUST** be able to read a vehicle number plate from a distance of 20.5 metres (67 feet – about five car lengths) in good daylight. From September 2001, you **MUST** be able to read a new style number plate from a distance of 20 metres (66 feet). If you need to wear glasses (or contact lenses) to do this, you **MUST** wear them at all times whilst driving.

The police have the power to require a driver, at any time, to undertake an eyesight test in good daylight.

Laws RTA 1988 sect 96 & MV(DL)R reg 40 & sch 8

82. At night or in poor visibility, do not use tinted glasses, lenses or visors or anything that restricts vision.

Alcohol and drugs

83. Do not drink and drive as it will seriously affect your judgement and abilities. You **MUST NOT** drive with a breath alcohol level higher than 35 µg /100ml or a blood alcohol level of more than 80 mg/100 ml. Alcohol will

- give a false sense of confidence
- reduce co-ordination and slow down reactions
- affect judgement of speed, distance and risk

- reduce your driving ability, even if you are below the legal limit
- take time to leave your body; you may be unfit to drive in the evening after drinking at lunchtime, or in the morning after drinking the previous evening. If you are going to drink, arrange another means of transport.

Law RTA 1988 sects 4, 5 & 11(2)

84. You **MUST NOT** drive under the influence of drugs or medicine. Check the instructions or ask your doctor or pharmacist. Using illegal drugs is highly dangerous. Never take them before driving; the effects are unpredictable, but can be even more severe than alcohol and may result in fatal or serious road accidents.

Law RTA 1988 sect 4

General rules, techniques & advice for all drivers & riders

This section should be read by all drivers, motorcyclists and cyclists. The rules in *The Highway Code* do not give you the right of way in any circumstance, but they advise you when you should give way to others. Always give way if it can help to avoid an accident.

Signals

85. Signals warn and inform other road users, including pedestrians (see page 391), of your intended actions. You should

- give clear signals in plenty of time, having checked it is not misleading to signal at that time

- use them, if necessary, before changing course or direction, stopping or moving off
- cancel them after use
- make sure your signals will not confuse others. If, for instance you want to stop after a side road, do not signal until you are passing the road. If you signal earlier it may

give the impression that you intend to turn into the road. Your brake lights will warn traffic behind you that you are slowing down

* use an arm signal to emphasise or reinforce your signal if necessary. Remember that signalling does not give you priority.

86. You should also
* watch out for signals given by other road users and proceed only when you are satisfied that it is safe
* be aware that an indicator on another vehicle may not have been cancelled.

87. You **MUST** obey signals given by police officers and traffic wardens (see page 392) and signs used by school crossing patrols.

Laws RTRA sect 28, RTA 1988 sect 35 and FTWO art 3

Traffic light signals and traffic signs

88. You **MUST** obey all traffic light signals (see page 390) and traffic signs giving orders, including temporary signals and signs (see pages 393 and 398) . Make sure you know, understand and act on all other traffic and information signs and road markings (see pages 394 – 400).

Laws RTA 1988 sect 36, TSRGD regs 10, 15, 16, 25, 26, 27, 28, 29, 36, 38 & 40

89. Police stopping procedures. If the police want to stop your vehicle they will, where possible, attract your attention by
* flashing blue lights or headlights or sounding their siren or horn
* directing you to pull over to the side by pointing and/or using the left indicator.

You **MUST** then pull over and stop as soon as it is safe to do so. Then switch off your engine.

Law RTA 1988 sect 163

90. Flashing headlights. Only flash your headlights to let other road users know that you are there. Do not flash your headlights in an attempt to intimidate other road users.

91. If another driver flashes his headlights never assume that it is a signal to go. Use your own judgement and proceed carefully.

92. The horn. Use only while your vehicle is moving and you need to warn other road users of your presence. Never sound your horn aggressively. You **MUST NOT** use your horn
* while stationary on the road
* when driving in a built up area between the hours of 11.30 pm and 7.00 am *except* when another vehicle poses a danger.

Law CUR reg 99

Lighting requirements

93. You **MUST**
* use headlights at night, except on restricted roads (those with street lights not more than 185 metres (600 feet) apart and which are generally subject to a speed limit of 30 mph)
* use headlights when visibility is seriously reduced (see Rule 201).
* ensure all sidelights and rear registration plate lights are lit at night.

Laws RVLR regs 24 & 25 & RV(R&L)R reg 19

94. You **MUST NOT**

- use any lights in a way which would dazzle or cause discomfort to other road users
- use front or rear fog lights unless visibility is seriously reduced. You **MUST** switch them off when visibility improves to avoid dazzling other road users.

Law RVLR reg 27

95. You should also

- use dipped headlights, or dim-dip if fitted, at night in built-up areas and in dull daytime weather, to ensure that you can be seen
- keep your headlights dipped when overtaking until you are level with the other vehicle and then change to main beam if necessary, unless this would dazzle oncoming traffic
- slow down, and if necessary stop, if you are dazzled by oncoming headlights.

96. Hazard warning lights. These may be used when your vehicle is stationary, to warn that it is temporarily obstructing traffic. Never use them as an excuse for dangerous or illegal parking.

You **MUST NOT** use hazard warning lights whilst driving unless you are on a motorway or unrestricted dual carriageway and you need to warn drivers behind you of a hazard or obstruction ahead. Only use them for long enough to ensure that your warning has been observed.

Law RVLR reg 27

Control of the vehicle

Braking

97. In normal circumstances. The safest way to brake is to do so early and lightly. Brake more firmly as you begin to stop. Ease the pressure off just before the vehicle comes to rest to avoid a jerky stop.

98. In an emergency. Brake immediately. Try to avoid braking so harshly that you lock your wheels. Locked wheels can lead to skidding.

99. Skids. Skidding is caused by the driver braking, accelerating or steering too harshly or driving too fast for the road conditions. If skidding occurs, ease off the brake or accelerator and try to steer smoothly in the direction of the skid. For example, if the rear of the vehicle skids to the right, steer quickly and smoothly to the right to recover.

Rear of car skids to the right   Driver steers to the right

100. ABS. The presence of an anti-lock braking system should not cause you to alter the way you brake from that indicated in Rule 97. However in the case of an emergency, apply the footbrake rapidly and firmly; do not release the pressure until the vehicle has slowed to the desired speed. The ABS should ensure that steering control will be retained.

101. Brakes affected by water. If you have driven through deep water your brakes may be less effective. Test them at the first safe opportunity by pushing gently on the brake pedal to make sure that they work. If they are not fully effective, gently apply light pressure while driving slowly. This will help to dry them out.

102. Coasting. This term describes a vehicle travelling in neutral or with the clutch pressed down. Do not coast, whatever the driving conditions. It reduces driver control because

- engine braking is eliminated
- vehicle speed downhill will increase quickly
- increased use of the footbrake can reduce its effectiveness
- steering response will be affected particularly on bends and corners
- it may be more difficult to select the appropriate gear when needed.

Speed limits

103. You **MUST NOT** exceed the maximum speed limits for the road and for your vehicle (see the table, right). Street lights usually mean that there is a 30 mph speed limit unless there are signs showing another limit.

Law RTRA sects 81, 86, 89 & sch 6

104. The speed limit is the absolute maximum and does not mean it is safe to drive at that speed irrespective of conditions. Driving at speeds too fast for the road and traffic conditions can be dangerous. You should always reduce your speed when

- the road layout or condition presents hazards, such as bends

- sharing the road with pedestrians and cyclists, particularly children, and motorcyclists
- weather conditions make it safer to do so
- driving at night as it is harder to see other road users.

Speed Limits

Type of vehicle	Built-up areas*	Elsewhere		Motorways
		Single carriage-ways	Dual carriage-ways	
	MPH	MPH	MPH	MPH
Cars & motorcycles (including car derived vans up to 2 tonnes maximum laden weight)	30	60	70	70
Cars towing caravans or trailers (including car derived vans and motorcycles)	30	50	60	60
Buses & coaches (not exceeding 12 metres in overall length)	30	50	60	70
Goods vehicles (not exceeding 7.5 tonnes maximum laden weight)	30	50	60	70[†]
Goods vehicles (exceeding 7.5 tonnes maximum laden weight)	30	40	50	60

These are the national speed limits and apply to all roads unless signs show otherwise.

*The 30 mph limit applies to all traffic on all roads in England and Wales (only Class C unclassified roads in Scotland) with street lighting unless signs show otherwise.

[†] 60 if articulated or towing a trailer

Typical Stopping Distances

	Thinking Distance
	Braking Distance

20 mph = 12 metres (40 feet) or 3 car lengths
6 metres | 6 metres

30 mph = 23 metres (75 feet) or 6 car lengths
9 metres | 14 metres

40 mph = 36 metres (120 feet) or 9 car lengths
12 metres | 24 metres

50 mph = 53 metres (175 feet) or 13 car lengths
15 metres | 38 metres

60 mph = 73 metres (240 feet) or 18 car lengths
18 metres | 55 metres

70 mph = 96 metres (315 feet) or 24 car lengths
21 metres | 75 metres

Stopping distances

105. Drive at a speed that will allow you to stop well within the distance you can see to be clear. You should

Rule 105: Use a fixed point to help measure a two second gap

• leave enough space between you and the vehicle in front so that you can pull up safely if it suddenly slows down or stops. The safe rule is never to get closer than the overall stopping distance. (see Typical Stopping Distances diagram, above)

• allow at least a two-second gap between you and the vehicle in front on roads carrying fast traffic. The gap should be at least doubled on wet roads and increased still further on icy roads

• remember, large vehicles and motorcycles need a greater distance to stop.

Lines & lane markings on the road

Diagrams of all lines are shown on page 78.

106. A broken white line. This marks the centre of the road. When this line lengthens and the gaps shorten, it means that there is a hazard ahead. Do not cross it unless you can see the road is clear well ahead and wish to overtake or turn off.

107. Double white lines where the line nearest to you is broken. This means you may cross the lines to overtake if it is safe, provided you can complete the manoeuvre before reaching a solid white line on your side. White arrows on the road indicate when you need to get back onto your side of the road.

108. Double white lines where the line nearest you is solid. This means you **MUST NOT** cross or straddle it unless it is safe and you need to enter adjoining premises or a side road. You may cross the line if necessary to pass a stationary vehicle, or overtake a pedal cycle, horse or road maintenance vehicle, if they are travelling at 10mph or less.
Laws RTA sect 36 & TSRGD regs 10 & 26

109. Areas of white diagonal stripes or chevrons painted on the road. These are to separate traffic lanes or to protect traffic turning right.
- If the area is bordered by a broken white line, you should not enter the area unless it is necessary and you can see that it is safe to do so.
- If the area is marked with diagonal stripes and bordered by solid white lines, you should not enter it except in an emergency.
- If the area is marked with chevrons and bordered by solid white lines you **MUST NOT** enter it except in an emergency.
Laws MT(E&W)R regs 5,9,10 & 16, MT(S)R regs 4,8,9 & 14, RTA sect 36 & TSRGD 10(1)

110. Lane dividers. These are short broken white lines which are used on wide carriageways to divide them into lanes. You should keep between them.

111. Reflective road studs may be used with white lines.
- White studs mark the lanes or the middle of the road.
- Red studs mark the left edge of the road.
- Amber studs mark the central reservation of a dual carriageway or motorway.
- Green studs mark the edge of the main carriageway at lay-bys, side roads and slip roads.

Multi-lane carriageways
Lane discipline
112. If you need to change lane, first use your mirrors and check your blind spots (the areas you are unable to see in the mirrors) to make sure you will not force another driver or rider to swerve or slow down. When it is safe to do so, signal to indicate your intentions to other road users and when clear move over.

113. You should follow the signs and road markings and get into lane as directed. In congested road conditions do not change lanes unnecessarily.

Single carriageway

114. Where a single carriageway has three lanes and the road markings or signs do not give priority to traffic in either direction
- use the middle lane only for overtaking or turning right. Remember, you have no more right to use the middle lane than a driver coming from the opposite direction
- do not use the right-hand lane.

115. Where a single carriageway has four or more lanes, use only the lanes that signs or markings indicate.

Dual carriageways

116. On a two-lane dual carriageway you should stay in the left-hand lane. Use the right-hand lane for overtaking or turning right. If you use it for overtaking move back to the left-hand lane when it is safe to do so.

117. On a three-lane dual carriageway, you may use the middle lane or the right-hand lane to overtake but return to the middle and then the left-hand lane when it is safe.

118. Climbing and crawler lanes. These are provided on some hills. Use this lane if you are driving a slow moving vehicle or if there are vehicles behind you wishing to overtake.

119. Cycle lanes. These are shown by road markings and signs. You **MUST NOT** drive or park in a cycle lane marked by a solid white line during its times of operation. Do not drive or park in a cycle lane marked by a broken white line unless it is unavoidable. You **MUST NOT** park in any cycle lane whilst waiting restrictions apply.
Law RTRA sects 5 & 8

120. Bus and tram lanes. These are shown by road markings and signs. You **MUST NOT** drive or stop in a tram lane or in a bus lane during its period of operation unless the signs indicate you may do so.
Law RTRA sects 5 & 8

121. One-way streets. Traffic **MUST** travel in the direction indicated by signs. Buses and/or cycles may have a contraflow lane. Choose the correct lane for your exit as soon as you can. Do not change lanes suddenly. Unless road signs or markings indicate otherwise, you should use
- the left-hand lane when going left
- the right-hand lane when going right
- the most appropriate lane when going straight ahead.

Remember – traffic could be passing on both sides.
Laws RTA 1988 sect 36 & RTRA sects 5 & 8

General advice

122. You **MUST NOT**
- drive dangerously
- drive without due care and attention
- drive without reasonable consideration for other road users.

Law RTA 1988 sects 2 & 3 as amended by RTA 1991

123. You **MUST NOT** drive on or over a pavement, footpath or bridleway except to gain lawful access to property.
Laws HA 1835 sect 72 & RTA sect 34

124. Adapt your driving to the appropriate type and condition of road you are on. In particular

- do not treat speed limits as a target. It is often not appropriate or safe to drive at the maximum speed limit
- take the road and traffic conditions into account. Be prepared for unexpected or difficult situations, for example, the road being blocked beyond a blind bend. Be prepared to adjust your speed as a precaution
- where there are junctions, be prepared for vehicles emerging
- in side roads and country lanes look out for unmarked junctions where nobody has priority
- try to anticipate what pedestrians and cyclists might do. If pedestrians, particularly children, are looking the other way, they may step out into the road without seeing you.

125. Be considerate. Be careful of and considerate towards other road users. You should

- try to be understanding if other drivers cause problems; they may be inexperienced or not know the area well
- be patient; remember that anyone can make a mistake
- not allow yourself to become agitated or involved if someone is behaving badly on the road. This will only make the situation worse. Pull over, calm down and, when you feel relaxed, continue your journey
- slow down and hold back if a vehicle pulls out into your path at a junction. Allow it to get clear. Do not over-react by driving too close behind it.

126. Safe driving needs concentration. Avoid distractions when driving such as

- loud music (this may mask other sounds)
- trying to read maps
- inserting a cassette or CD or tuning a radio
- arguing with your passengers or other road users
- eating and drinking.

Mobile phones and in-car technology

127. You **MUST** exercise proper control of your vehicle at all times. You **MUST NOT** use a hand-held mobile phone, or similar device, when driving or when supervising a learner driver, except to call 999 or 112 in a genuine emergency when it is unsafe or impractical to stop.

Never use a hand-held microphone when driving. Using hands free equipment is also likely to distract your attention from the road. It is far safer not to use any telephone while you are driving – find a safe place to stop first.
Laws RTA 1988 sects 2 & 3 & CUR regs 104 & 110

128. There is a danger of driver distraction being caused by in-vehicle systems such as route guidance and navigation systems, congestion warning systems, PCs, multi-media, etc.

Do not operate, adjust or view any such system if it will distract your attention while you are driving; you **MUST** exercise proper control of your vehicle at all times. If necessary find a safe place to stop first.
Laws RTA 1988 sects 2 & 3 & CUR reg 104

In slow moving traffic

129. You should

- reduce the distance between you and the vehicle ahead to maintain traffic flow
- never get so close to the vehicle in front that you cannot stop safely
- leave enough space to be able to manoeuvre if the vehicle in front breaks down or an emergency vehicle needs to get past
- not change lanes to the left to overtake
- allow access into and from side roads, as blocking these will add to congestion.

Rule 129: Do not block access to a side road

Driving in built up areas

130. Narrow residential streets. You should drive slowly and carefully on streets where there are likely to be pedestrians, cyclists and parked cars.

In some areas a 20 mph maximum speed limit may be in force. Look out for

- vehicles emerging from junctions
- vehicles moving off
- car doors opening
- pedestrians
- children running out from between parked cars
- cyclists and motorcyclists.

131. Traffic calming measures. On some roads there are features such as road humps, chicanes and narrowings which are intended to slow you down. When you approach these features reduce your speed. Allow cyclists and motorcyclists room to pass through them. Maintain a reduced speed along the whole of the stretch of road within the calming measures. Give way to oncoming traffic if directed to do so by signs. You should not overtake other moving vehicles whilst in these areas.

Rule 131: Chicanes may be used to slow traffic down

Country roads

132. Take extra care on country roads and reduce your speed at approaches to bends, which can be sharper than they appear, and at minor junctions and turnings, which may be partially hidden. Be prepared for pedestrians, horse riders and cyclists walking or riding in the road. You should also reduce your speed where country roads enter villages.

133. Single-track roads. These are only wide enough for one vehicle. They may have special passing places. If you see a vehicle coming towards you, or the driver behind wants to overtake, pull into a passing place on your left, or wait opposite a passing place on your right. Give way to vehicles coming uphill whenever you can. If necessary, reverse until you reach a passing place to let the other vehicle pass.

134. Do not park in passing places.

Using the road

General rules

135. **Before moving off** you should
- use all mirrors to check the road is clear
- look round to check the blind spots (the areas you are unable to see in the mirrors)
- signal if necessary before moving out
- look round for a final check. Move off only when it is safe to do so.

Rule 135: Check the blind spot
before moving off

136. **Once moving** you should
- keep to the left, unless road signs or markings indicate otherwise. The exceptions are when you want to overtake, turn right or pass parked vehicles or pedestrians in the road
- keep well to the left on right-hand bends. This will improve your view of the road and help avoid the risk of colliding with traffic approaching from the opposite direction
- keep both hands on the wheel, where possible. This will help you to remain in full control of the vehicle at all times
- be aware of other vehicles especially cycles and motorcycles. These are more difficult to see than larger vehicles and their riders are particularly vulnerable. Give them plenty of room, especially if you are driving a long vehicle or towing a trailer
- select a lower gear before you reach a long downhill slope. This will help to control your speed

- when towing, remember the extra length will affect overtaking and manoeuvring. The extra weight will also affect the braking and acceleration.

Mirrors

137. All mirrors should be used effectively throughout your journey. You should

- use your mirrors frequently so that you always know what is behind and to each side of you
- use them in good time before you signal or change direction or speed
- be aware that mirrors do not cover all areas and there will be blind spots. You will need to look round and check.

Remember: Mirrors - Signal - Manoeuvre

Overtaking

138. Before overtaking you should make sure

- the road is sufficiently clear ahead
- the vehicle behind is not beginning to overtake you
- there is a suitable gap in front of the vehicle you plan to overtake.

139. Overtake only when it is safe to do so. You should

- not get too close to the vehicle you intend to overtake
- use your mirrors, signal when it is safe to do so, take a quick sideways glance into the blind spot area and then start to move out
- not assume that you can simply follow a vehicle ahead which is overtaking; there may only be enough room for one vehicle
- move quickly past the vehicle you are

overtaking, once you have started to overtake. Allow plenty of room. Move back to the left as soon as you can but do not cut in

- take extra care at night and in poor visibility when it is harder to judge speed and distance

- give way to oncoming vehicles before passing parked vehicles or other obstructions on your side of the road
- only overtake on the left if the vehicle in front is signalling to turn right, and there is room to do so
- stay in your lane if traffic is moving slowly in queues. If the queue on your right is moving more slowly than you are, you may pass on the left
- give motorcyclists, cyclists and horse riders at least as much room as you would a car when overtaking (see Rules 188, 189 and 191).

Remember: Mirrors - Signal - Manoeuvre

Rule 139: Do not cut in too quickly

140. Large vehicles. Overtaking these is more difficult. You should

- drop back to increase your ability to see ahead. Getting too close to large vehicles will obscure your view of the road ahead and there may be another slow moving vehicle in front
- make sure that you have enough room to complete your overtaking manoeuvre before committing yourself. It takes longer to pass a large vehicle. If in doubt do not overtake
- not assume you can follow a vehicle ahead which is overtaking a long vehicle. If a problem develops, they may abort overtaking and pull back in.

141. You **MUST NOT** overtake

- if you would have to cross or straddle double white lines with a solid line nearest to you (but see Rule 108)
- if you would have to enter an area designed to divide traffic, if it is surrounded by a solid white line
- the nearest vehicle to a pedestrian crossing, especially when it has stopped to let pedestrians cross
- if you would have to enter a lane reserved for buses, trams or cycles during its hours of operation
- after a 'No Overtaking' sign and until you pass a sign cancelling the restriction.

Laws RTA 1988 sect 36, TSRGD regs 10,22,23 & 24, ZPPPCRGD reg 24

142. DO NOT overtake if there is any doubt, or where you cannot see far enough ahead to be sure it is safe. For example, when you are approaching

- a corner or bend
- a hump bridge
- the brow of a hill.

143. DO NOT overtake where you might come into conflict with other road users. For example

- approaching or at a road junction on either side of the road
- where the road narrows
- when approaching a school crossing patrol
- between the kerb and a bus or tram when it is at a stop
- where traffic is queuing at junctions or road works
- when you would force another vehicle to swerve or slow down
- at a level crossing
- when a vehicle is indicating right, even if you believe the signal should have been cancelled. Do not take a risk; wait for the signal to be cancelled.

144. Being overtaken. If a driver is trying to overtake you, maintain a steady course and speed, slowing down if necessary to let the vehicle pass. Never obstruct drivers who wish to pass. Speeding up or driving unpredictably while someone is overtaking you is dangerous. Drop back to maintain a two-second gap if someone overtakes and pulls into the gap in front of you.

145. Do not hold up a long queue of traffic, especially if you are driving a large or slow moving vehicle. Check your mirrors frequently, and if necessary, pull in where it is safe and let traffic pass.

Road junctions

146. Take extra care at junctions. You should

- watch out for cyclists, motor- cyclists and pedestrians as they are not always easy to see
- watch out for pedestrians crossing a road into which you are turning. If they have started to cross they have priority, so give way
- watch out for long vehicles which may be turning at a junction ahead; they may have to use the whole width of the road to make the turn (see Rule 196)
- not assume, when waiting at a junction, that a vehicle coming from the right and signalling left will actually turn. Wait and make sure
- not cross or join a road until there is a gap large enough for you to do so safely.

147. You **MUST** stop behind the line at a junction with a 'Stop' sign and a solid white line across the road. Wait for a safe gap in the traffic before you move off.

Laws RTA 1988 sect 36 & TSRGD regs 10 & 16

148. The approach to a junction may have a 'Give Way' sign or a triangle marked on the road. You **MUST** give way to traffic on the main road when emerging from a junction with broken white lines across the road.

Laws RTA 1988 sect 36 & TSRGD regs 10(1), 16(1) & 25

149. Dual carriageways. When crossing or turning right, first assess whether the central reservation is deep enough to protect the full length of your vehicle.

- If it is, then you should treat each half of the carriageway as a separate road. Wait in the central reservation until there is a safe gap in the traffic on the second half of the road.
- If the central reservation is too shallow for the length of your vehicle, wait until you can cross both carriageways in one go.

Rule 149: Assess your vehicle's length and do not obstruct traffic

150. Box junctions. These have criss-cross yellow lines painted on the road (see page 80). You **MUST NOT** enter the box until your exit road or lane is clear. However, you may enter the box and wait when you want to turn right, and are only stopped from doing so by oncoming traffic, or by other vehicles waiting to turn right. At signalled roundabouts you **MUST NOT** enter the box unless you can cross over it completely without stopping.

Law TSRGD regs 10(1) & 29(2)

Rule 150: Enter a box junction only if your exit road is clear

Junctions controlled by traffic lights

151. You **MUST** stop behind the white 'Stop' line across your side of the road unless the light is green. If the amber light appears you may go on only if you have already crossed the stop line or are so close to it that to stop might cause an accident.
Laws RTA 1988 sect 36 & TSRGD regs 10 & 36

152. You **MUST NOT** move forward over the white line when the red light is showing. Only go forward when the traffic lights are green if there is room for you to clear the junction safely or you are taking up a position to turn right. If the traffic lights are not working, proceed with caution.
Laws RTA 1988 sect 36 & TSRGD regs 10 & 36

153. Green filter arrow. This indicates a filter lane only. Do not enter that lane unless you want to go in the direction of the arrow. You may proceed in the direction of the green arrow when it, or the full green light shows. Give other traffic, especially cyclists, time and room to move into the correct lane.

154. Advanced stop lines. Some junctions have advanced stop lines or bus advance areas to allow cycles and buses to be positioned ahead of other traffic. Motorists, including motorcyclists, **MUST** stop at the first white line reached, and should avoid encroaching on the marked area. If your vehicle has proceeded over the first white line at the time that the signal goes red, you **MUST** stop at the second white line, even if your vehicle is in the marked area. Allow cyclists and buses time and space to move off when the green signal shows.
Laws RTA 1988 sect 36 & TSRGD regs 10 & 43(2)

Rule 154: Do not encroach on the area marked for cyclists

Turning right

155. Well before you turn right you should

- use your mirrors to make sure you know the position and movement of traffic behind you
- give a right-turn signal

- take up a position just left of the middle of the road or in the space marked for traffic turning right
- leave room for other vehicles to pass on the left, if possible.

Rule 155: Position your vehicle correctly to avoid obstructing traffic

156. Wait until there is a safe gap between you and any oncoming vehicle. Watch out for cyclists, motorcyclists and pedestrians. Check your mirrors and blind spot again to make sure you are not being overtaken, then make the turn. Do not cut the corner. Take great care when turning into a main road; you will need to watch for traffic in both directions and wait for a safe gap.
Remember: Mirrors - Signal - Manoeuvre

157. When turning at a cross roads where an oncoming vehicle is also turning right, there is a choice of two methods

- turn right side to right side; keep the other vehicle on your right and turn behind it. This is generally the safest method as you have a clear view of any approaching traffic when completing your turn
- left side to left side, turning in front of each other. This can block your view of oncoming vehicles, so take extra care.

Road layout, markings or how the other vehicle is positioned can determine which course should be taken.

Rule 157: Turning right side to right side   Turning left side to left side

Turning left

158. Use your mirrors and give a left-turn signal well before you turn left. Do not overtake just before you turn left and watch out for traffic coming up on your left before you make the turn, especially if driving a large vehicle. Cyclists and motorcyclists in particular may be hidden from your view.

Rule 158: Do not cut in on cyclists

159. When turning
- keep as close to the left as is safe and practical
- give way to any vehicles using a bus lane, cycle lane or tramway from either direction.

Roundabouts

160. On approaching a roundabout

take notice and act on all the information available to you, including traffic signs, traffic lights and lane markings which direct you into the correct lane. You should

- use **Mirrors - Signal - Manoeuvre** at all stages
- decide as early as possible which exit you need to take
- give an appropriate signal (see Rule 162). Time your signals so as not to confuse other road users
- get into the correct lane
- adjust your speed and position to fit in with traffic conditions
- be aware of the speed and position of all the traffic around you.

Rule 160: Follow the correct procedure at roundabouts

161. When reaching the roundabout

you should

- give priority to traffic approaching from your right, unless directed otherwise by signs, road markings or traffic lights
- check whether road markings allow you

to enter the roundabout without giving way. If so, proceed, but still look to the right before joining
- watch out for vehicles already on the roundabout; be aware they may not be signalling correctly or at all
- look forward before moving off to make sure traffic in front has moved off.

162. Signals and position, unless signs or markings indicate otherwise.

When taking the first exit
- signal left and approach in the left-hand lane
- keep to the left on the roundabout and continue signalling left to leave.

When taking any intermediate exit
- select the appropriate lane on approach to and on the roundabout, signalling as necessary
- stay in this lane until you need to alter course to exit the roundabout
- signal left after you have passed the exit before the one you want.

When taking the last exit or going full circle
- signal right and approach in the right-hand lane
- keep to the right on the roundabout until you need to change lanes to exit the roundabout
- signal left after you have passed the exit before the one you want.

When there are more than three lanes at the entrance to a roundabout, use the most appropriate lane on approach and through it.

163. In all cases watch out for and give plenty of room to

- pedestrians who may be crossing the approach and exit roads
- traffic crossing in front of you on the roundabout, especially vehicles intending to leave by the next exit
- traffic which may be straddling lanes or positioned incorrectly
- motorcyclists
- cyclists and horse riders who may stay in the left-hand lane and signal right if they intend to continue round the roundabout
- long vehicles (including those towing trailers) which might have to take a different course approaching or on the roundabout because of their length. Watch out for their signals.

164. Mini-roundabouts. Approach these in the same way as normal roundabouts. All vehicles **MUST** pass round the central markings except large vehicles which are physically incapable of doing so. Remember, there is less space to manoeuvre and less time to signal. Beware of vehicles making U-turns.
Laws RTA 1988 sect 36 & TSRGD regs 10(1) & 16(1)

165. At double mini-roundabouts treat each roundabout separately and give way to traffic from the right.

166. Multiple roundabouts. At some complex junctions, there may be a series of mini-roundabouts at the intersections. Treat each mini-roundabout separately and follow the normal rules.

Rule 166: Treat each roundabout separately

Pedestrian crossings

167. You **MUST NOT** park on a crossing or in the area covered by the zig-zag lines. You **MUST NOT** overtake the moving vehicle nearest the crossing or the vehicle nearest the crossing which has stopped to give way to pedestrians.
Laws ZPPPCRGD regs 18, 20 & 24, RTRA sect 25(5), TSRGD regs 10, 27 & 28

168. In queuing traffic, you should keep the crossing clear.

Rule 168: Keep the crossing clear

169. You should take extra care where the view of either side of the crossing is blocked by queuing traffic or incorrectly parked vehicles. Pedestrians may be crossing between stationary vehicles.

170. Allow pedestrians plenty of time to cross and do not harass them by revving your engine or edging forward.

171. Zebra crossings. As you approach a zebra crossing
- look out for people waiting to cross and be ready to slow down or stop to let them cross
- you **MUST** give way when someone has moved onto a crossing
- allow more time for stopping on wet or icy roads
- do not wave people across; this could be dangerous if another vehicle is approaching
- be aware of pedestrians approaching from the side of the crossing.

Law ZPPPCR reg 25

Signal-controlled crossings

172. Pelican crossings. These are signal-controlled crossings where flashing amber follows the red 'Stop' light. You **MUST** stop when the red light shows.

Rule 172: Allow pedestrians to cross when the amber light is flashing

When the amber light is flashing, you **MUST** give way to any pedestrians on the crossing.

If the amber light is flashing and there are no pedestrians on the crossing, you may proceed with caution.

Laws ZPPPCRGD regs 23 & 26 & RTRA sect 25(5)

173. Pelican crossings which go straight across the road are one crossing, even when there is a central island. You **MUST** wait for pedestrians who are crossing from the other side of the island.

Law ZPPPCRGD reg 26 & RTRA sect 25(5)

174. Give way to pedestrians who are still crossing after the signal for vehicles has changed to green.

175. Toucan and puffin crossings. These are similar to pelican crossings, but there is no flashing amber phase.

Reversing

176. Choose an appropriate place to manoeuvre. If you need to turn your car around, wait until you find a safe place. Try not to reverse or turn round in a busy road; find a quiet side road or drive round a block of side streets.

177. Do not reverse from a side road into a main road. When using a driveway, reverse in and drive out if you can.

178. Look carefully before you start reversing. You should
- use all your mirrors
- check the 'blind spot' behind you (the part of the road you cannot see easily in the mirrors)

Rule 178: Check all round when reversing

- check there are no pedestrians, particularly children, cyclists, or obstructions in the road behind you
- look mainly through the rear window
- check all around just before you start to turn and be aware that the front of your vehicle will swing out as you turn
- get someone to guide you if you cannot see clearly.

179. You **MUST NOT** reverse your vehicle further than necessary.
Law CUR reg 106

Road users requiring extra care

180. The most vulnerable road users are pedestrians, cyclists, motorcyclists and horse riders. It is particularly important to be aware of children, elderly and disabled people, and learner and inexperienced drivers and riders.

Pedestrians

181. In urban areas there is a risk of pedestrians, especially children, stepping unexpectedly into the road. You should drive with the safety of children in mind at a speed suitable for the conditions.

182. Drive carefully and slowly when

- in crowded shopping streets or residential areas
- driving past bus and tram stops; pedestrians may emerge suddenly into the road
- passing parked vehicles, especially ice

cream vans; children are more interested in ice cream than traffic and may run into the road unexpectedly
- needing to cross a pavement; for example, to reach a driveway. Give way to pedestrians on the pavement
- reversing into a side road; look all around the vehicle and give way to any pedestrians who may be crossing the road

Rule 181: Watch out for children in busy areas

- turning at road junctions; give way to pedestrians who are already crossing the road into which you are turning
- the pavement is closed due to street repairs and pedestrians are directed to use the road.

183. Particularly vulnerable pedestrians. These include
- children and elderly pedestrians who may not be able to judge your speed and could step into the road in front of you. At 40 mph your vehicle will probably kill any pedestrians it hits. At 20 mph there is only a 1 in 20 chance of the pedestrian being killed. So kill your speed
- elderly pedestrians who may need more time to cross the road. Be patient and allow them to cross in their own time. Do not hurry them by revving your engine or edging forward
- blind and partially sighted people who may be carrying a white cane (white with a red band for deaf and blind people) or using a guide dog
- people with disabilities. Those with hearing problems may not be aware of your vehicle approaching. Those with walking difficulties require more time.

184. Near schools. Drive slowly and be particularly aware of young cyclists and pedestrians. In some places, there may be a flashing amber signal below the 'School' warning sign which tells you that there may be children crossing the road ahead. Drive very slowly until you are clear of the area.

185. Drive carefully when passing a stationary bus showing a 'School Bus' sign (see page 401) as children may be getting on or off.

186. You **MUST** stop when a school crossing patrol shows a 'Stop' for children sign (see page 393).
Law RTRA sect 28

Motorcyclists and cyclists
187. It is often difficult to see motorcyclists and cyclists especially when they are coming up from behind, coming out of junctions and at roundabouts. Always look out for them when you are emerging from a junction.

Rule 187: Look out for motorcyclists at junctions

188. When passing motorcyclists and cyclists, give them plenty of room (see Rule 139). If they look over their shoulder whilst you are following them it could mean that they may soon attempt to turn right. Give them time and space to do so.

189. Motorcyclists and cyclists may suddenly need to avoid uneven road surfaces and obstacles such as draincovers or oily, wet or icy patches on the road. Give them plenty of room.

Other road users

190. Animals. When passing animals, drive slowly. Give them plenty of room and be ready to stop. Do not scare animals by sounding your horn or revving your engine.

Look out for animals being led or ridden on the road and take extra care and keep your speed down at left-hand bends and on narrow country roads. If a road is blocked by a herd of animals, stop and switch off your engine until they have left the road. Watch out for animals on unfenced roads.

191. Horse riders. Be particularly careful of horses and riders, especially when overtaking. Always pass wide and slow. Horse riders are often children, so take extra care and remember riders may ride in double file when escorting a young or inexperienced horse rider. Look out for horse riders' signals and heed a request to slow down or stop. Treat all horses as a potential hazard and take great care.

192. Elderly drivers. Their reactions may be slower than other drivers. Make allowance for this.

193. Learners and inexperienced drivers. They may not be so skilful at reacting to events. Be particularly patient with learner drivers and young drivers. Drivers who have recently passed their test may display a 'new driver' plate or sticker.

Other vehicles

194. Emergency vehicles. You should look and listen for ambulances, fire engines, police or other emergency vehicles using flashing blue, red or green lights, headlights or sirens.

When one approaches do not panic. Consider the route of the emergency vehicle and take appropriate action to let it pass. If necessary, pull to the side of the road and stop, but do not endanger other road users.

195. Powered vehicles used by disabled people. These small vehicles travel at a maximum speed of 8 mph. On a dual carriageway they **MUST** have a flashing amber light, but on other roads you may not have that advance warning.
Law RVLR reg 17(1)

196. Large vehicles. These may need extra road space to turn or to deal with a hazard that you are not able to see. If you are following a large vehicle, such as a bus or articulated lorry, be prepared to stop and wait if it needs room or time to turn.

Rule 196: Long vehicles need extra room

197. Large vehicles can block your view. Your ability to see and to plan ahead will be improved if you pull back to increase your separation distance.

198. Buses, coaches and trams. Give priority to these vehicles when you can do so safely, especially when they signal to pull away from stops. Look out for people getting off a bus or tram and crossing the road.

199. Electric vehicles. Be careful of electric vehicles such as milk floats and trams. Trams move quickly but silently and cannot steer to avoid you.

200. Vehicles with flashing amber lights. These warn of a slow-moving vehicle (such as a road gritter or recovery vehicle) or a vehicle which has broken down, so approach with caution.

Driving in adverse weather conditions

201. You **MUST** use headlights when visibility is seriously reduced, generally when you cannot see for more than 100 metres (328 feet). You may also use front or rear fog lights but you **MUST** switch them off when visibility improves (see Rule 211).
Law RVLR regs 25 & 27

Wet weather
202. In wet weather, stopping distances will be at least double those required for stopping on dry roads (see pages 359). This is because your tyres have less grip on the road. In wet weather

- you should keep well back from the vehicle in front. This will increase your ability to see and plan ahead
- if the steering becomes unresponsive, it probably means that water is preventing the tyres from gripping the road. Ease off the accelerator and slow down gradually
- the rain and spray from vehicles may make it difficult to see and be seen.

Icy and snowy weather
203. In winter check the local weather forecast for warnings of icy or snowy weather. **DO NOT** drive in these conditions unless your journey is essential. If it is, take great care. Carry a spade, warm clothing, a warm drink and emergency food in case your vehicle breaks down.

204. Before you set off
- you **MUST** be able to see, so clear all snow and ice from all your windows
- you **MUST** ensure that lights and number plates are clean
- make sure the mirrors are clear and the windows are de-misted thoroughly.
Laws CUR reg 30 & RVLR reg 23

Rule 204: Make sure your windscreen is completely clear

205. When driving in icy or snowy weather
- drive with care, even if the roads have been gritted
- keep well back from the vehicle in front as stopping distances can be ten times greater than on dry roads
- take care when overtaking gritting vehicles, particularly if you are riding a motorcycle
- watch out for snowploughs which may throw out snow on either side. Do not overtake them unless the lane you intend to use has been cleared
- be prepared for the road conditions changing over relatively short distances.

206. Drive extremely carefully when the roads are icy. Avoid sudden actions as these could cause a skid. You should
- drive at a slow speed in as high a gear as possible; accelerate and brake very gently
- drive particularly slowly on bends where skids are more likely. Brake progressively on the straight before you reach a bend. Having slowed down, steer smoothly round the bend, avoiding sudden actions
- check your grip on the road surface when there is snow or ice by choosing a safe place to brake gently. If the steering feels unresponsive this may indicate ice

and your vehicle losing its grip on the road. When travelling on ice, tyres make virtually no noise.

Windy weather

207. High sided vehicles are most affected by windy weather, but strong gusts can also blow a car, cyclist or motorcyclist off course. This can happen at open stretches of road exposed to strong cross winds, or when passing bridges or gaps in hedges.

208. In very windy weather your vehicle may be affected by turbulence created by large vehicles. Motorcyclists are particularly affected, so keep well back from them when they are overtaking a high-sided vehicle.

Fog

209. Before entering fog check your mirrors then slow down. If the word 'Fog' is shown on a roadside signal but the road is clear, be prepared for a bank of fog or drifting patchy fog ahead. Even if it seems to be clearing, you can suddenly find yourself in thick fog.

210. When driving in fog you should
- use your lights as required in Rule 201
- keep a safe distance behind the vehicle in front. Rear lights can give a false sense of security
- be able to pull up within the distance you can see clearly. This is particularly important on motorways and dual carriageways, as vehicles are travelling faster
- use your windscreen wipers and demisters

- beware of other drivers not using headlights
- not accelerate to get away from a vehicle which is too close behind you
- check your mirrors before you slow down. Then use your brakes so that your brake lights warn drivers behind you that you are slowing down
- stop in the correct position at a junction with limited visibility and listen for traffic. When you are sure it is safe to emerge, do so positively and do not hesitate in a position that puts you directly in the path of approaching vehicles.

211. You **MUST NOT** use front or rear fog lights unless visibility is seriously reduced (see Rule 201) as they dazzle other road users and can obscure your brake lights. You **MUST** switch them off when visibility improves.
Law RVLR regs 25 & 27

Hot weather

212. Keep your vehicle well ventilated to avoid drowsiness. Be aware that the road surface may become soft or if it rains after a dry spell it may become slippery. These conditions could affect your steering and braking.

Waiting & parking

213. You **MUST NOT** wait or park where there are restrictions shown by
- yellow lines along the edge of the carriageway (see page 399)
- school entrance markings on the carriageway.

The periods when restrictions apply are shown on upright signs, usually at intervals along the road, parallel to the kerb.
Law RTRA sects 5&8

Parking

214. Use off-street parking areas, or bays marked out with white lines on the road as parking places, wherever possible. If you have to stop on the road side

- stop as close as you can to the side
- do not stop too close to a vehicle displaying a Blue Badge, remember, they may need more room to get in or out
- you **MUST** switch off the engine, headlights and fog lights
- you **MUST** apply the handbrake before leaving the vehicle
- you **MUST** ensure you do not hit anyone when you open your door
- it is safer for your passengers (especially children) to get out of the vehicle on the side next to the kerb
- lock your vehicle.

Laws CSDPA sect 21, CUR reg 98, 105 & 107, RVLR reg 27, RTA 1988 sect 42

Rule 214: Check before opening your door

215. You **MUST NOT** stop or park on
- the carriageway or the hard shoulder of a motorway except in an emergency (see Rule 244)
- a pedestrian crossing, including the area marked by the zig-zag lines (see Rule 167)
- a Clearway (see page 393)
- a Bus Stop Clearway within its hours of operation
- taxi bays as indicated by upright signs and markings
- an Urban Clearway within its hours of operation, except to pick up or set down passengers (see page 393)
- a road marked with double white lines, except to pick up or set down passengers
- a bus, tram or cycle lane during its period of operation
- a cycle track
- red lines, in the case of specially designated 'red routes', unless otherwise indicated by signs.

Laws MT(E&W)R regs 7 & 9, MT(S)R regs 6 & 8, ZPPPCRGD regs 18 & 20, RTRA sects 5 & 8, TSRGD regs 10, 26, 27 & 29(1), RTA 1988 sects 36 & 21(1)

216. You **MUST NOT** park in parking spaces reserved for specific users, such as Blue Badge holders or residents, unless entitled to do so.
Laws CSDPA sect 21 & RTRA sects 5 & 8

217. DO NOT park your vehicle or trailer on the road where it would endanger, inconvenience or obstruct pedestrians or other road users. For example, do not stop
- near a school entrance
- anywhere you would prevent access for Emergency Services
- at or near a bus stop or taxi rank
- on the approach to a level crossing
- opposite or within 10 metres (32 feet) of a junction, except in an authorised parking space
- near the brow of a hill or hump bridge
- opposite a traffic island or (if this would cause an obstruction) another parked vehicle
- where you would force other traffic to enter a tram lane
- where the kerb has been lowered to help wheelchair users
- in front of an entrance to a property
- on a bend.

218. DO NOT park partially or wholly on the pavement unless signs permit it. Parking on the pavement can obstruct and seriously inconvenience pedestrians, people in wheelchairs, the visually impaired and people with prams or pushchairs.

219. Controlled Parking Zones. The zone entry signs indicate the times when the waiting restrictions within the zone are in force. Parking may be allowed in some places at other times. Otherwise parking will be within separately signed and marked bays.

220. Goods vehicles. Vehicles with a maximum laden weight of over 7.5 tonnes (including any trailer) **MUST NOT** be parked on a verge, pavement or any land situated between carriageways, without police permission. The only exception is when parking is essential for loading and unloading, in which case the vehicle **MUST NOT** be left unattended.
Law RTA 1988 sect 19

221. Loading and unloading. Do not load or unload where there are yellow markings on the kerb and upright signs advise restrictions are in place (see page 400). This may be permitted where parking is otherwise restricted. On red routes, specially marked and signed bays indicate where and when loading and unloading is permitted.
Law RTRA sects 5 & 8

Parking at night
222. You **MUST NOT** park on a road at night facing against the direction of the traffic flow unless in a recognised parking space.
Laws CUR reg 101 & RVLR reg 24

223. All vehicles **MUST** display parking lights when parked on a road or a lay-by on a road with a speed limit greater than 30 mph.
Law RVLR reg 24

224. Cars, goods vehicles not exceeding 1525kg unladen, invalid carriages and motorcycles may be parked without lights on a road (or lay-by) with a speed limit of 30 mph or less if they are
- at least 10 metres (32 feet) away from any junction, close to the kerb and facing in the direction of the traffic flow
- in a recognised parking place or lay-by. Other vehicles and trailers, and all vehicles with projecting loads, **MUST NOT** be left on a road at night without lights.
Law RVLR reg 24

225. Parking in fog. It is especially dangerous to park on the road in fog. If it is unavoidable, leave your parking lights or sidelights on.

226. Parking on hills. If you park on a hill you should
- park close to the kerb and apply the handbrake firmly
- select a forward gear and turn your steering wheel away from the kerb when facing uphill
- select reverse gear and turn your steering wheel towards the kerb when facing downhill
- use 'park' if your car has an automatic gearbox.

Motorways

Many other Rules apply to motorway driving, either wholly or in part: Rules 43, 67–105, 109–113, 118, 122 126–128, 135, 137, 194, 196, 200, 201–212, 248–252, 254–264.

General

227. Prohibited vehicles. Motorways
MUST NOT be used by pedestrians, holders of provisional car or motorcycle driving licences unless exempt, riders of motorcycles under 50cc, cyclists and horse riders. Certain slow-moving vehicles and those carrying oversized loads (except by special permission), agricultural vehicles and most invalid carriages are also prohibited.

Laws HA 1980 sects 16, 17 & sch 4, MT(E&W)R reg 4, MT(E&W)(A)R, R(S)A sects 7 ,8 & sch 3 & MT(S)R reg 10

228. Traffic on motorways usually travels faster than on other roads, so you have less time to react. It is especially important to use your mirrors earlier and look much further ahead than you would on other roads.

Motorway signals

229. Motorway signals (see page 390) are used to warn you of a danger ahead. For example, there may be an accident, fog, or a spillage, which you may not immediately be able to see.

230. Signals situated on the central reservation apply to all lanes. On very busy stretches, signals may be overhead with a separate signal for each lane.

231. Amber flashing lights. These warn of a hazard ahead. The signal may show a temporary maximum speed limit, lanes that are closed or a message such as 'Fog'. Adjust your speed and look out for the danger until you pass a signal which is not flashing or one that gives the 'All clear' sign and you are sure it is safe to increase your speed.

232. Red flashing lights. If red lights on the overhead signals flash above your lane (there may also be a red 'X') you **MUST NOT** go beyond the signal in that lane. If red lights flash on a signal in the central reservation or at the side of the road, you **MUST NOT** go beyond the signal in any lane.

Laws RTA 1988 sect 36 & TSRGD regs 10 & 38

Driving on the motorway
Joining the motorway

233. When you join the motorway you will normally approach it from a road on the left (a slip road) or from an adjoining motorway. You should

- give priority to traffic already on the motorway
- check the traffic on the motorway and adjust your speed to fit safely into the traffic flow in the left-hand lane
- not cross solid white lines that separate lanes

- stay on the slip road if it continues as an extra lane on the motorway
- remain in the left-hand lane long enough to adjust to the speed of traffic before considering overtaking.

On the motorway

234. When you can see well ahead and the road conditions are good, you should

- drive at a steady cruising speed which you and your vehicle can handle safely and is within the speed limit (see table on page 358)
- keep a safe distance from the vehicle in front and increase the gap on wet or icy roads, or in fog (see Rules 105 & 210).

235. You **MUST NOT** exceed 70 mph, or the maximum speed limit permitted for your vehicle (see page 358). If a lower speed limit is in force, either permanently or temporarily, at roadworks for example, you **MUST NOT** exceed the lower limit. On some motorways, mandatory motorway signals (which display the speed within a red ring) are used to vary the maximum speed limit to improve traffic flow. You **MUST NOT** exceed this speed limit. *Law RTRA sects 17, 86, 89 & sch 6*

236. The monotony of driving on a motorway can make you feel sleepy. To minimise the risk, follow the advice in Rule 80.

237. You **MUST NOT** reverse, cross the central reservation, or drive against the traffic flow. If you have missed your exit, or ~ave taken the wrong route, carry on to the ~xt exit.
MT(E&W)R regs 6, 7 & 10 & MT(S)R 5, 7 & 9

Lane discipline

238. You should drive in the left-hand lane if the road ahead is clear. If you are overtaking a number of slower moving vehicles it may be safer to remain in the centre or outer lanes until the manoeuvre is completed rather than continually changing lanes. Return to the left-hand lane once you have overtaken all the vehicles or if you are delaying traffic behind you. Slow moving or speed restricted vehicles should always remain in the left-hand lane of the carriageway unless overtaking. You **MUST NOT** drive on the hard shoulder except in an emergency or if directed to do so by signs. *Laws MT(E&W)R regs 5, 9 & 16(1)(a) & MT(S)R regs 4, 8 & 14(1)(a)*

239. The right-hand lane of a motorway with three or more lanes **MUST NOT** be used (except in prescribed circumstances) if you are driving

- any vehicle drawing a trailer
- a goods vehicle with a maximum laden weight over 7.5 tonnes
- a passenger vehicle with a maximum laden weight exceeding 7.5 tonnes constructed or adapted to carry more than eight seated passengers in addition to the driver.

Laws MT(E&W)R reg 12 & MT(S)R reg 11

240. Approaching a junction. Look well ahead for signals or signs. Direction signs may be placed over the road. If you need to change lanes, do so in good time. At some junctions a lane may lead directly off the motorway. Only get in that lane if you wish to go in the direction indicated on the overhead signs.

Overtaking

241. Do not overtake unless you are sure it is safe to do so. Overtake only on the right. You should
- check your mirrors
- take time to judge the speeds correctly
- make sure that the lane you will be joining is sufficiently clear ahead and behind
- take a quick sideways glance into the blind spot area to verify the position of a vehicle that may have disappeared from your view in the mirror
- remember that traffic may be coming up behind you very quickly. Check your mirrors carefully. When it is safe to do so, signal in plenty of time, then move out
- ensure you do not cut in on the vehicle you have overtaken
- be especially careful at night and in poor visibility when it is harder to judge speed and distance.

242. Do not overtake on the left or move to a lane on your left to overtake. In congested conditions, where adjacent lanes of traffic are moving at similar speeds, traffic in left-hand lanes may sometimes be moving faster than traffic to the right. In these conditions you may keep up with the traffic in your lane even if this means passing traffic in the lane to your right. Do not weave in and out of lanes to overtake.

243. You **MUST NOT** use the hard shoulder for overtaking.
Laws MT(E&W)R regs 5 & 9 & MT(S)R regs 4 & 8

Stopping

244. You **MUST NOT** stop on the carriageway, hard shoulder, slip road, central reservation or verge except in an emergency, or when told to do so by the police, an emergency sign or by flashing red light signals.
Laws MT(E&W)R regs 7(1), 9, 10 & 16 & MT(S)R regs 6(1), 8, 9 & 14

245. You **MUST NOT** pick up or set down anyone, or walk on a motorway, except in an emergency.
Laws RTRA sect 17 & MT(E&W)R reg 15

Leaving the motorway

246. Unless signs indicate that a lane leads directly off the motorway, you will normally leave the motorway by a slip road on your left. You should
- watch for the signs letting you know you are getting near your exit
- move into the left-hand lane well before reaching your exit
- signal left in good time and reduce your speed on the slip road as necessary.

247. On leaving the motorway or using a link road between motorways, your speed may be higher than you realise - 50 mph may feel like 30 mph. Check your speedometer and adjust your speed accordingly. Some slip-roads and link roads have sharp bends, so you will need to slow down.

Breakdowns & accidents

Breakdowns

248. If your vehicle breaks down, think first of other road users and

- get your vehicle off the road if possible
- warn other traffic by using your hazard warning lights if your vehicle is causing an obstruction
- put a warning triangle on the road at least 45 metres (147 feet) behind your broken down vehicle on the same side of the road, or use other permitted warning devices if you have them. Always take great care when placing them, but never use them on motorways
- keep your sidelights on if it is dark or visibility is poor
- do not stand (or let anybody else stand), between your vehicle and oncoming traffic
- at night or in poor visibility do not stand where you will prevent other road users seeing your lights.

Additional rules for the motorway

249. If your vehicle develops a problem, leave the motorway at the next exit or pull into a service area. If you cannot do so, you should

- pull on to the hard shoulder and stop as far to the left as possible, with your wheels turned to the left
- try to stop near an emergency telephone (situated at approximately one mile intervals along the hard shoulder)
- leave the vehicle by the left-hand door and ensure your passengers do the same.

You **MUST** leave any animals in the vehicle or, in an emergency, keep them under proper control on the verge

- do not attempt even simple repairs
- ensure that passengers keep away from the carriageway and hard shoulder, and that children are kept under control
- walk to an emergency telephone on your side of the carriageway (follow the arrows on the posts at the back of the hard shoulder) – the telephone is free of charge and connects directly to the police. Use these in preference to a mobile phone (see Rule 257)

Rule 249: Keep well back from the hard shoulder

- give full details to the police; also inform them if you are a vulnerable motorist such as a woman travelling alone
- return and wait near your vehicle (well away from the carriageway and hard shoulder)

- if you feel at risk from another person, return to your vehicle by a left-hand door and lock all doors. Leave your vehicle again as soon as you feel this danger has passed.

Laws MT(E&W)R reg 14 & MT(S)R reg 12

250. Before you rejoin the carriageway after a breakdown, build up speed on the hard shoulder and watch for a safe gap in the traffic. Be aware that other vehicles may be stationary on the hard shoulder.

251. If you cannot get your vehicle on to the hard shoulder

- do not attempt to place any warning device on the carriageway
- switch on your hazard warning lights
- leave your vehicle only when you can safely get clear of the carriageway.

Disabled drivers

252. If you have a disability which prevents you from following the above advice you should

- stay in your vehicle
- switch on your hazard warning lights
- display a 'Help' pennant or, if you have a car or mobile telephone, contact the emergency services and be prepared to advise them of your location.

Obstructions

253. If anything falls from your vehicle (or any other vehicle) on to the road, stop and retrieve it only if it is safe to do so.

254. Motorways. On a motorway do not try to remove the obstruction yourself. Stop at the next emergency telephone and call the police.

Accidents

255. Warning signs or flashing lights. If you see or hear emergency vehicles in the distance be aware there may be an accident ahead.

256. When passing the scene of an accident do not be distracted or slow down unnecessarily (for example if an accident is on the other side of a dual carriageway). This may cause another accident or traffic congestion, but see Rule 257.

257. If you are involved in an accident or stop to give assistance

- use your hazard warning lights to warn other traffic
- ask drivers to switch off their engines and stop smoking
- arrange for the emergency services to be called immediately with full details of the accident location and any casualties (on a motorway, use the emergency telephone which allows easy location by the emergency services. If you use a mobile phone, first make sure you have identified your location from the marker posts on the side of the hard shoulder)
- move uninjured people away from the vehicles to safety; on a motorway this should, if possible, be well away from the traffic, the hard shoulder and the central reservation

- do not move injured people from their vehicles unless they are in immediate danger from fire or explosion
- do not remove a motorcyclist's helmet unless it is essential to do so
- be prepared to give first aid as shown on pages 410-411
- stay at the scene until emergency services arrive.

If you are involved in any other medical emergency on the motorway you should contact the emergency services in the same way.

Accidents involving dangerous goods

258. Vehicles carrying dangerous goods in packages will be marked with plain orange reflective plates. Road tankers and vehicles carrying tank containers of dangerous goods will have hazard warning plates (see page 401).

259. If an accident involves a vehicle containing dangerous goods, follow the advice in Rule 257 and, in particular
- switch off engines and **DO NOT SMOKE**
- keep well away from the vehicle and do not be tempted to try to rescue casualties as you yourself could become one
- call the emergency services and give as much information as possible about the labels and markings on the vehicle.
  DO NOT use a mobile phone close to a vehicle carrying flammable loads.

Documentation

260. If you are involved in an accident which causes damage or injury to any other person, vehicle, animal or property, you **MUST**
- stop
- give your own and the vehicle owner's name and address, and the registration number of the vehicle, to anyone having reasonable grounds for requiring them
- if you do not give your name and address at the time of the accident, report the accident to the police as soon as reasonably practicable, and in any case within 24 hours.

Law RTA 1988 sect 170

261. If another person is injured and you do not produce your insurance certificate at the time of the accident to a police officer or to anyone having reasonable grounds to request it, you **MUST**
- report the accident to the police as soon as possible and in any case within 24 hours
- produce your insurance certificate for the police within seven days.

Law RTA 1988 sect 170

Road works

262. When the 'Road Works Ahead' sign is displayed, you will need to be more watchful and look for additional signs providing more specific instructions.

- You **MUST NOT** exceed any temporary maximum speed limit.
- Use your mirrors and get into the correct lane for your vehicle in good time and as signs direct
- Do not switch lanes to overtake queuing traffic
- Do not drive through an area marked off by traffic cones.
- Watch out for traffic entering or leaving the works area, but do not be distracted by what is going on there.
- Bear in mind that the road ahead may be obstructed by the works or by slow moving or stationary traffic.

Law RTRA sect 16

Additional rules for high speed roads

263. Take special care on motorways and other high speed dual carriageways.

- One or more lanes may be closed to traffic and a lower speed limit may apply.
- Works vehicles that are slow moving or stationary with a large 'Keep Left' or 'Keep Right' sign on the back are sometimes used to close lanes for repairs.
- Check mirrors, slow down and change lanes if necessary.
- Keep a safe distance from the vehicle in front (see Rule 105).

264. Contraflow systems mean that you may be travelling in a narrower lane than normal and with no permanent barrier between you and oncoming traffic. The hard shoulder may be used for traffic, but be aware that there may be broken down vehicles ahead of you. Keep a good distance from the vehicle ahead and observe any temporary speed limits.

Railway level crossings

265. A level crossing is where a road crosses a railway line. Approach and cross it with care. Never drive on to a crossing until the road is clear on the other side and do not get too close to the car in front. Never stop or park on, or near, a crossing.

Controlled crossings

266. Most crossings have traffic light signals with a steady amber light, twin flashing red stop lights (see pages 390 and 395) and an audible alarm for pedestrians. They may have full, half or no barriers.

- You **MUST** always obey the flashing red stop lights.
- You **MUST** stop behind the white line across the road.
- Keep going if you have already crossed the white line when the amber light comes on.
- You **MUST** wait if a train goes by and the red lights continue to flash. This means another train will be passing soon.
- Only cross when the lights go off and barriers open.
- Never zig-zag around half-barriers, they lower automatically because a train is approaching.
- At crossings where there are no barriers, a train is approaching when the lights show.

Laws RTA 1988 sect 36 & TSRGD regs 10 & 40

Rule 266: Stop when the traffic lights show

267. Railway telephones. If you are driving a large or slow-moving vehicle, or herding animals, a train could arrive before you are clear of the crossing. You **MUST** obey any sign instructing you to use the railway telephone to obtain permission to cross. You **MUST** also telephone when clear of the crossing.

Laws RTA 1988 sect 36 & TSRGD regs 10 & 16(1)

268. Crossings without traffic lights. Vehicles should stop and wait at the barrier or gate when it begins to close and not cross until the barrier or gate opens.

User-operated gates or barriers

269. Some crossings have 'Stop' signs and small red and green lights. You **MUST NOT** cross when the red light is showing, only cross if the green light is on. If crossing with a vehicle, you should

- open the gates or barriers on both sides of the crossing
- check that the green light is still on and cross quickly
- close the gates or barriers when you are clear of the crossing.

Laws RTA 1988 sect 36 & TSRGD regs 10 & 52(2)

270. If there are no lights, follow the procedure in Rule 269. Stop, look both ways and listen before you cross. If there is a railway telephone, always use it to contact the signal operator to make sure it is safe to cross. Inform the signal operator again when you are clear of the crossing.

Open crossings

271. These have no gates, barriers, attendant or traffic lights but will have a 'Give Way' sign. You should look both ways, listen and make sure there is no train coming before you cross.

Accidents and breakdowns

272. If your vehicle breaks down, or if you have an accident on a crossing you should

- get everyone out of the vehicle and clear of the crossing immediately
- use a railway telephone if available to tell the signal operator. Follow the instructions you are given

- move the vehicle clear of the crossing if there is time before a train arrives. If the alarm sounds, or the amber light comes on, leave the vehicle and get clear of the crossing immediately.

Tramways

273. You **MUST NOT** enter a road, lane or other route reserved for trams. Take extra care where trams run along the road. The width taken up by trams is often shown by tram lanes marked by white lines, yellow dots or by a different type of road surface. Diamond-shaped signs give instructions to tram drivers only.
Law RTRA sects 5 & 8

274. Take extra care where the track crosses from one side of the road to the other and where the road narrows and the tracks come close to the kerb. Tram drivers usually have their own traffic signals and may be permitted to move when you are not. Always give way to trams. Do not try to race or overtake them.

275. You **MUST NOT** park your vehicle where it would get in the way of trams or where it would force other drivers to do so.
Law RTRA sects 5 & 8

276. Tram stops. Where the tram stops at a platform, either in the middle or at the side of the road, you **MUST** follow the route shown by the road signs and markings. At stops without platforms you **MUST NOT** drive between a tram and the left-hand kerb when a tram has stopped to pick up passengers.
Law RTRA sects 5 & 8

277. Look out for pedestrians, especially children, running to catch a tram approaching a stop.

278. Cyclists and motorcyclists should take extra care when riding close to or crossing the tracks, especially if the rails are wet. It is safest to cross the tracks directly at right angles.

Light signals controlling traffic

Traffic Light Signals

RED means 'Stop'. Wait behind the stop line on the carriageway

RED AND AMBER also means 'Stop'. Do not pass through or start until GREEN shows

GREEN means you may go on if the way is clear. Take special care if you intend to turn left or right and give way to pedestrians who are crossing

AMBER means 'Stop' at the stop line. You may go on only if the AMBER appears after you have crossed the stop line or are so close to it that to pull up might cause an accident

A GREEN ARROW may be provided in addition to the full green signal if movement in a certain direction is allowed before or after the full green phase. If the way is clear you may go but only in the direction shown by the arrow. You may do this whatever other lights may be showing. White light signals may be provided for trams

Flashing red lights

Alternately flashing red lights mean YOU MUST STOP

At level crossings, lifting bridges, airfields, fire stations, etc

Motorway signals

Do not proceed further in this lane

Change lane

Reduced visibility ahead

Lane ahead closed

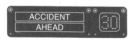

Temporary maximum speed limit and information message

Leave motorway at next exit

Temporary maximum speed limit

End of restriction

Lane control signals

Green arrow – lane available to traffic facing the sign.
Red crosses – lane closed to traffic facing the sign.
White diagonal arrow – change lanes in direction shown

Signals to other road users

Direction indicator signals

I intend to move out to the right or turn right

I intend to move in to the left or turn left or stop on the left

Brake light signals

I am applying the brakes

Reversing light signals

I intend to reverse

These signals should not be used except for the purposes described.

Arm signals

For use when direction indicator signals are not used, or when necessary to reinforce direction indicator signals and stop lights. *Also for use by pedal cyclists and those in charge of horses.*

| I intend to move in to the left or turn left | I intend to move out to the right or turn right | I intend to slow down or stop |

Signals by authorised persons

Stop

Traffic approaching
from the front

Traffic approaching from
both front and behind

Traffic approaching
from behind

To beckon traffic on

From the side

From the front

From behind*

Arm signals to persons controlling traffic

want to go straight on

I want to turn left;
use either hand

I want to turn right

bilingual signs appear on emergency services vehicles and clothing

Traffic signs

Signs giving orders
Signs with red circles are mostly prohibitive. Plates below signs qualify their message.

School crossing patrol

Maximum speed

National speed limit applies

Stop and give way

Entry to 20 mph zone

End of 20 mph zone

Give way to traffic on major road

No vehicles except bicycles being pushed

No entry for vehicular traffic

No right turn

No left turn

No U-turns

Give priority to vehicles from opposite direction

No overtaking

No motor vehicles

Manually operated temporary STOP and GO signs

No buses (over 8 passenger seats)

No cycling

No vehicles carrying explosives

No towed caravans

No vehicle or combination of vehicles over length shown

No vehicles over height shown

No vehicles over width shown

No vehicles over maximum gross weight shown (in tonnes)

No goods vehicles over maximum gross weight shown (in tonnes) except for loading and unloading

No waiting

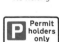
Permit holders only

Parking restricted to permit holders

No stopping (Clearway)

No stopping during times shown except for as long as necessary to set down or pick up passengers

No stopping during period indicated except for buses

Note: Although *The Highway Code* shows many of the signs commonly in use, a comprehensive explanation of our signing system is given in the Department's booklet *Know Your Traffic Signs*, which is on sale at booksellers. The booklet also illustrates and explains the vast majority of signs the road user is likely to encounter. The signs illustrated in *The Highway Code* are not all drawn to the same scale. In Wales, bilingual versions of some signs are used including Welsh and English versions of place names. Some older designs of signs may still be seen on the roads.

Signs with blue circles but no red border mostly give positive instruction.

Route to be used by pedal cycles only

Turn left ahead (right if symbol reversed)

Turn left (right if symbol reversed)

Keep left (right if symbol reversed)

Ahead only

One-way traffic (note: compare circular 'Ahead only' sign)

Segregated pedal cycle and pedestrian route

Minimum speed

End of minimum speed

Mini-roundabout (roundabout circulation – give way to vehicles from the immediate right)

Vehicles may pass either side to reach same destination

With-flow bus and cycle lane

Contra-flow bus lane

With-flow pedal cycle lane

Pedestrian crossing point over tramway

Trams only

Buses and cycles only

Warning signs Mostly triangular

Distance to 'STOP' line ahead

Crossroads

Junction on bend ahead

T-junction

Staggered junction

Distance to 'Give Way' line ahead

The priority through route is indicated by the broader line.

Sharp deviation of route to left (or right if chevrons reversed)

Double bend first to left (symbol may be reversed)

Bend to right (or left if symbol reversed)

Roundabout

Uneven road

Plate below some signs

Dual carriage-way ends

Road narrows on right (left if symbol reversed)

Road narrows on both sides

Two-way traffic crosses one-way road

Two-way traffic straight ahead

Traffic signals not in use

Slippery road

Steep hill downwards

Steep hill upwards

Gradients may be shown as a ratio i.e. 20% = 1:5

Warning signs – continued

No footway for 400 yds

Pedestrians in road ahead

Frail (or blind or disabled if shown) pedestrians likely to cross road ahead

Patrol

School crossing patrol ahead (some signs have amber lights which flash when children are crossing)

Pedestrian crossing

Queues likely

Traffic queues likely ahead

Cycle route ahead

Side winds

Hump bridge

Ice

Risk of ice

Ford

Worded warning sign

Risk of grounding

STOP when lights show

Light signals ahead at level crossing, airfield or bridge

Level crossing with barrier or gate ahead

Level crossing without barrier or gate ahead

Level crossing without barrier

Trams crossing ahead

Cattle

Wild animals

Wild horses or ponies

Accompanied horses or ponies

Quayside or river bank

Opening or swing bridge ahead

Low-flying aircraft or sudden aircraft noise

Falling or fallen rocks

14'-6"   4.4 m

Available width of headroom indicated

Tunnel ahead

Safe height 16'-6"

Overhead electric cable; plate indicates maximum height of vehicles which can pass safely

Humps for ½ mile

Distance over which road humps extend

Hidden dip

Other danger; plate indicates nature of danger

Soft verges for 2 miles

Soft verges

DIrection signs Mostly rectangular Signs on motorways – blue backgrounds

At a junction leading directly
into a motorway
(junction number may be shown
on a black background)

On approaches to junctions
(junction number on black background)

Route confirmatory sign
after junction

Downward pointing arrows mean 'Get in lane' The left-hand lane leads to a different destination from the other lanes.

The panel with the inclined arrow indicates the destinations which can be reached by leaving the motorway at the next junction

Signs on primary routes – green backgrounds

On approaches to junctions

On approaches to junctions

Blue panels indicate that the motorway starts at the junction ahead. Motorways shown in brackets can also be reached along the route indicated.
White panels indicate local or non-primary routes leading from the junction ahead. Brown panels show the route to tourist attractions.
The name of the junction may be shown at the top of the sign.
The aircraft symbol indicates the route to an airport. A symbol may be included to warn of a hazard or restriction along that route.

Route confirmatory sign
after junction

At the junction

On approach to a junction
in Wales (bilingual)

Signs on non-primary and local routes – black borders

On approaches to junctions

Green panels indicate that the primary route starts at the junction ahead. Route numbers on a blue background show the direction to a motorway. Route numbers on a green background show the direction to a primary route.

At the junction

Direction to toilets with
access for the disabled

Other direction signs

Picnic site

Ancient monument in the care of English Heritage

Direction to camping and caravan site

Advisory route for lorries

Tourist attraction

Route for pedal cycles forming part of a network

Route for pedestrians

Diversion route

Recommended route for pedal cycles to place shown

Symbols showing emergency diversion route for motorway and other main road traffic

Holiday route

Direction to a car park

Information signs All rectangular

Start of motorway and point from which motorway regulations apply

Area in which cameras are used to enforce traffic regulations

Traffic has priority over oncoming vehicles

No through road for vehicles

Hospital ahead with Accident and Emergency facilities

End of motorway

   Tourist information point

Parking place for solo motorcycles

Advance warning of restriction or prohibition ahead

Motorway service area sign showing the operator's name

Entrance to controlled parking zone

End of controlled parking zone

Bus lane on road at junction ahead

'Countdown' markers at exit from motorway (each bar represents 100 yards to the exit). Green-backed markers may be used on primary routes and white-backed markers with black bars on other routes. At approaches to concealed level crossings white-backed markers with red bars may be used. Although these will be erected at equal distances the bars do not represent 100 yard intervals.

Recommended route for pedal cycles

Appropriate traffic lanes at junction ahead

With-flow bus lane ahead which pedal cycles and taxis may also use

Road works signs

Road works

Loose chippings

Road works
1 mile ahead

End of road works
and any temporary
restrictions

Temporary lane closure
(the number and position
of arrows and red bars
may be varied according
to lanes open and closed)

Temporary hazard
at road works

Lane restrictions at
road works ahead

One lane crossover
at contraflow
road works

Signs used on the back of slow-
moving or stationary vehicles
warning of a lane closed ahead by
a works vehicle. There are no
cones on the road.

Slow-moving or
stationary works vehicle
blocking a traffic lane.
Pass in the direction
shown by the arrow.

Mandatory
speed
limit ahead

Road markings Across the carriageway

Stop line at signals or
police control

Stop line at 'Stop' sign

Stop line for pedestrians
at a level crossing

Give way to traffic on major road

Give way to traffic from the right
at a roundabout

Give way to traffic from the right
at a mini-roundabout

Along the carriageway

Edge line

Centre line See
Rule 106

Hazard warning
line See Rule 106

Double white lines
See Rules 107 and 108

Diagonal hatching
See Rule 109

Lane line See
Rule 110

Along the edge of the carriageway

Waiting restrictions

Waiting restrictions indicated by yellow lines apply to the carriageway, pavement and verge. You may stop to load or unload (unless there are also loading restrictions as described below) or while passengers board or alight. Double yellow lines mean no waiting at any time, unless there are signs that specifically indicate seasonal restrictions. The times at which the restrictions apply for other road markings are shown on nearby plates or on entry signs to controlled parking zones. If no days are shown on the signs, the restrictions are in force every day including Sundays and Bank Holidays. White bay markings and upright signs (see below) indicate where parking is allowed.

Red Route stopping controls

Red lines are used on some roads instead of yellow lines. In London the double and single red lines used on Red Routes indicate that stopping to park, load/unload or to board and alight from a vehicle (except for a licensed taxi or if you hold a Blue Badge) is prohibited. The red lines apply to the carriageway, pavement and verge. The times that the red line prohibitions apply are shown on nearby signs, but the double red line ALWAYS means no stopping at any time. On Red Routes you may stop to park, load/unload in specially marked boxes and adjacent signs specify the times and purposes and duration allowed. A box MARKED IN RED indicates that it may only be available for the purpose specified for part of the day (eg between busy peak periods). A box MARKED IN WHITE means that it is available throughout the day.

RED AND SINGLE YELLOW LINES CAN ONLY GIVE A GUIDE TO THE RESTRICTIONS AND CONTROLS IN FORCE AND SIGNS, NEARBY OR AT A ZONE ENTRY, MUST BE CONSULTED.

No waiting
at any time

No waiting during
times shown on sign

Waiting is limited to the times
and duration shown

No stopping
at any time

No stopping during
times shown on sign

Parking is limited at the
times for duration shown

Only loading may take place
at the times shown for up to a
maximum duration of 20 mins

On the kerb or at the edge of the carriageway

Loading restrictions on roads other than Red Routes

Yellow marks on the kerb or at the edge of the carriageway indicate that loading or unloading is prohibited at the times shown on the nearby black and white plates. You may stop while passengers board or alight. If no days are indicated on the signs the restrictions are in force every day including Sundays and Bank Holidays.
ALWAYS CHECK THE TIMES SHOWN ON THE PLATES.

Lengths of road reserved for vehicles loading and unloading are indicated by a white 'bay' marking with the words 'Loading Only' and a sign with the white on blue 'trolley' symbol. This sign also shows whether loading and unloading is restricted to goods vehicles and the times at which the bay can be used. If no times or days are shown it may be used at any time. Vehicles may not park here if they are not loading or unloading.

No loading or unloading at any time

No loading or unloading at the times shown

Loading bay

Other road markings

Keep entrance clear of stationary vehicles, even if picking up or setting down children

Warning of 'Give Way' just ahead

Parking space reserved for vehicles named

See Rule 215

See Rule 120

Box junction See Rule 150

Do not block that part of the carriageway indicated

Indication of traffic lanes

Vehicle markings

Large goods vehicle rear markings

Motor vehicles over 7500 kilograms maximum gross weight and trailers over 3500 kilograms maximum gross weight

School bus (displayed in front or rear window of bus or coach)

The vertical markings are also required to be fitted to builders' skips placed in the road, commercial vehicles or combinations longer than 13 metres (optional on combinations between 11 and 13 metres)

Left

Right

LONG VEHICLE

LONG VEHICLE

or

LONG VEHICLE

Hazard warning plates

2YE
1089
Newtown-on-Moors
(0123) 45678

Certain tank vehicles carrying dangerous goods must display hazard information panels The panel illustrated is for flammable liquid.

Diamond symbols indicating other risks include:

The above panel will be displayed by vehicles carrying certain dangerous goods in packages

Toxic substance

Oxidizing substance

Non-flammable compressed gas

Radioactive substance

Spontaneously combustible substance

Corrosive substance

Projection markers

Side marker

End marker

Both required when load or equipment (eg crane jib) overhangs front or rear by more than two metres

Annexes

1. Choosing & maintaining your bicycle

Make sure that

- you choose the right size of cycle for comfort and safety
- lights and reflectors are kept clean and in good working order
- tyres are in good condition and inflated to the pressure shown on the tyre
- gears are working correctly
- the chain is properly adjusted and oiled
- the saddle and handlebars are adjusted to the correct height.

You **MUST**

- ensure your brakes are efficient
- at night, use lit front and rear lights and have an efficient red rear reflector.

PCUR regs 6 & 10 & RVLR no 18

2. Motorcycle licence requirements

If you have a provisional motorcycle licence, you **MUST** satisfactorily complete a Compulsory Basic Training (CBT) course. You can then ride on the public road, with L plates (in Wales either D plates, L plates or both can be used), for up to two years.

To obtain your full motorcycle licence you **MUST** pass a motorcycle theory test and then a practical test.

Law RTA 1988 sect 97

If you have a full car licence you may ride motorcycles up to 125cc and 11kW power output, with L plates (and/or D plates in Wales), on public roads, but you **MUST** first satisfactorily complete a CBT course if you have not already done so.

If you have a full moped licence and wish to obtain full motorcycle entitlement you will be required to take a motorcycle theory test if you did not take a separate theory test when you obtained your moped licence. You **MUST** then pass a practical motorcycle test.

Note that if CBT was completed for the full moped licence there is no need to repeat it, but if the moped test was taken before 1/12/90 CBT will need to be completed before riding a motorcycle as a learner.

Law MV(DL)R reg 42(1) & 69(1)

Light motorcycle licence (A1): you take a test on a motorcycle of between 75 and 125cc. If you pass you may ride a motorcycle up to 125cc with power output up to 11kW.

Standard motorcycle licence (A): if your test vehicle is between 120 and 125cc and capable of more than 100 km/h you will be given a standard (A) licence. You will then be restricted to motorcycles of up to 25 kW for two years. After two years you may ride any size machine.

Direct or Accelerated Access enables riders over the age of 21, or those who reach 21 before their two-year restriction ends, to ride larger motorcycles sooner. To obtain a licence to do so they are required to
- have successfully completed a CBT course
- pass a theory test, if they are required to do so
- pass a practical test on a machine with power output of at least 35kW.

To practise, they can ride larger motorcycles, with L plates (and/or D plates in Wales), on public roads, but only when accompanied by an approved instructor on another motorcycle in radio contact.

You **MUST NOT** carry a pillion passenger or pull a trailer until you have passed your test.
Law MV(DL)R reg 16

Moped Licence Requirements

Mopeds are up to 50cc with a maximum speed of 50 km/h.

To ride a moped, learners **MUST**
- be 16 or over
- have a provisional moped licence
- complete CBT training.

You **MUST** first pass the theory test for motorcycles and then the moped practical test to obtain your full moped licence. If you passed your driving test before 1 February 2001 you are qualified to ride a moped without L plates (and/or D plates in Wales), although it is recommended that you complete CBT before riding on the road. If you passed your driving test after this date you **MUST** complete CBT before riding a moped on the road.
Laws MV(DL)R reg 43

Note. For motorcycle and moped riders wishing to upgrade, the following give exemption from taking the motorcycle theory test
- full A1 motorcycle licence
- full moped licence, if gained after 1/7/96.
Laws MV(DL)R reg 42

3. Motor vehicle documentation & learner driver requirements

Documents

Driving licence. You **MUST** have a valid signed driving licence for the category of vehicle you are driving. You **MUST** inform the Driver and Vehicle Licensing Agency (DVLA) if you change your name and/or address
Law RTA 1988 sect 87

Insurance. You **MUST** have a valid insurance certificate covering you for third party liability. Before driving any vehicle, make sure that it has this cover for your use or that your own insurance gives you adequate cover. You **MUST NOT** drive a vehicle without insurance.
Law RTA 1988 sect 143

MOT. Cars and motorcycles **MUST** normally pass an MOT test three years from the date of the first registration and every year after that. You **MUST NOT** drive a vehicle without an MOT certificate, when it should have one. Driving an unroadworthy vehicle may invalidate your insurance. Exceptionally, you may drive to a pre-arranged test appointment or to a garage for repairs required for the test.
Law RTA 1988 sects 45, 47, 49 & 53

403

Vehicle Registration Document.
Registration documents are issued for all motor vehicles used on the road, describing them (make, model, etc.) and giving details of the registered keeper. You **MUST** notify the Driver and Vehicle Licensing Agency in Swansea as soon as possible when you buy or sell a vehicle, or if you change your name or address.

For registration documents issued after 27 March 1997 the buyer and seller are responsible for completing the registration documents. The seller is responsible for forwarding them to DVLA. The procedures are explained on the back of the registration documents.
Law RV(R&L)R regs 10, 12 & 13

Vehicle Excise Duty. All vehicles used or kept on the roads **MUST** have a valid Vehicle Excise Duty disc (tax disc) displayed at all times. Any vehicle exempt from duty **MUST** display a nil licence.
Law VERA sect 29

Production of documents. You **MUST** be able to produce your driving licence and counterpart, a valid insurance certificate and (if appropriate) a valid MOT certificate, when requested by a police officer. If you cannot do this you may be asked to take them to a police station within seven days.
Law RTA 1988 sects 164 & 165

Learner drivers
Learners driving a car **MUST** hold a valid provisional licence. They **MUST** be supervised by someone at least 21 years old who holds a full EC/EEA licence for that type of car (automatic or manual) and has held one for at least three years.
Law MV(DL)R reg 16

Vehicles. Any vehicle driven by a learner MUST display red L plates. In Wales, either red D plates, red L plates, or both, can be used. Plates **MUST** conform to legal specifications and **MUST** be clearly visible to others from in front of the vehicle and from behind. Plates should be removed or covered when not being driven by a learner (except on driving school vehicles).
Law MV(DL)R reg 16 & sched 4

You **MUST** pass the theory test (if one is required) and then a practical driving test for the category of vehicle you wish to drive before driving unaccompanied.
Law MV(DL)R reg 40

4. The road user & the law

Road traffic law
The following list can be found abbreviated throughout the Code. It is not intended to be a comprehensive guide, but a guide to some of the important points of law. For the precise wording of the law, please refer to the various Acts and Regulations (as amended) indicated in the Code.

Abbreviations are listed below. Most of the provisions apply on all roads throughout Great Britain, although there are some exceptions.

Chronically Sick & Disabled Persons Act 1970	CSDPA
Functions of Traffic Wardens Order 1970	FTWO
Highway Act 1835 or 1980 (as indicated)	HA
Horses (Protective Headgear for Young Riders) Regulations 1992	H(PHYR)R
Motor Cycles (Protective Helmets) Regulations 1980	MC(PH)R
Motorways Traffic (England & Wales) Regulations 1982	MT(E&W)R
Motorways Traffic (Scotland) Regulations 1995	MT(S)R
Motor Vehicles (Driving Licences) Regulations 1999	MV(DL)R
Motor Vehicles (Wearing of Seat Belts) Regulations 1993	MV(WSB)R
Motor Vehicles (Wearing of Seat Belts by Children in Front Seats) Regulations 1993	MV(WSBCFS)R
Pedal Cycles (Construction & Use) Regulations 1983	PCUR
Public Passenger Vehicles Act 1981	PPVA
Road Traffic Act 1988 or 1991 (as indicated)	RTA
Road Traffic (New Drivers) Act 1995	RT(ND)A
Road Traffic Regulation Act 1984	RTRA
Road Vehicles (Construction & Use) Regulations 1986	CUR
Road Vehicles Lighting Regulations 1989	RVLR
Road Vehicles (Registration & Licensing) Regulations 1971	RV(R&L)R
Roads (Scotland) Act 1984	R(S)A
Traffic Signs Regulations & General Directions 2002	TSRGD
Vehicle Excise and Registration Act 1994	VERA
Zebra, Pelican and Puffin Pedestrian Crossings Regulations and General Directions 1997	ZPPPCRGD

The definition of a road in England and Wales is 'any highway and any other road to which the public has access and includes bridges over which a road passes'.

In Scotland, there is a similar definition which is extended to include any way over which the public have a right of passage. It is important to note that references to 'road' therefore generally include footpaths, bridle-ways and cycle tracks and many roadways and driveways on private land (including many car parks). In most cases, the law will apply to them and there may be additional rules for particular paths or ways. Some serious driving offences, including drink-driving offences, also apply to all public places, for example public car parks.

5. Penalties

Parliament has set the maximum penalties for road traffic offences. The seriousness of the offence is reflected in the maximum penalty. It is for the courts to decide what sentence to impose according to circumstances.

The penalty table on page 88 indicates some of the main offences, and the associated penalties.

Penalty table

Offence — Maximum penalties

	IMPRISONMENT	FINE	DISQUALIFICATION	PENALTY POINTS
*Causing death by dangerous driving	10 years	Unlimited	Obligatory–2 years minimum	3–11 (if exceptionally not disqualified)
*Dangerous driving	2 years	Unlimited	Obligatory (if exceptionally not disqualified)	3–11
Causing death by careless driving under the influence of drink or drugs	10 years	Unlimited	Obligatory–2 years minimum	3–11 (if exceptionally not disqualified)
Careless or inconsiderate driving	-	£2,500	Discretionary	3–9
Driving while unfit through drink or drugs or with excess alcohol; or failing to provide a specimen for analysis	6 months	£5,000	Obligatory	3–11 (if exceptionally not disqualified)
Failing to stop after an accident or failing to report an accident	6 months	£5,000	Discretionary	5–10
Driving when disqualified	6 months (12 months in Scotland)	£5,000	Discretionary	6
Driving after refusal or revocation of licence on medical grounds	6 months	£5,000	Discretionary	3–6
Driving without insurance	-	£5,000	Discretionary	6–8
Driving otherwise than in accordance with a licence	-	£1,000	Discretionary	3–6
Speeding	-	£1,000 (£2,500 for motorway offences)	Discretionary	3–6 or 3 (fixed penalty)
Traffic light offences	-	£1,000	Discretionary	3
No MOT certificate	-	£1,000	-	-
Seat belt offences	-	£500	-	-
Dangerous cycling	-	£2,500	-	-
Careless cycling	-	£1,000	-	-
Cycling on pavement	-	£500	-	-
Failing to identify driver of a vehicle	-	£1,000	Discretionary	3

* Where a court disqualifies a person on conviction for one of these offences, it must order an extended retest. The courts also have discretion to order a retest for any other offence which carries penalty points: an extended retest where disqualification is obligatory, and an ordinary test where disqualification is not obligatory.

There is a wide range of other more specific offences which, for the sake of simplicity, are not shown here.

The penalty points and disqualification system is described below.

Penalty points the disqualification

The penalty point system is intended to deter drivers from following unsafe driving practices. The court **MUST** order points to be endorsed on the licence according to the fixed number or the range set by Parliament. The accumulation of penalty points acts as a warning to drivers that they risk disqualification if further offences are committed.

A driver who accumulates 12 or more penalty points within a three year period must be disqualified. This will be for a minimum period of six months, or longer if the driver has previously been disqualified.

For every offence which carries penalty points the court has a discretionary power to order the licence holder to be disqualified. This may be for any period the court thinks fit, but will usually be between a week and a few months.

In the case of serious offences, such as dangerous driving and drink-driving, the court **MUST** order disqualification. The minimum period is 12 months, but for repeat offenders or where the alcohol level is high, it may be longer.

For example, a second drink-drive offence in the space of 10 years will result in a minimum of three years' disqualification.

Furthermore, in some serious cases, the court **MUST** (in addition to imposing a fixed period of disqualification) order the offender to be disqualified until they pass a driving test. In other cases the court has a discretionary power to order such disqualification. The test may be an ordinary length test or an extended test according to the nature of the offence.
Laws RTRA sects.28,29,34,35 and 36

New drivers. Special rules apply to drivers within two years of the date of passing their driving test if they passed the test after 1 June 1997 and held nothing but a provisional (learner) licence before passing the test.

If the number of penalty points on their licence reaches six or more as a result of offences they commit before the two years are over (including any they committed before they passed the test), their licence will be revoked. They must then reapply for a provisional licence and may drive only as learners until they pass a theory and practical driving test.
Law RT(ND)A

Note. This applies even if they pay by fixed penalty. Drivers who already have a full licence for one type of vehicle are not affected by this when they pass a test to drive another type.

Other consequences of offending

Where an offence is punishable by imprisonment then the vehicle used to commit the offence may be confiscated.

In addition to the penalties a court may decide to impose, the cost of insurance is likely to rise considerably following conviction for a serious driving offence. This is because insurance companies consider such drivers are more likely to have an accident.

Drivers disqualified for drinking and driving twice within 10 years, or once if they are over two and a half times the legal limit, or those who refused to give a specimen, also have to satisfy the Driver and Vehicle Licensing Agency's Medical Branch that they do not have an alcohol problem and are otherwise fit to drive before their licence is returned at the end of their period of disqualification.

Persistent misuse of drugs or alcohol may lead to the withdrawal of a driving licence.

6. Vehicle maintenance, safety & security

Vehicle maintenance

Take special care that lights, brakes, steering, exhaust system, seat belts, demisters, wipers and washers are all working. Also

- lights, indicators, reflectors, and number plates **MUST** be kept clean and clear
- windscreens and windows **MUST** be kept clean and free from obstructions to vision
- lights **MUST** be properly adjusted to prevent dazzling other road users. Extra attention needs to be paid to this if the vehicle is heavily loaded
- exhaust emissions **MUST NOT** exceed prescribed levels
- ensure your seat, seat belt, head restraint and mirrors are adjusted correctly before you drive
- items of luggage are securely stowed.

Law: many regulations within CUR cover the above equipment and RVLR regs 23 & 27

Warning displays

Make sure that you understand the meaning of all warning displays on the vehicle instrument panel. Do not ignore warning signs, they could indicate a dangerous fault developing.

- When you turn the ignition key, warning lights will be illuminated but will go out when the engine starts (except the handbrake warning light). If they do not, or if they come on whilst you are driving, stop and investigate the problem, as you could have a serious fault.
- If the charge warning light comes on while you are driving, it may mean that the battery isn't charging. This must also be checked as soon as possible to avoid loss of power to lights and other electrical systems.

Tyres

Tyres **MUST** be correctly inflated and be free from certain cuts and other defects. **Cars, light vans and light trailers MUST** have a tread depth of at least 1.6mm across the central three-quarters of the breadth of the

tread and around the entire circumference.
Motorcycles, large vehicles and passenger carrying vehicles MUST have a tread depth of at least 1mm across three-quarters of the breadth of the tread and in a continuous band around the entire circumference.
Mopeds should have visible tread.
Laws CUR reg 27

If a tyre bursts while you are driving, try to keep control of your vehicle. Grip the steering wheel firmly and allow the vehicle to roll to a stop at the side of the road.

If you have a flat tyre, stop as soon as it is safe to do so. Only change the tyre if you can do so without putting yourself or others at risk – otherwise call a breakdown service.

Tyre pressures. Check weekly. Do this before your journey, when tyres are cold. Warm or hot tyres may give a misleading reading.

Your brakes and steering will be adversely affected by under-inflated or over-inflated tyres. Excessive or uneven tyre wear may be caused by faults in the braking or suspension systems, or wheels which are out of alignment. Have these faults corrected as soon as possible.

Fluid levels

Check the fluid levels in your vehicle at least weekly. Low brake fluid may result in brake failure and an accident. Make sure you recognise the low fluid warning lights if your vehicle has them fitted.

Before winter

Ensure that the battery is well maintained and that there are appropriate anti-freeze agents in your radiator and windscreen bottle.

Other problems

If your vehicle
- pulls to one side when braking, it is most likely to be a brake fault or incorrectly inflated tyres. Consult a garage or mechanic immediately
- continues to bounce after pushing down on the front or rear, its shock absorbers are worn. Worn shock absorbers can seriously affect the operation of a vehicle and should be replaced
- smells of anything unusual such as burning rubber, petrol or electrical; investigate immediately. Do not risk a fire.

Overheated engines or fire

Most engines are water cooled. If your engine overheats you should wait until it has cooled naturally. Only then remove the coolant filler cap and add water or other coolant.

If your vehicle catches fire, get the occupants out of the vehicle quickly and to a safe place. Do not attempt to extinguish a fire in the engine compartment, as opening the bonnet will make the fire flare. Call the fire brigade.

Petrol stations

Never smoke or use a mobile phone on the forecourt of petrol stations as these are major fire risks and could cause an explosion.

Vehicle security
When you leave your vehicle you should
- remove the ignition key and engage the steering lock
- lock the car, even if you only leave it for a few minutes
- close the windows completely
- never leave children or pets in an unventilated car
- take all contents with you, or lock them in the boot. Remember, for all a thief knows a carrier bag may contain valuables. Never leave vehicle documents in the car.

For extra security fit an anti-theft device such as an alarm or immobiliser. If you are buying a new car it is a good idea to check the level of built-in security features. Consider having your registration number etched on all your car windows. This is a cheap and effective deterrent to professional thieves.

7. First aid on the road

In the event of an accident, you can do a number of things to help, even if you have had no training.

1. Deal with danger

Further collisions and fire are the main dangers following an accident. Approach any vehicle involved with care. Switch off all engines and, if possible, warn other traffic. Stop anyone from smoking.

2. Get help

Try to get the assistance of bystanders. Get someone to call the appropriate emergency services as soon as possible. They will need to know the exact location of the accident and the number of vehicles involved.

3. Help those involved

DO NOT move casualties still in vehicles unless further danger is threatened. **DO NOT** remove a motorcyclist's helmet unless it is essential. **DO NOT** give the casualty anything to eat or drink. **DO** try to make them comfortable and prevent them from getting cold, but avoid unnecessary movement. **DO** give reassurance confidently to the casualty. They may be shocked but prompt treatment will minimise this.

4. Provide emergency care

Follow the *ABC of First aid*

A is for **Airway** – check for and relieve any obstruction to breathing. Remove any obvious obstruction in the mouth. Breathing may begin and colour improve.

B is for **Breathing** – if breathing does not begin when the airway has been cleared, lift the chin and tilt the head very gently backwards. Pinch the casualty's nostrils and blow into the mouth until the chest rises; withdraw, then repeat regularly once every four seconds until the casualty can breathe unaided.

C is for **Circulation** – prevent blood loss to maintain circulation. If bleeding is present apply firm hand pressure over the wound, preferably using some clean material, without pressing on any foreign body in the wound. Secure a pad with a bandage or length of cloth. Raise the limb to lessen the bleeding, provided it is not broken.

5. Be prepared

Always carry a first aid kit. You could save a life by learning emergency aid and first aid from a qualified organisation, such as the local ambulance services, the St John Ambulance Association and Brigade, St Andrew's Ambulance Association, the British Red Cross or any suitable qualified body.

Index

annex one
LIST OF TEST CENTRES

England

Aldershot
Barnstaple
Barrow
Basildon
Basingstoke
Bath
Berwick-upon-Tweed
Birkenhead
Birmingham
Blackpool
Bolton
Boston
Bournemouth
Bradford
Brighton
Bristol
Bury St Edmunds
Cambridge
Canterbury
Carlisle
Chatham
Chelmsford
Cheltenham
Chester
Chesterfield
Colchester
Coventry
Crawley
Derby
Doncaster
Dudley

Durham
Eastbourne
Exeter
Fareham
Gloucester
Grantham
Grimsby
Guildford
Harlow
Harrogate
Hastings
Hereford
Huddersfield
Hull
Ipswich
Isle of Wight
Isles of Scilly
King's Lynn
Leeds
Leicester
Lincoln
Liverpool
London
– Croydon
– Ilford
– Kingston
– Southgate
– Southwark
– Staines
– Uxbridge
Lowestoft
Luton

Manchester
Mansfield
Middlesbrough
Milton Keynes
Morpeth
Newcastle
Northampton
Norwich
Nottingham
Oldham
Oxford
Penzance
Peterborough
Plymouth
Portsmouth
Preston
Reading
Redditch
Runcorn
Salford
Salisbury
Scarborough
Scunthorpe
Sheffield
Shrewsbury
Sidcup
Slough
Solihull
Southampton
Southend-on-Sea
Southport
St Helens

Stevenage
Stockport
Stoke-on-Trent
Stratford-upon-Avon
Sunderland
Sutton Coldfield
Swindon
Taunton
Torquay
Truro
Watford
Weymouth
Wigan
Wolverhampton
Worcester
Workington
Worthing
Yeovil
York

Scotland
Aberdeen
Ayr
Dumfries
Dundee
Dunfermline
Edinburgh
Elgin
Fort William
Gairloch
Galashiels
Glasgow
Clydebank
Greenock
Helmsdale

Huntly
Inverness
Isle of Arran
Isle of Barra
Isle of Benbecula
Isle of Islay, Bowmore
Isle of Mull, Salen
Isle of Tiree
Kirkwall
Kyle of Lochalsh
Lerwick
Motherwell
Oban
Pitlochry
Portree
Stirling
Stornoway
Stranraer
Tarbert, Argyllshire
Tongue
Ullapool
Wick

Wales
Aberystwyth
Bangor
Builth Wells
Cardiff
Haverfordwest
Merthyr Tydfil
Newport
Rhyl
Swansea

Northern Ireland
Ballymena
Belfast
Londonderry
Newry
Omagh
Portadown

annex two
SERVICE STANDARDS

We judge our performance against the following standards (printed in our Business Plan) which we review each year

- 90% of customers will be satisfied with the overall level of service received
- 95% of calls to booking offices will make contact with our automated call-handling system without receiving an engaged tone
- after a call has gone through our automated call-handling system, we will answer 90% of all incoming calls to booking offices in no more than 20 seconds
- we will give 95% of candidates an appointment at their preferred centre within two weeks of their preferred date
- we will keep 99.5% of appointments
- we will answer 97% of all letters and e-mails within 10 working days
- we will pay 95% of all refunds within 15 days of receiving a valid claim.

Complaints guide - We aim to give our customers the best possible service. Please tell us when

- we've done well
- when you aren't satisfied.

Your comments can help us to improve the service we offer.

If you have any questions about your theory test please contact us using the numbers below.

For DSA
Tel 0870 01 01 372, fax 0870 01 04 372

For DVTA (in Northern Ireland)
Tel 0845 600 6700, fax 0870 01 04 372

If you have any complaints about how your theory test was carried out, or any aspect of our customer service, please call the Customer Services section on 0870 600 0067. Alternatively you can write to the Customer Services Manager at the following address:

Customer Services
Driving Theory Test
PO Box 381
Manchester M50 3UW

If you're dissatisfied with the reply you can write to the Managing Director at the same address.

If you're still not satisfied, you can take up your complaint with:

The Chief Executive
Driving Standards Agency
56 Stanley House
Talbot Street
Nottingham NG1 5GU

In Northern Ireland you should write to

The Chief Executive
Driver and Vehicle Testing Agency
Balmoral Road
Belfast BT12 6QL

None of this removes your right to take your complaint to your Member of Parliament, who may decide to raise your case personally with the DSA or DVTA Chief Executive, the Minister or the Parliamentary Commissioner for Administration (the Ombudsman). Please refer to our leaflet *Service Standards - putting things right*.

DSA is a Trading Fund and we are required to cover our costs from the driving test fee.

We don't have a quota for test passes or fails and if you demonstrate the standard required, you'll pass your test.

Refunding fees and expenses - DSA will normally refund the test fee, or rearrange another test at no further cost to you, if

• we cancel your test
• you cancel and give us at least three clear working days' notice
• you keep the test appointment but the test doesn't take place, or isn't finished, for a reason that isn't your fault.

We'll also repay you the expenses that you had to pay on the day of the test if we cancelled your test at short notice.

We'll consider reasonable claims for

• the cost of travelling to and from the test centre

• any standard pay or earnings you lost through taking unpaid holiday leave (usually for half a day), after tax and national insurance contributions.

Please write to the address below and send a receipt showing travel costs and an employer's letter, which shows what earnings you lost. If you think you're entitled to fees and expenses write to:

Customer Services
Driving Theory Test
PO Box 381
Manchester M50 3UW

This reimbursement policy doesn't affect your existing legal rights.

DVTA has a different reimbursement policy.

annex three
PHOTOGRAPHIC ID IN NORTHERN IRELAND

Forms of photographic identification acceptable at both theory and practical tests in Northern Ireland are listed below

- your passport, or document of like nature. Your passport doesn't have to be British

- an employer's identity or workplace pass bearing your photograph and signature

- Trade Union Card bearing your photograph and signature

- Student Union Card with reference to either the NUS or an education establishment or a course reference number. The card must bear your photo and signature

- School Bus Pass bearing the name of the issuing authority and your photograph and signature.

These are subject to review and may change. Visit www.dvtani.gov.uk for the latest information or refer to your test appointment letter.

Any form of photographic identification presented must be recognisably you and, unless you can bring associated paperwork like a marriage certificate, must be in the same name as you booked your test.

If you don't have any of these you can bring a signed photograph, together with a statement that it's a true likeness of you. Both the statement and the back of the photograph must be signed by the same person. They can be any of the following

- Member of Parliament
- medical practitioner
- teacher (qualified)
- Justice of the Peace
- civil servant (established)
- police officer
- bank official
- minister of religion
- barrister or solicitor.

WIN AN iPOD NANO!*

The publishers of The Official DSA Theory Test book are offering you the chance to win an iPod nano.

To enter, answer the three questions on the next page then tell us **in 25 words or less** how learning to drive will make a difference to your life. Then send this form to:

Theory Test Competition 2006, TSO, Freepost, ANG 4748, Norwich NR3 1YX

One winner will be drawn per calendar month from February 2006 to September 2006. The winners will be entrants with all the correct answers and the most apt and original 25 word essay, as decided by the judges.

Your opinion is important to us. In order to help us to continually improve our products please could you answer these **optional** questions:

Name the shop or website that you bought this product from?

. . . .

How would you improve this, or any other, DSA publication?

. . . .
. . . .
. . . .
. . . .

* Terms and conditions apply

Questions

1 Between what times must you not use your horn?

. . . .

2 You should switch your rear foglights on when visibility drops below what distance?

. . . .

3 When can you wait in a yellow box junction?

. . . .

. . . .

Learning to drive will change my life . . . .

. . . .

. . . .

. . . .

. . . .

Name . . . .

Address . . . .

. . . .

. . . .

Daytime telephone number. . . . .

E-mail address . . . .

I have read, accept and agree to be bound by the Competition Rules

Signature: . . . .   **Date:** . . . .

Competition Rules

1　Only one entry accepted per purchase.

2　All entries must be on official entry forms. No photocopies will be accepted.

3　Each entry is valid for one month's draw only.

4　The competition will run from February 2006 to September 2006. One prize shall be awarded per calendar month. All entries must be received by 29 September 2006. No responsibility can be taken by the Promoter for lost, late, misdirected or stolen entries.

5　The monthly prize will be one 2GB Apple iPod Nano or another make and model of a similar value to be selected by the Promoter (£139 at the time of going to press). Colour is subject to availability. There will be no cash alternatives.

6　Only entrants over the age of 17 and resident in the UK are eligible.

7　The winning entries will be decided on the last business day of each month from February 2006 to September 2006 from all correct entries received during that month. The winner will be notified within 2 weeks of each monthly prize draw.

8　The winner will be contacted via the email address or telephone number they provide. The Promoter will not be held responsible if the winner cannot be contacted by the means they gave.

9　Each month the winner's name will be published on the Promoter's website at www.tso.co.uk.

10　The prize will be made available within six weeks of each monthly prize draw.

11　By accepting any Prize, entrants consent to the use for promotional and other related purposes (without further payment and except as prohibited by law) of their name, address, likeness and Prize information. The winner may be required to participate in the Promoter's reasonable marketing and promotional activities. By entering into this competition you consent to participate in the Promoter's reasonable marketing and promotional activities. Each winning entrant agrees that all rights including copyright in all works created and submitted by such entrant as part of the competition shall be owned by the Promoter absolutely without the need for further payment being made to such entrant. Each such entrant further agrees to waive unconditionally and irrevocably all moral rights pursuant to the Copyright, Designs and Patents Act of 1988 and under any similar law in force from time to time anywhere in the world in respect of all such works.

12　The Promoter reserves the right to cancel this competition at any stage, if deemed necessary in its opinion, and if circumstances arise outside of its control.

13　Entrants will be deemed to have accepted these rules and to agree to be bound by them when entering this competition.

14　This competition is not open to employees or contractors of the Promoter or the Driving Standards Agency or any person directly involved in the organisation or running of the competition, or their direct family members. The judge's decision is final in every situation including any not covered above and no correspondence will be entered into.

15　The Promoter is The Stationery Office Limited, St Crispins, Duke Street, Norwich, NR3 1PD (the publishers of The Official DSA Theory Test for Car Drivers and The Highway Code book).